Developing Children's Critical Thinking through Picturebook'

This accessible text will show students and class teachers how they can enable their pupils to become critical thinkers through the medium of picturebooks. By introducing children to the notion of making meaning together through thinking and discussion, Roche focuses on carefully chosen picturebooks as a stimulus for discussion, and shows how they can constitute an accessible, multimodal resource for adding to literacy skills, while at the same time developing in pupils a far wider range of literary understanding.

By allowing time for thinking about and digesting the pictures as well as the text, and then engaging pupils in classroom discussion, this book highlights a powerful means of developing children's oral language ability, critical thinking, and visual literacy, while also acting as a rich resource for developing children's literary understanding. Throughout, Roche provides rich data and examples from real classroom practice.

This book also provides an overview of recent international research on doing 'interactive read alouds', on what critical literacy means, on what critical thinking means and on picturebooks themselves.

Lecturers on teacher education courses for early years or primary levels, classroom teachers, pre-service education students, and all those interested in promoting critical engagement and dialogue about literature will find this an engaging and very insightful text.

Mary Roche is Senior Lecturer in Education at St. Patrick's College, Thurles, Ireland.

Developing Children's Critical Thinking through Picturebooks

A guide for primary and early years students and teachers

Mary Roche

Routledge
Taylor & Francis Group

LONDON AND NEW YORK

First published 2015
by Routledge
2 Park Square, Milton Park, Abingdon, Oxon OX14 4RN

and by Routledge
711 Third Avenue, New York, NY 10017

Routledge is an imprint of the Taylor & Francis Group, an informa business

© 2015 M. Roche

British Library Cataloguing in Publication Data
A catalogue record for this book is available from the British Library

Library of Congress Cataloging-in-Publication Data
Roche, Mary.
Developing children's critical thinking through picturebooks : a guide for primary and early years students and teachers / Mary Roche.
pages cm
ISBN 978-0-415-72768-6 (hardback) – ISBN 978-0-415-72772-3 (paperback) – ISBN 978-1-315-76060-5 (e-book) 1. Thought and thinking–Study and teaching (Elementary) 2. Critical thinking–Study and teaching (Elementary) 3. Picture books for children–Educational aspects.
I. Title.
LB1590.3.R636 2014
370.15'2–dc23
2014006304

ISBN: 978-0-415-72768-6 (hbk)
ISBN: 978-0-415-72772-3 (pbk)
ISBN: 978-1-315-76060-5 (ebk)

Typeset in Bembo
by Cenveo Publisher Services

Children are made readers on the laps of their parents.

Emilie Buchwald

For my parents Nora and Paddy who gave me a love of reading and a strong sense of social justice.

Contents

List of figures

The figures are all from the picturebook *Once Upon an Ordinary School Day* (McNaughton, C. and Kitamura, S. (2004) Andersen Press). They have been reproduced with permission from Andersen Press.

Acknowledgements

I would like particularly to thank my sister Jean who painstakingly read the whole book chapter by chapter and made very intelligent and helpful suggestions. A special thanks goes also to my nephew George and my niece Sophie who love reading and discussing picturebooks and from whom I learned so much. I am indebted to several other people as well: Emma and Sarah for their loving encouragement; the 'St Pats Picturebook Gang' – Aine, Assumpta, Ciara, Deirdre, Duncan, Jennifer, Karen, Marian, Michelle, Nora and Sarah, with whom I've had so much fun and learning; the many children who earnestly and joyfully discussed picturebooks with me over the years; the teachers who allowed me into their classrooms and pre-schools when I had retired from primary teaching; and my college colleagues and friends who shared insights and anecdotes about reading picturebooks with their own children. Most of all, I would like to thank my husband Charlie who read the manuscript, made great suggestions, provided endless cups of coffee and technical expertise, and who was completely supportive throughout.

Credits and permissions

I wish to acknowledge the cooperation and support of:

Mathilde Coffy, Rights Manager, Andersen Press who gave me permission to use the illustrations and material from *Once Upon an Ordinary School Day* by Colin McNaughton (author) and Satoshi Kitamura (illustrator).

NCCA (Aistear) who gave me permission to use material from the podcasts I prepared for the Aistear Toolkit.

The editor at *Inis* Magazine (Children's Books Ireland) who gave me permission to quote from my picturebook reviews.

Sarah Tuckwell, Editorial Assistant at Routledge Education who was wonderfully patient and professional.

Front Cover image: Detail from 'Bí ag Léamh' (1994) copyright S Roche, used with the artist's permission.

Thank you all.

List of abbreviations

CT&BT	Critical Thinking and Book Talk
RRSG	Rand Reading Study Group
CPD	Continuing Professional Development
NCCA	National Council for Curriculum and Assessment
RE	Religious Education
SPHE	Social, Personal and Health Education
RSE	Relationships and Sexuality
SESE	Social, Environmental and Scientific Education

Introduction
Becoming a reader

Books have been part of my life for as long as I can remember. As a small child, on my mom's lap, I saw very early how characters can reach out from the page and invite you into their world. I was captivated by *Pookie, the Rabbit with Wings* and *Fingerling* – a tiny gnome-like character who had special powers. I loved them dearly: they became part of my reality and I was only too happy to accept the invitation to enter their world. Mom and I read the comic strip 'Count Curly Wee' in the newspaper together every day. I loved the rhythm and rhyme of it. I can remember being about three and loving the texture and feel of a Blackie edition of *Puss in Boots,* as my mom and I scrutinised the pictures together, talking about them and marvelling at the exotic 'Marquis of Carabas'. Lois Lowry (1997) wrote about 'how private, powerful, and memorable a moment it is, in the life of a child, when the shape of letters takes on meaning and a door of the world opens' (np). I remember reading C–U–P and calling it 'soup'. At three I was well on my way to a lifetime of pleasure in reading and 'C–U–P soup' was my very memorable and powerful moment, because everyone clapped and laughed.

And when I was old enough to join the local library and discovered Enid Blyton, I was so hungry for her books that I'd take my allocation of two and hide those I hadn't yet read behind books in the adult section, much to the amusement of Queenie, the library assistant, who'd replace them as soon as I'd left. My dad worked there too, and a favourite treat was to be allowed into the 'store' where the smell of old books was intoxicating. For the little me then, and the much bigger me now, reading a good book means being transported to another time and place, completely oblivious to all else.

I have been excited all my life by literature and, more recently, by the realisation of the power that being literate bestows. As a young child, with the incredible good fortune to be born to parents who loved and valued language, stories, art and books, I quickly became a voracious reader. This continued throughout my school and college days, and then I became a teacher who was passionate about introducing great books to children. Maxine Greene (1978 p 27) wrote that 'there are always persons who turn toward teaching because they see themselves as people committed to arousing others to critical thinking or to conscientization (Freire 1972) or even to bringing about social change'. Teaching children to love books and reading, to be excited by reading and discussion, to be engaged and questioning and interactive in their reading and in their responses to books, is what I love to do. And in that work I am animated by a humanitarian love of democratic practices and by democracy itself – conceptual frameworks that are located in values of hope, care, freedom and social justice.

Values

As teachers, as *people*, our actions reflect the beliefs we hold. Through becoming involved in self-study action research for my master's and doctoral work, I began the lifelong practice of what Mason (2002) calls 'the discipline of noticing'. This noticing includes becoming aware of, and naming, the beliefs and values that, as Jack Whitehead (2012) says 'give meaning and purpose to our lives in education', questioning them in light of new learning, theorising our practice anew each time, and remaining alert to the fact that as we develop professionally we must 'outgrow our former selves' (Harste *et al.* 1984).

Prior to my postgraduate studies, on which I embarked as a fulltime teacher in my forties – and for much of my reading life – I had been an uncritical consumer of text. I was engaged and enthused and excited by texts, my imagination was fired, and I absorbed values and attitudes about life and living through devouring novels, but I was largely uncritical. I either liked a book or didn't and I rarely questioned why. I had had very little practice in critical thinking during my own experiences of being a pupil. I had no experience of classroom discussion at all, and no 'productive and analytical literate practices' (Comber 2003). That was how schooling was in the 1950s and 1960s when I was a pupil. As a teacher-researcher, I sought ways of teaching children to develop a capacity for reading between the lines and 'generating alternative explanations' (Leland *et al.* 2005). I wanted to encourage them to take an active role in questioning and challenging their own and each other's views, as well as critically examining books, and the overt and covert ideologies and messages about life and living that they might contain: in short I wanted my students to become critically literate agents in their own learning (Roche 2000, 2007, 2011). And throughout this process I was a learner also: through examining the values I held about dialogue and critical thinking, I learned to become more critical and I began to recognise and challenge practices that can serve to silence and disempower children as real literate beings.

Comber (2003 p 14, cited in Leland *et al.* 2005) suggests that the absence of 'productive and analytical practices' from some children's literate repertoires is an urgent *equity issue* throughout schooling (my emphasis). She argues that early childhood is 'a crucial site of practice' because it is during that period that children form initial relationships with schooling and formal learning; it is there where they are first constituted as learners and there where most children are first constituted as readers (p 14).

Leland *et al.* (2005 op. cit.) develop this point by critiquing some classrooms as replication and repetition settings. They suggest that what is missing from these sites is the involvement of young people in any deep processes of 'critique and analysis':

> In contrast, children who experience a critical approach to literacy learn to 'read between the lines' and generate alternative explanations regarding the author's intent. They are encouraged to take an active role in questioning both the texts themselves and the beliefs and personal experiences they bring to them.
>
> (p 259)

Would I be a different type of person, or a different literate being had I been exposed as a child to the kinds of critical literacy practices that Leland *et al.* (2005) talk about above? Who can say? What I would like to do, by writing this book, is to deepen understanding about more equitable forms of literacy pedagogy.

What this book is about

This book, then, is meant to serve as a guide to those who wish to introduce children to good literature, big ideas, critical engagement, and the notion of making meaning together through thinking and discussion. It is about creating what Leland *et al.* (2013) call 'real readers', by which is meant readers who know how to read, who can read for enjoyment and understanding, who can look beneath the surface and challenge any assumptions and premises that may be hidden there and who can also examine their own assumptions and discuss them with others. It is about creating critical thinkers who can think for themselves. It is about creating readers who enjoy reading and who enjoy discussion and dialogue about books. These are the key purposes of the book and will inform most chapters.

This book is for classroom teachers, pre-service education students, literacy students, parents, and all those interested in promoting critical engagement and dialogue about literature. It is also aimed at people who are the kinds of wholehearted, open-minded and responsible thinkers that Dewey (1934) encouraged us to be. Meek (in Taylor 2004) says:

> ... school pedagogy is difficult to shift. The most neglected point of all is the understanding that, from what they are invited to read and the nature of both the invitation and the text, both children and adults construct a view of the required task, and of the chances of success.
>
> (p 350)

So, although I would be delighted to think I may have an educative influence in the learning of teachers and 'shifting' school pedagogy as Meek (op. cit.) described, this book is not for people who want templates and reproducibles and 'truths' about how to teach. There are guidelines and observations, and there is some advice, but ultimately, you are being invited to examine what you understand by 'literacy' and to challenge yourself, if necessary, to move beyond possibly narrow visions.

In this book you will be introduced to 'Critical Thinking and Book Talk' (CT&BT) – an approach to literacy that emphasises what I consider to be some of the neglected aspects of the field. These neglected aspects include, among others, the development of oral language, critical thinking, love of reading, and the development of the ability to respond to literature in an authentic fashion through dialogue and discussion. We will examine the phenomenon known as 'picturebooks' and you will be guided through a rationale for the CT&BT teaching approach as well as shown how to begin such work in your own setting – whether at home or in a classroom. We will look at examples from both contexts. My hope is that you will recognise the potential of helping children to develop both their language and their critical thinking skills under your guidance as an effective facilitator.

'Thinking Time' and CT&BT

I was first introduced to classroom discussion and dialogic pedagogy in the mid-1990s when I came across the work of Philomena Donnelly who had adapted an American programme called 'Philosophy for Children' (P4C) (Lipman 1982) to suit an Irish classroom context. Donnelly's model, *Thinking Time* (Donnelly 1994) which is focused on philosophising, is now well known in Ireland, and for many years I used her methodology in my classroom. It was through using her pioneering classroom approach that I gradually refined what I was doing to concentrate more on critical thinking and critical literacy, using picturebooks as stimuli. Initially, my reason for doing so was to clarify what I was doing for timetabling purposes, and also to fulfil my school's mandate that all teachers were expected to reflect on and improve their teaching of literacy and numeracy. CT&BT differs from Donnelly's programme in that Donnelly does not use any one resource for stimulating philosophical dialogue. When I began to develop this model, I chose picturebooks as resources (as opposed to chapter books) and I introduced them to infant, middle and senior primary classes (since then to preschoolers, secondary students and undergraduates). Naively, initially I felt that because picturebooks are usually short, attractive and encourage visual literacy they would provide a useful 'prop'. As I developed my own knowledge about picturebooks, I realised that they are hugely complex and amazing in their own right. And, as I used high quality picturebooks more and more and saw the enjoyment and the engagement of the children and recognised that they were improving their oral language skills, their reading and their thinking, I was convinced of the immense potential picturebooks held as literacy learning tools, as well as sources of pleasure.

How this book is organised

The book is organised in two main sections.

- Section 1: 'The Why' (Chapters 1 to 5) looks primarily at some of the theoretical and conceptual frameworks of CT&BT, although there are many examples of classroom and home practice throughout.
- Section 2: 'The How' (Chapters 6 and 7) largely deals with the practical aspects of doing CT&BT.

Chapter 1 examines the rationale for doing Critical Thinking and Book Talk (CT&BT). It outlines the 'why' factor, beginning with a critique of how literacy – in many current educational contexts – appears to be becoming narrowed down to a set of measurable skills of decoding and encoding. It provides a brief overview of the CT&BT approach and an explanation of why critical thinking and critical literacy are needed now more than ever.

Chapter 2 looks at the whole idea of comprehension and meaning-making. It examines different perspectives on literacy and looks at the role of picturebooks in developing visual literacy. Taking one picturebook as an example, we look at how children, education students and teachers respond to the same images.

Chapter 3 looks at dialogue and interactive readalouds and examines some of the preparation and planning that are needed. We look at some of the features of picturebooks as they are applied in interactive readalouds in both a home setting and in workshops for teachers.

Chapter 4 focuses on oral language development. We realise that although reading aloud is a wonderful practice to adopt, we also need to be aware that it is largely through the thinking, interaction and dialogue around the picturebooks that language and vocabulary are built and consolidated.

Chapter 5 examines the phenomenon known as picturebooks. We look at some of the theory of picturebooks and examine some of the features that distinguish this kind of children's literature from all others.

Chapter 6 features several case studies demonstrating the use of picturebooks with various age groups in the primary school. We see how holding discussions about picturebooks allows children to become real people to us. We look at actual classroom practice and examine some of the practical issues that can arise.

Chapter 7 builds on this practical aspect and shows how to go about setting up CT&BT in a classroom. You will be introduced to some of the pedagogical framing issues.

Chapter 8 the conclusion, provides a summary of the main ideas.

It should be noted that each chapter can be read in its own right and you may want to skip some chapters or read them out of sequence. Another point to note is that where I have used children's dialogue I have used their own colloquialisms and grammar without using 'sic'. I have only used real names in a few cases: most names have been changed and, here and there, only initials are used.

Recommended reading

Fox, M. (2008) *Reading Magic: why reading aloud to our children will change their lives forever*. Orlando, New York and London: Harcourt.

Hall, K. (2004) *Literacy and Schooling: towards renewal in primary education policy*. Aldershot: Ashgate.

Hunt, P. (ed.) (2009) *Understanding Children's Literature*. Abingdon. Oxon: Routledge.

Leland, C., Lewison, M. and Harste, J. (2013) *Teaching Children's Literature: it's critical!* New York and London: Routledge.

Eccleshare, J. (ed.) (2009) *1001 Children's Books You Must Read Before You Grow Up*. London: Cassell Illustrated.

Meek, M. (1988) *How Texts Teach What Children Learn*. Stroud, Glos: Thimble Press.

Chapter 1

'Critical Thinking and Book Talk'

The 'why' factor

Narrowing visions of literacy

As pressure mounts to improve 'learning outcomes' in literacy and numeracy, there is a danger that the notion of literacy may narrow to '*decoding*' and '*encoding*', and the teaching of discrete sets of skills and competencies. Or that the idea of 'engagement with literature' may narrow to teaching '*comprehension strategies*' such as inference and prediction. Or that a focus on devices such as *plot, setting, characters and theme* will suffice as bases for developing literary 'meaning-making' in children. These are all important aspects of literacy. But we must not stop there. The '*Critical Thinking and Book Talk*' (*CT&BT*) (Roche 2010) approach, using carefully chosen picturebooks as stimuli for thinking, engagement and discussion, can constitute an accessible, multimodal resource for adding to these skills, while at the same time developing a far wider range of literary understanding than focusing solely on those skills permits.

When I first began trying to create a democratic educational experience for my pupils by using more dialogic pedagogies, my aim was to create the kind of classroom where, as Leland *et al.* (2005) describe,

> ...children expand their understandings of the purposes of literacy and begin to see how literacy relates to their interactions with others. The instructional approaches and the culture that children experience in these settings play a major role in shaping their emerging identities as cultural and literate beings.
>
> (p 258)

This necessitated that I first become critical and I now believe that my best teachers were the children I worked with, along with my own reflections and theorising of what was happening as I struggled with ideas of critical literacy. As I became more critical I also realised how texts position readers. Janks (2010) states that all texts are positioned and positioning in that all texts work to position their readers. The ideal reader then, from the point of view of the writer (or speaker), Janks says, 'is the one who buys into the text and its meanings'.

> They are positioned by the writer's points of view, and the linguistic (and other semiotic) choices made by the writer are designed to produce effects that position the reader. We can play with the word 'design' by saying that texts have designs on us as readers, listeners or viewers. They entice us into their way of seeing and understanding the world into their version of reality.
>
> (Janks op.cit. p 61)

If texts position readers, I realised, then surely literacy *pedagogies* can also serve to position learner-readers. Leland *et al.* (2005, citing Comber 2003 p 13) suggest that, as early as preschool, children are acquiring qualitatively different repertoires of literacy practice. 'While some children are involved in communicative practices that engage them in production, analysis, and response, others appear to be experiencing "piecemeal recycled literacies of replication and repetition"' (Comber op. cit.). Leland *et al.* (op. cit.) state that common activities in the latter group 'include filling in blanks, copying letters or words, and coloring in pictures'. This is problematic, they say, because it means that 'some children are beginning their academic careers with a limited and ultimately dysfunctional view of what literacy is for and what it can do in the world' (Leland *et al.* 2005 p 259).

What infant teacher among us has not at some point worried about the mindless prescription of workbooks that often accompany literacy textbooks: workbooks that are less about literacy and more about keeping children quiet? I know of several schools where the staff members have collectively decided to stop using commercially produced workbooks and have instead devised their own approaches to formative assessment and literacy skills consolidation. Children in these schools are not judged by how neatly they can 'stay inside the lines' or join dots, or connect cats to kittens with crayon lines. They are not positioned as passive consumers whose only choice is, perhaps, deciding what colours to use. Children in these schools are seen as active agents in their own learning.

If children can be thus positioned as different kinds of literate beings by the pedagogies they encounter, what about the teachers? Having been a teacher for many years I saw how 'basal' reading texts and their accompanying regurgitative-style workbooks could interrupt and ultimately stultify reading for pleasure. By basal texts I mean the kinds of textbooks that are generated by school book publishers and linked to the English curriculum content. In Janks' (op. cit.) language we can ask 'How do such texts position teachers?' In my own case I saw how such programmes can contribute to reducing teachers to mere technicians delivering other people's ideas. For example, 'teacher-proof' manuals often accompany these commercial basal reading schemes: manuals where even the teacher's questions are decided in advance and where there seems to be no place for children's questions; manuals where 'activities' for the children are designed by someone who does not know their different talents; manuals where comprehension is reduced to often meaningless regurgitation. And in each class that I taught during the early part of my career I recognised children who were like the little reader I had been, who had read their textbooks during the summer holidays as soon as they were bought, and who then sat in class, frustrated and bored in equal measure, as these same texts were ploughed through relentlessly, line by line. Occasionally some new insights were developed but not often enough to create any kind of learning excitement. Discussion, in the classrooms in which I was a pupil, was a non-event. We passively imbibed the teachers'/ textbook designers' 'standard one-right answers' and kept our own gradually dwindling ideas to ourselves. Our teachers were deeply committed and professional but transmission pedagogy prevailed.

However, as I developed as a teacher, I also saw the opposite. As one who used picturebooks for enjoyment and as springboards for discussion, I saw how a whole classroom could be animated in sharing ideas and learning from each other, practising what Littleton and Mercer (2013) call 'interthinking'. I could see the learning taking place; the recognition in the eyes, the buzz of excitement and engagement. I could take advantage of such 'light bulb' moments – teaching moments. And often I could see myself learning too, about the book, yes, but also about the people who populated my classrooms and whom

I got to know and love as individuals through hearing them think out loud. It was what led me to develop *Critical Thinking and Book Talk*.

I am not advocating that we mount white chargers and launch a crusade against basal reading schemes. I am not suggesting that we stop teaching reading skills such as phonics either. I would hope that after reading this book you might be persuaded to make space in your classrooms, potential classrooms, libraries, nurseries or homes for good quality picturebooks. Even more importantly – I am hoping that you will make space for discussing these books with your children.

In a *Guardian* newspaper report entitled 'Children missing out on the joys of a good book' (Brown, 7 July 2013, p 14) Maggie Brown states that '82% of [250] teachers blame the government's "target-driven" education policies for the fact that fewer children are reading for pleasure. Two-thirds of the teachers polled said they lacked time in the school day to introduce a variety of books and saw this as a "major barrier to being able to develop a love of reading"'. The reasons why fewer children may be reading for pleasure are many and complex, but interactive reading, such as will be explained later in the CT&BT approach, might go some small way towards addressing this problem.

A simple enough process

- *That story was so cool! Let's do it again.* (George, aged 3)
- *Thinking is a bit like swimming because it takes you a while to get good at it but soon you can go deeper.* (Marlee, aged 9)
- *I knew I was really getting good at thinking cos I could see loads of different ideas. Like, normally, you'd never do that kind of thinking by yourself – but it really happens when we all tell our thoughts and give each other ideas.* (Heidi, aged 10)
- *I was a bit cynical when you started the philosophy tutorial by showing us* Once Upon an Ordinary School Day *but afterwards at lunch everyone at our table was talking about it and we were amazed at how a children's storybook opened up all kinds of discussions about the whole complexity of education – like what constitutes 'ordinary' in teaching and learning.* (Ruth, a student teacher, Year 1 undergraduate)
- *You have no idea what you've started! My whole family has been continuously debating what* The Wolf *[Barbelet 1992] represents since we discussed it at our workshop last Wednesday.* (Deirdre, teacher with several years' experience)

These quotes represent a cross section of responses from people who have been exposed to the 'Critical Thinking and Book Talk' approach to reading picturebooks together and discussing them. I think you'll agree that enjoyment and engagement are evident. On the surface it is a simple enough approach: all you need is a good picturebook and a child or a group of children who can see the pictures and hear the story. The discussion will be prompted by a question from the adult, who is a participant in the process, or by questions the book has raised for the children. In a classroom situation, the children take turns democratically in sharing ideas, agreeing or disagreeing respectfully with each other and with the teacher. It will obviously be a less formal process at home.

It certainly seems simple. As the quotes above show, student teachers seem to 'get' it. Children of all ages seem to enjoy it. Many teachers seem instinctively to recognise the common sense of this dialogic practice. But while they support the idea conceptually, especially when shown videos of classes engaged in dialogue, many teachers say that they lack specific knowledge about suitable 'good' books, and more general knowledge about critical thinking, questioning and leading discussions. Most confess they know little or nothing about decoding images. Throughout my many years of working with teachers the statement that has been made most often and most plaintively is 'But you seem to know instinctively what questions to ask. You see things in the story and in the pictures that I'd never see! You know when to stay quiet'. My response is: you learn to do it by doing it. There is a skill involved. Like any other skill you need to do it to get better at it. You wouldn't consider that you could learn to cycle just by watching videos about cycling, reading books about cycling or attending talks about cycling. At some point you would need to get up on your bicycle. However, we will also see a little later that, as well as this seemingly simple skill-based premise, there are several other factors to be considered.

Staying with the skills-base idea for a moment however, it can be argued that, as they engage in the process of talking and thinking, children will develop several sets of skills too. They learn tolerance for diverse points of view as well as the social skills of turn-taking, listening actively and courteous response – all traits of civilised social citizens. Margaret Meek wrote in 1988 that 'everyone knows that the most significant things about reading are the most obvious' and she goes on to say, citing Smith (1979) that 'children learn to read by reading' (p 3). Children learn to talk by talking and listening. They learn to think by thinking. They have been doing so since birth and perhaps even before birth. Both skills are developed to a greater or lesser degree by encouragement, modelling, and enthusiasm on the part of more experienced other readers, talkers and thinkers as Vygotsky (1978) argued.

More knowledgeable others and experience through interaction

Vygotsky focused on the connections between people and the sociocultural context in which they act and interact in shared experiences (Crawford, 1996). Wertsch (1988) consolidates Vygotsky's (1978) claim that higher mental functioning in individuals has social origins. Vygotsky (op. cit.) suggests that social interaction plays a fundamental role in the process of cognitive development. He also suggested that 'more knowledgeable others' (MKO) scaffold an individual's learning. The MKO refers to anyone who has a better understanding or a higher ability level than the learner. Although normally a teacher or an older adult, the MKO could also be peers or younger people. We will see examples of children acting as MKOs throughout this book because this is what happens during CT&BT classroom discussions. Children can act as MKOs for peers through modelling better thinking, or demonstrating a more articulate speaking ability, or simply by being more socially competent and confident. CT&BT discussions can also be a demonstration or application of Vytgotsky's (1978) 'Zone of Proximal Development' (ZPD). The ZPD is the distance between a student's ability to perform a task under adult guidance and/or with peer collaboration and the student's ability to solve the problem independently. According to Vygotsky, it was in this zone or space that learning occurred.

Many schools still hold primarily to transmission or instruction models of teaching in which a teacher or lecturer 'transmits' information to students. These are largely monologic classrooms with the dominant monologue being that of the teacher. Children answer in response to teacher-directed closed questions. Constructivists like Vygotsky promote learning contexts in which students play an active role in learning. This will entail having a dialogic classroom where views are exchanged equitably. The idea of teacher-as-expert and student-as-empty-vessel is less visible in such classrooms. Teachers can and should be learners. This means that the roles of teacher and learner might have to shift in order to facilitate the creation of a classroom culture of trust and on-going participation in community. Education is a social process, as Dewey (1963) said:

> The principle that development of experience comes about through interaction means that education is essentially a social process. This quality is realized in the degree in which individuals form a community group. *It is absurd to exclude the teacher from membership in the group.* As the most mature member of the group he has a peculiar responsibility for the conduct of the interactions and intercommunications which are the very life of the group as a community.
>
> (p 58, my emphasis)

Caring relationships

Human relationships are at the heart of every classroom. The pedagogical relationship must be grounded in reciprocal care and trust according to Noddings (1992). Caring sees the creation of trusting relationships as the foundation for building an effective academic and social climate for schooling (Chaskin and Rauner 1995, Erickson 1993). Lin (2001), citing Noblit *et al.* (1995), suggests that caring may not be visible or explicit in an educational environment 'yet it guides the interactions and organization of schools and classrooms' (p 2). Noddings argues throughout her work that authentic human liberation and social justice can be achieved by 'caring people in caring communities' (Bergman 2004 p 151). Noddings (1992) also suggests that the need to be cared for is a universal human need, if we are to grow and arrive at some level of acceptability in our culture and community.

A caring pedagogical relationship can help dissolve traditional power relationships between teachers and students. From years of discussing picturebooks with children I began to see very clearly the interconnectedness of my students' lives with mine, and our connectedness to others in society, through our dialectical and dialogical engagement. Buber (1965) wrote about the teaching situation as being always a situation 'that has never been before and will never come again. It demands of you a reaction which cannot be prepared beforehand. It demands nothing of what is past. It demands presence, responsibility; it demands you' (p 114). Greene (1978) argues for teachers to seek 'to institute the kind of dialogue that might move the young to pose their own worthwhile questions, to tell their own stories, to reach out in their being together to learn how to learn' (p 32). (See also Roche 2007, 2011.)

Research (e.g. Alexander 2006, 2010; Mercer 2000; Murphy 2004; Wells 1986; Roche 2007, 2011) shows that learning grows and knowledge is produced in classrooms that are dialogic communities. In a CT&BT discussion a teacher can collaborate with his or her students in order to help facilitate meaning-construction. Learning can become an exercise in reciprocity for both students and teacher. We will explore this idea further below.

So where does critical thinking fit in?

> The National Literacy Strategy ... emphasised language as a body of skills to be taught and tested and failed to recognise literacy as a *highly complex, socio-cultural practice,* made real in social interaction and relationships.
>
> (Cremin *et al.* 2007 p 56 my emphasis)

Critical thinking is necessary for making sense and meaning of our lives and our world. Without it we risk being mere receivers and consumers of others' knowledge. Critical *thinking* is essential for critical *literacy*. Critical thinking about literacy enables us to see it as the 'highly complex socio-cultural practice' that Cremin *et al.* (op. cit.) describe above. Many educators (Comber 2001; Evans 2004; Gee, 1993; Leland *et al.* 2013; Stephens, 1992; Vasquez 2010) see critical thinking and critical literacy as requirements for challenging the taken-for-granted assumptions, values and norms of the world. Others (Ayers, Brookfield, Freire, and many other critical pedagogues) think that we should not only challenge such norms but transform them. 'The drama of education is always a narrative of transformation' according to educationalist Bill Ayers blog (nd).

Critical thinking and critical literacy are central aspects of critical pedagogy. Pedagogy – critical or otherwise – is rooted in social relationships. The social relationship of a classroom involves the teacher with the pupils and the pupils with the teacher and with each other. Shor (1992) defines critical pedagogy as teaching so as to engender.

> habits of thought, reading, writing, and speaking which go beneath surface meaning … to understand the deep meaning, root causes, social context, ideology, and personal consequences of any action, event, object, process, organization, experience, text, subject matter, policy, mass media, or discourse.
>
> (p 129)

These ideas are repeated in the work of many critical pedagogues like Kincheloe, McLaren, Giroux and others, all of whom draw on the work of Paulo Freire. People can of course, reflect and think alone. Critical thinking is not limited to school settings. However, I believe that if the habit of thinking critically is started in early years' settings, it may lead to the development of more reflective and critical adults.

Freire (1972) critiqued a 'banking' model of education which is often referred to as a 'transmission' model and which is also grounded in a particular view of the pedagogical relationship. A banking or transmission model is premised on seeing knowledge as a fixed body of truths that exists 'out there' separate from the knower and is grounded in a particular positioning of the teacher in relation to the pupil. Delivering a fixed body of truths positions some people as powerful and some as less powerful or even powerless. It ignores or devalues the *embodiedness* of the learner. When we work with students, we are not teaching a group of disembodied, clone-like 'brains' or 'heads': we are working with warm bodies, unique *people*: funny and goofy, or angry and stubborn, or gentle and dreamy, insightful knowers, just like ourselves. Where a banking model of education exists, knowledge is perceived as a commodity to be deposited or transmitted into pupils' empty heads by an expert knower (teacher); it is stored there until exam time, when it is withdrawn or 'regurgitated'. This is a one-size-fits-all model that ignores the uniqueness of each learner, and Freire sees this kind of school experience as a form of oppression by a power figure on a largely powerless one. Throughout his work he argued for a *problematising* form of education where students would seek to interrogate and understand authentic and meaningful issues and create their own knowledge rather than unquestioningly to absorb the knowledge of others: in other words that students needed to be 'problem-posers'.

A problematising form of education and critical literacy

A problematising form of education is built on the idea that, like life itself, knowledge construction is a hugely complex process and is dependent on social interaction. Knowledge is more than information: it is a process of meaning-making and is always incomplete, fluid and dynamic. Freire (1972) suggested that teaching with such a view of knowledge is a more humanising form of pedagogy than the traditional transmission model. It builds on freedom of speech and thought, empowerment, dialogue and discussion. Literacy, he felt, provides the key to freedom and liberation from oppression. No small wonder then that, in totalitarian regimes, those who create literature are often first to be sent for 'reeducation' or worse. No small wonder either, that in male-dominated, fundamentalist societies, education for women is considered dangerous for 'stability'. Discussion does not feature here. Education in such regimes is centred on compliance through dominance and control.

For Freire, literacy involved reading the word (naming) in order to read the world. If the oppressed could recognise how their world was constructed (named) then they could learn how to liberate themselves by renaming it. Freire argued that all forms of privilege and injustice, and all forms of power, particularly the power of text, must be interrogated. The field of critical literacy draws heavily on the work of Freire.

Critical literacy is not just important for those who live in oppressive regimes. We all need to be critically literate. Comber (2001 p 2) argues that being critically literate is essential in everyday daily life even in 'our western, developed, media-driven world'. Stating that critical literacies must include what she calls 'an ongoing analysis of textual practices' that must be negotiated in the more 'mundane and ordinary' aspects of daily life, she suggests asking several questions 'that could be important catalysts in the process':

> How do particular texts work? What effects do they have on the reader? Who has produced the text, under what circumstances, and for which readers? What's missing from this account? How could it be told differently? Critical literacy means practicing the use of language in powerful ways to get things done in the world.
>
> (p 2)

Children that I encouraged to become critically literate began to see problems in traditional stories very quickly. Some 5 year olds said:

- *The little red hen needs to get new friends. Simple.*
- *Cinderella should have said No! She let everyone boss her around, even the godmother and the prince.*
- *The three little pigs are heroes for killing the wolf and then he's called a baddie cos he wants to kill them. That's not very fair!*
- *Goldilocks is so stupid. She shouldn't have gone into the house: worse things than bears could have been in there.*
- *There's a lot of violence in them stories.*

Older children (age 7–8) discussing Anthony Browne's *Gorilla* said:

- *Where's the mother? That girl needs her mother cos that Dad is useless.*
- *Yeah he's in a world of his own and so's Hannah and that's very lonely.*

- *He [Browne] does that a lot – he makes you see how lonely people are even when they're with other people. Remember in the* Voices in the Park *book?*

Discussing the image of the Orang-utan in Browne's *Zoo*, a group of 7–8-year-old boys said:

- *I think it's a witch's dog.*
- *Oh I think I know now – his wife might be dying.*
- *I know! He might be in some kind of trouble.*
- *I recognise that – it's an orange skin. Maybe he ate a poisoned orange.*
- *I think it's a laundry-chute or maybe a letterbox.*
- *What might be making him so sad?*
- *They took him away and they put him in a different place.*
- *He's young because he is crying.*
- *No, they're not his grey hairs – they're off a dog or some other white animal.*

Discussing the image of the 'boy in the cage' from *Zoo* the same group said:

- *It's sad because he looks like nobody cares about him.*
- *I think it's interesting and sad both…interesting because it's such a sad picture but such happy colours.*
- *I think he's about 7 or 8.*
- *12, I'd say.*
- *I was going to say that it's very difficult to figure out because you don't know why he's in there.*
- *Maybe he's not in there, maybe it's the shadows of the bars of a cage.*
- *His Mum and Dad probably own a zoo and he works there and he's tired.*
- *No. He's not just tired. I'd say he's very sad.* (See also Roche 2000 Appendix 4.5)

We will see in a later chapter how a group of 8 and 9 year olds with more experience of critical literacy contrasted Browne's *Zoo* and Burningham's *Oi! Get off our Train*.

Reasons for promoting critical thinking and critical literacy

We will examine a few of the arguments that various educators have made for promoting critical thinking and critical literacy. For example, Margaret Meek has been promoting 'meaning-making' all through her publications, and asks what it means to be literate:

> My purpose is not a neutral one … there are two models of literacy on offer in our schools: a utilitarian one …and a supercharged model which allows its possessors to choose and control all that they read and write. This powerful literacy includes the ability, the habit even, of being critical, that is, of making judgements, especially about the writing of others. My belief is that, until …all children in school have access to, and are empowered by, critical literacy …then we are failing to educate the next generation properly.
>
> (Meek 1991 p 10)

Victor Quinn (1997) taught critical thinking because he wanted to 'interrupt the tabloid culture' (p 5) while Postman and Weingartner (1972) suggested that schools 'must serve as the principal medium for developing in youth the attitudes and skills of social, political and cultural criticism' (p 2). Robert Fisher (2006) (in Jones and Hodson, 2006) suggests that dialogic teaching aimed at improving thinking helps develop 'habits of intelligent behaviour' which include being: '*curious* (asking deep and interesting questions); *collaborative* (through engaging in discussion); *critical* (through giving reasons and evidence); *creative* (through generating and building on ideas); and *caring* (through developing awareness of self and care of others)' (pp 33–4). These 'habits', he says, can contribute to the development of a thoughtful and deliberative citizenry. Fisher was building on the work of Matthew Lipman (1977) who set up the Philosophy for Children movement. And, as we said already, Paulo Freire saw critical literacy as a means for students and their teachers to learn to 'read the world'.

Critical thinking, then, would seem to be an essential component for promoting active citizenry and a well-functioning democracy.

Critical thinking and democracy

These are not new ideas: they are as old, or older, than Socrates. In Roche (2007) I referred to how, in the last century, Russell (1932) explains how there is often 'too great a love for conformity both in the herd and in the bureaucrat' (p 144). Russell saw these two factors as grounds for 'the harm that is done to education by politics' (ibid.). Like Russell I believe that it is better to produce free-thinking individuals than conformist citizens. Having engaged in dialogic pedagogy for the last two decades, and having been informed by reading critical pedagogy literatures, I now understand education to be a deeply political concept, rather than a neutral enterprise. I now realise that if we could bring about the development of a population of educated, independent thinkers, passionate about having 'a spirit of dialogue' and 'sharing opinions without hostility' in a 'coherent' way (Bohm 1998 pp 6–7) it could have potential significance for the formation of an open and democratic society: '...a genuine culture could arise in which opinions and assumptions are not defended incoherently. And that kind of culture is necessary for the society to work and ultimately for the society to survive' (Bohm op.cit. p 7).

The work of Erich Fromm is relevant to these arguments also. Fromm (1979) worried that people had lost the ability to think for themselves and had become used to collective 'herd' thinking. He argued that people must exercise their freedom in thinking for themselves. When we look at the media-driven society in which we live, we see that children are constantly being bombarded with messages about how to live as part of the socially acceptable herd, what it is to be a girl or a boy, how to be popular, cool, accepted. They are being initiated into 'herd thinking' and 'groupthink' (Janis 1972) at a very early stage. Groupthink is a term used to describe how individuals feel pressured into agreeing with the consensus of a group, often against their own better judgement. The group can then make faulty judgements because of lack of consideration of alternative points of view. I believe that children need to be able to think critically so as to make informed choices about what to believe and what not to believe. They need to be able to think for themselves so as to resist 'herd thinking' and 'groupthink'.

According to Vivian Vasquez (2007) it is very difficult to be a young person today:

> Day in and day out children take in multi-modal bits of information consisting of words and images that sometimes conflict and at other times are complementary.

Often this textual information works to position them in ways that offer up ideals for who they can and cannot be in the world today, who they should and should not be as well as what they should and should not do or think. Given this complex world, we cannot afford for children not to engage in some tough conversations if they are to learn to become critical analysts of the world who are able to make informed decisions as they engage with the world around them.

(p 6)

In a chapter entitled 'The future of critical literacy' Hilary Janks also (2010 pp 203–34) provides a serious overview of the 'on-going socio-historical imperative for critical literacy'. She speaks about how information becomes altered through 'spin' and how necessary critical literacy is: 'in a world of spin critical literacy helps us to understand whose interests are served by the stories we are told and the stories we tell' (p 204). However, she concludes on a hopeful note when she says: 'Critical literacy work in classrooms can be simultaneously serious and playful. We should teach it with a subversive attitude, self-irony and a sense of humour' (p 234).

This last point is really important I believe. We are working with young children: we must choose our texts with care and pose our questions sensitively. We must never destroy their innocence or make them anxious about the world or the future.

What exactly is critical thinking?

Critical thinking means thinking for yourself. It is the opposite of receiving information passively which is, sadly, what happens in a lot in classrooms, especially those premised on a transmission model as we saw earlier. Critical thinking requires effort because it involves active engagement with ideas. It means looking at something from all sides and weighing up the evidence before adopting a particular stance or point of view. It does not mean that you simply reject the thinking of others. Instead, you examine it and come to conclusions as to whether you agree or disagree with their ideas. It means, too, that you are able to provide reasons for your judgements. It can also mean that, for some questions, more than one answer is acceptable; there can be more than one 'right' answer, or maybe no single 'right answer' but, rather, several that can move us towards a more complete answer. This is a very empowering realisation for children, as is the idea that the teacher does not hold all the answers – which is equally liberating for the teacher. And, for teachers, it is important to realise that higher-order and open-ended questions cannot demand a quick answer. We all need time to think and process ideas.

Giving children time to think about a question is hugely important. Teachers who believe in and contribute to a form of 'hurry-along curriculum' (Dadds 2001) deny their pupils the 'luxury' of thinking time. These are teachers who focus on coverage rather than discovery and understanding. Their lessons are predominantly teacher-focused rather than learner-focused. They are often conscientious, dedicated teachers, but they rely on getting the syllabus covered rather than teaching for understanding. Changing from 'teaching for coverage' to 'teaching for understanding' can be done. I did it. It took time and a lot of critical engagement. My experience has been that even small changes in teaching approaches can build up over time to become substantial changes in thinking and in practice.

Reading a picturebook together critically will demand a lot of time for thinking. There are different approaches you could take, and you will need to suit the approach to the age and number of the children and to what you want to happen. First of all the picturebook you choose has to have some relevance for the child's life, because critical literacy begins with exploring issues that prompt children to think and talk about social issues that have meaning for them. One approach would be to read the story aloud during one literacy session. Then children could be given an opportunity to examine the pictures during the next. However, this approach denies children the opportunity to make meaning from the pictures and story simultaneously, which is something that Goodman (1998 cited in Evans 1998 p xi) critiqued: '...teachers are often so overly focused on teaching children to read that they forget that learning is taking in and interpreting the meanings of the whole not just the print in books'.

Another approach might entail arranging for several small groups of children to examine the book together before reading it aloud to the class. Alternatively, if you have a visualiser attached to a whiteboard or to a computer and data projector, you could project the pictures as you read to the class which could enable children to look more closely at details. A parent or a teacher in a one-to-one situation will obviously find this step of 'looking closely' much easier. Teachers might take the picturebook as a unit for a week's work and take time each day to examine the book before holding the discussion on the Friday, for example. You must decide what works best in your particular context. Teachers of single mainstream classes will need to adopt a different approach to teachers in multi-class settings, for example.

Deirdre, a teaching friend, told me how her class of 8- and 9-year-old boys took nearly two weeks to digest Anthony Browne's *The Tunnel* (1992). Deirdre scanned the images and displayed them using the whiteboard as she read the story aloud.

They actually only paid cursory attention to the text. The real engagement for them was studying the illustrations. They spent ages examining each picture, discussing it, going back to check details on previous pictures, explaining to me and to each other what they thought the various elements of the pictures meant. It was a real eye-opener for me. Up to now I always focused almost exclusively on the text and the narrative. You could say that the CT&BT approach has given us permission to linger! (Extract from conversation with DL, 6 July 2013)

Whatever you do, let the children have time to study the illustrations. Let them examine all of the images, including the covers front and back, the endpapers and the introductory pages. It always surprises me that so many people skip over the opening pages in order to 'get on with the story'. Check out videos of picturebooks being read aloud on YouTube for examples of what I mean. Generally, these videos do not show attention being given to the cover or endpapers, or to any of the front matter. The covers and preliminary pages are very important for setting the scene and providing clues and cues as to what the story is about. They have been carefully chosen and considered by the author, the illustrator and the publisher. Referring to this 'peritext' Sipe and McGuire (2006) state that teachers generally only pay cursory attention, if any to it, which they feel is an omission:

In the field of children's publishing, illustrators, authors, editors, and book designers have paid special attention to the ways in which the front and back covers, dust jacket, endpapers, half-title and title pages, and dedication page all work together with the text and accompanying illustrations to produce a unified effect. These features are often referred to as the 'peritext' of the picturebook ...Although all books obviously have some of these features, such as covers and a title page, in picturebooks all peritextual features are especially planned and designed so that there is an aesthetic coherence to the entire book...

(p 291)

An example from practice with preschoolers

When I introduced *Penguin* by Polly Dunbar (2007) to the children in a preschool setting, I began by naming some of these features. Cover, front/back, author, illustrator, blurb, spine, endpapers and dedication were new words for many of the children. I pointed to the 'front cover' and we discussed what we saw, causing huge excitement in 3-year-old Lily who told me gleefully she had that book at home. Lily is a very shy child and rarely spoke out but seeing a familiar book cover gave her the confidence to join in the discussion. She spoke with clarity and projected her voice well, which she hadn't done previously.

Penguin's endpapers, front and back, show lots of little stars but on different coloured backgrounds – pale green at the front and pale blue at the back. When I asked the children why Polly Dunbar might have chosen these as endpapers, Greg told me it could be wrapping paper because his birthday present had been wrapped in starry paper. (He had also possibly seen the small picture of a gift-wrapped carton on the title page.) Emily listened to Greg and added 'I think that stars are very happy things cos so are birthdays'. Paul said 'you get stars for being a good boy and ...that boy in the story is getting something'. Lily (who had the book at home) demonstrated close looking when she pointed out that Ben, the little boy in the story, had green pyjamas with stars on them. Other children looked puzzled by the way the conversation was going but were intrigued. Gradually I introduced some new language. 'Blurb' was a new word that those preschool children loved and later, as they examined a selection of picturebooks, some children pointed to sections of print on the back covers of books enquiring 'What does my blurb say, please?'

'What has this got to do with critical thinking?' you might ask. By suggesting to the children that they might listen to the story and look at the pictures and then decide afterwards if they thought Polly Dunbar's blurb worked well, or if their understandings of the stars on the endpapers were probable, they are being invited into a dialogue. It is open ended and there are several possibilities for being 'right'. When the teacher says 'I wonder *why* Polly Dunbar chose stars for the endpapers', children can offer guesses, opinions and explanations. By the time they discuss the pictures and the story they are already aware that their thoughts and ideas matter. They are also learning that artists and authors and publishers make choices and that everything they see in the book has been deliberately put there by someone.

> Illustrations have a crucial role to play in enabling children to gain meaning from books and, apart from wordless texts, they work in partnership with print in picture books. Alongside the words, illustrations provide a starting point from which the reader gets meaning and to which the reader gives meaning.
>
> (Evans 1998 p xv)

This is a very important lesson and could provide the foundation for critical and visual literacy. By carefully posing open-ended questions, yes and no answers can be avoided, but even where they occur, you can gently nudge the child into providing a reason. This is important especially when children start a discussion with 'I liked the part where' because, by asking them for reasons, they are encouraged to think critically.

The task of making meaning

Each reader brings her/himself to the task of making meaning. Wolfgang Iser, who in the 1970s spoke about the nature of the relationship between readers and texts, highlighted that every text contains 'gaps' that readers must creatively fill for themselves and that, rather than asking what texts *mean,* we should instead ask what texts *do* to readers. Louise Rosenblatt argued in 1938 and again in 1978, that reading entails a transaction between a reader and a text, and that every reader brings a unique viewpoint to a text. While these and other theories of reader response have since been critiqued, it still remains the case that no two readers will form the same impressions of, or make the same associations with, a text or with the illustrations. Nikolajeva and Scott (2006) say:

> If words and images fill each other's gaps wholly, there is nothing left for the reader's imagination, and the reader remains somewhat passive. The same is true if the gaps are identical in words and images (or if there are no gaps at all) …However as soon as words and images provide alternative information or contradict each other in some way, we have a variety of readings and interpretations.
>
> (p 17)

As teachers of literacy, we need to keep this thought to the forefront of our minds and realise that each child will make meaning that is personal to her. By asking open-ended questions teachers can aid children's processes of articulating personal responses to texts.

Critical literacy as a social practice

Jewett and Smith (2003), drawing on Luke and Freebody (1999), argue that 'effective literacy draws on a repertoire of practices that allow learners, as they engage in reading and writing activities, to act as code breakers, meaning makers, text users, and text critics' (p 69). They suggest that the first three of these practices, i.e. code breakers, meaning makers, text users, are adopted in most classrooms. However, the 'text critic' element is not as widespread, they say, especially in elementary classrooms:

> In this domain, learners 'critically analyze and transform texts by acting on knowledge that texts are not ideologically natural or neutral – that they represent particular points of views while silencing others and influence people's ideas'. In other words, the reader learns to look beyond the words on the page and into the province of how the text 'works' – linguistically, politically, culturally, and socially – to position the reader.
>
> (Jewett and Smith op.cit. p 69)

Stephens and Watson (1994) state that reading literature is a socially and culturally constructed event framed by the ideologies of the teacher and the text (p 1). Factors like gender, race and social class help determine the way we read and the meaning we take from texts (p 6), and each reader also experiences 'an individual aesthetic experience that underlies interpretation' (p 8). The 'impact of a reader's imagination on the text's implications produces a significance which is greater than the represented situation might otherwise seem to possess' (p 10) and they encourage teachers to demonstrate 'the active nature of reading' to children (ibid). Leland *et al.* (2013) state that:

> readers who are able to size up the situation and draw their own conclusions become *agents of text* since they retain the power to make their own rational decisions about what to believe. Those who don't engage in critical reading are more likely to become *victims of text* since they tacitly accept assumptions that might not stand up to further scrutiny.
>
> (Leland *et al.* 2013 p 4, emphasis in original)

But children do not become agents of text without a concerted effort on the part of a parent, or caregiver, school staff or teacher. The work of helping children to become 'agents of text', which is one of the underpinning reasons for the CT&BT approach to literacy, rests on several assumptions.

Underpinning values and assumptions

My earlier statement that 'all' that's needed is a good picturebook and some children to discuss it, is actually not completely true. There are some significant assumptions and values underpinning this teaching approach. They are:

- values about 'the other';
- values about knowledge;
- values about professional development or teacher-as-learner.

The first underpinning assumption: to do with recognising the other

The CT&BT teaching approach rests firmly on the assumption that the adult will recognise the child as a real **person** – a real person who is likeable and who deserves respect for their uniqueness – not generally a problem for a parent, but one which may be challenging for teachers. Such a stance is influenced by our ontological values. If we recognise the child as a real person, 'a real and concrete other' (Benhabib 1987), an embodied learner, a unique thinker and knower, in the sense of Buber's (1965) *Ich-du* or *I-Thou* relationship, or Freire's 'humanising pedagogy', then we will likely have no difficulty talking *with* and *to* that child.

The contrary applies also: if we see the child as 'a generalised and abstract other' (Benhabib op. cit.) – in the sense of Buber's (1965) (op. cit.) *I-it* relationship – then we might be tempted to talk *at* and *down to* the child. This kind of language is often seen in curricular documents or policies or lesson plans: 'the pupils will be enabled to…' or 'the pupils will demonstrate that they can…' – which pupil? all? some? or just John or Jane? Griffiths (2003), writing about social justice in education, speaks about the importance of hearing individual voices and 'little stories' which do not reduce all the characters to 'ciphers' – where people are spoken about as 'the PhD candidate' or 'the black schoolgirl' or the 'white teacher' (p 81). Engaging children in dialogue will involve getting to know John and Jane well, as 'particular people in specific contexts' (Griffiths op. cit.). It will involve being interested in them and wanting to hear how they make sense and meaning of the world. It goes without saying that we also, of course, want them to have the richest and most beneficial learning experiences possible while they are in our care.

Even if you find this kind of pedagogical relationship difficult at the beginning, the very process of doing CT&BT discussions allows you to see how individual children think and feel, through listening to their words. I certainly found it to be the case in my own research. In my MA dissertation (Roche 2000) I described how I worked in an all male, inner-city school. When classes were allocated I was dismayed. I resented and actually disliked the class of boys I had been given: I knew they were challenging and difficult. I had begun my MA and I wanted a quiet, biddable group who would make my data gathering easy. However, as I engaged my boisterous group in weekly discussions, I began to see them for the warm, funny, complex and endearing people they were. Here are some examples from my work with them:

- Jack, a silent 7-year-old boy who had never contributed in class, surprised me by calmly distinguishing thinking from dreaming in a discussion when he said '*Well, you can kind of control your thinking. You make your brain work when you think – but dreaming kind of happens by itself. It's still your brain working but its carrying on all by itself when you're having a break*'.
- Don, an 8-year-old boy with educational difficulties, told me that fishes think about lorries, and gave me a very good reason: '*when you be's coming up the North Main Street (where the petshop is) the fish be's looking out the side cos his eyes are at the side and he sees all the lorries, and he be's saying to himself "I wonder what all those big things are"*'. It took a classroom discussion to remind me of how much prior knowledge children have.
- Arty, an 8-year-old boy with behaviour problems, told me that he knew that God was the same size as a giraffe because the church doors were the same as the giraffe house in Fota (a local wildlife park).
- Kevin, a 7 year old, whose mother told me how he applied the discussion skill of turn-taking, using a bar of soap as a 'talking object', at home in the bath with his brother.
- Colm, an 8 year old who, when the Inspector participated in a discussion about aliens, earnestly and respectfully said '*I disagree with the eh…Customer… the first time you said there was no such thing as aliens and then next time round you said maybe all the aliens aren't bad…like…which is it?*'
- Or James who '*disagreed with that whole story*' (Adam and Eve) because '*Miss, snakes don't talk – they only goes "Sssss"*'.

I could provide countless examples of times when my pupils became 'real people' to me as they articulated their thoughts. It is significant and salutary to note that, were it not for the fact that I needed data for my MA, I probably wouldn't have persevered with the discussions because it took quite a long time to get the class used to the habits of courteous interaction. Just look at what I would have missed had I given up.

Teachers who have engaged wholeheartedly in the CT&BT process refer to the way in which this educational approach had a significant effect on the classroom dynamic. All refer to the way it enabled them to see their children differently.

- *I didn't want to teach this class of 11 and 12 year old girls. I had seen them come up through the school and heard the staffroom talk and frankly, they were a nightmare class. And so I took them on resentfully. Then I was introduced to CT&BT by Mary and tried it out with the class and without my even realising it things changed.* (EM a teacher of 10 years' experience)
- *This version of classroom discussion has had a significant and positive effect on the dynamics in my classroom. It fostered a warm, respectful and supportive relationship between the children and each other and the children and me. I have used this format of classroom discussion ever since. I have found it to be an enriching and empowering way of **being** with my pupils and only wish that I had known of it much earlier in my teaching career.* (Excerpt from written evaluation MO'S, a teacher of over 30 years' experience; emphasis in original) (See also Roche 2007 Appendix B2)

A second underpinning assumption: to do with knowledge

Another of the assumptions I spoke about earlier, is related to classroom culture and atmosphere. It involves recognising the child as a **knower** who has thoughts and ideas worth listening to – an epistemological stance. If we see knowledge as a commodity or a product, something 'out there', abstracted from a knower, a reified package that can be transmitted or delivered from a knowing expert to a non-knower – in the sense of Freire's (1972) 'banking model' – then we will be very unlikely to see any value of discussing picturebooks with children as a means of generating knowledge. Such a stance would also mean that we would find it difficult to imagine teachers learning from what their pupils say.

I will describe later on how I read Dosh and Mike Archer's *Yellow Bird, Black Spider* to several different third classes (9–10 year olds) and how each class drew different meanings from the book. (Interestingly, there was always a general acceptance that both bird and spider were male: in itself this gendering of the characters could provide a basis for critical literacy – why do we assume maleness?) In each class, I learned that the bird was right to assert *his* independence. But each class gave different reasons for it. In one class, a child said that she thought that the book was written by the Archers to explain freedom: freedom to be yourself, freedom to decide what to wear and how to live, and freedom to take control. I gained a whole new understanding of the book from listening to these discussions. The discussion about 'different kinds of freedom' that ensued was amazing in its sophistication. Then, just as I was comfortable with the idea of the bird being a symbol of personal freedom and the spider an annoying pedant who tried to make him conform, I was confounded and forced to think again when another child said 'But if the bird has the right to be himself, shouldn't the spider have to right to be himself too? Can't there be two "rights"?'

If we recognise knowledge as a process – an always incomplete, partial, evolving and dynamic process – and socially constructed – then we can engage in discussion as a form of 'problem-posing' (Freire 1972) and see our discussions as a way of becoming 'a community of enquiry'. In my own PhD work (Roche 2007), and drawing again on Fromm's (1979) ideas, I saw that my CT&BT approach was embedded in the idea of 'being' rather than predominately located in an ethic of 'having'. As I developed my teaching approach, I began to realise that I had to develop my own capacity to *be* critical enough so that I encourage others to *be* critical. It was not just about *having* skills – despite my earlier assertions about learning by doing. This kind of work embraces knowledge, skills and dispositions – the cognitive and the affective domains. It encompasses the idea of working together to construct knowledge and make meaning together. And each group of children brought their own particular ways of knowing to the process.

As I developed my ideas with the children I taught, I tried to embody my values about the pedagogical relationship as 'us and we', thinking together as a community of enquiry through dialogue. The notion of community of enquiry is used in Lipman's Philosophy for Children movement and originates in the work of C.S. Peirce (1955). The concept is located in the idea that people are participants, not spectators in knowledge making and was a core concept of Dewey's educational work. Dewey, who in his old age met Lipman, believed in cooperative intelligence through problem solving (1934). Throughout his work, Dewey argued for schools to become democratic and participatory communities, wherein all members could learn and develop. Those who engage in this kind of work quickly see that thinking together in a community of enquiry can become an exercise of freedom where each person's ideas are listened to and responded to with respect.

A third underpinning assumption: to do with professional development

The notion of teacher-as-learner was referred to earlier. If you decide to try the CT&BT approach, you will need to become au fait with a wide range of picturebooks and be able to choose them with some discretion – especially if you are a teacher with limited funds. You will need to read and re-read the books yourself several times before introducing it to your class. Serafini (2012) emphasises this strongly when he says:

> In addition to the knowledge necessary to support sophisticated discussion of picture books, teachers need to be able to organize effective learning experiences, foster a sense of community, facilitate discussions, structure curriculum into coherent units of study, and draw upon effective instructional practices to extend students' exposure and exploration of the texts and images they encounter. It is the blend of one's pedagogical knowledge with a deeper understanding of the textual and visual elements of children's literature itself that will truly enhance our discussions of these texts.
>
> (p 459)

In other words you don't just bring along a book, read it aloud and let the children have a chat. You will need to examine the pictures, doing what Doonan (1992) calls 'close looking', rather than merely skimming over the pictures so as to 'get on with the text and the story'. You could also engage in some professional reading – there is a huge range of literature about picturebooks and I will include some of those that I found most helpful at the end of Chapter 5.

You will need to THINK too. And this last is very important, as well as being very hard work. You cannot encourage critical thinking in children unless you can think critically yourself. However, you need to be keenly aware that by pre-reading the book and studying the pictures you will form *your* ideas about the book. It is really, really difficult to refrain from imposing these ideas on the children. You must guide and facilitate, not dominate.

You will also need to develop the skill of listening attentively, which is again, premised on the values and assumptions outlined above. If, like me, you are an inveterate talker, then that skill of staying quiet so as to really *hear* a child will demand effort too. This was something I struggled with for many years. Even when I thought I was being attentive to children, video evidence showed me that I was a complete 'living contradiction' (Whitehead 1989). My colleague, Karen, who is a teacher and a literacy expert, confided to me recently during a workshop on CT&BT, that she had to try very hard not to speak so as to allow children time to expand on their thoughts in a discussion about *Yellow Bird, Black Spider*. Other teachers agree:

- *When reflecting on my own practice around book talk, I realised that in the past I've done way too much of the talking. CT&BT has taught me to shut up and let the children really talk and it's wonderful!* (Email from KW, 12 May 2013)
- *It was so difficult! I began to realise how I stay in teacher-as-teller mode even during readalouds. I wanted the children to reach the same conclusions as I had. I struggled not to interrupt with a 'Yes, but..' statement. This methodology is great for making me aware of the power difference in my class and the urge I seem to have for control and that's no harm at all!* (Conversation with EM, 27 May 2013)
- *They just weren't getting it. I really wanted them to see the point of the story and we were nearly at the end and I found myself forcing my ideas on them and saying things like 'Look. This is what's going on...' and I realised that I have probably been doing that a LOT.* (Conversation with CL, 27 May 2013)
- *I have found the CT&BT to be an approach that provides the optimal learning environment in which to explore literature with children. Its strength lies in its simplicity, but equally its capacity to facilitate profound, enjoyable and meaningful discussion around books. Moreover, it re-creates what those of us who enjoy talking about books actually do — we read without interruption and then reflect upon and question those elements that captured our interest and imagination. When we do this in the company of others, we are exposed to other ways of seeing and knowing, we listen and expand upon our existing knowledge and understanding. As someone who loves to read and talk about books, I thought that I had always strived to do this in my classroom, but having implemented the CT&BT approach I realise now that I wasn't always doing that. I recognise now that I was doing most of the talking and questioning! In contrast, the CT&BT approach prioritises the children's talk, reflections and questioning and the democratic exchange of perspectives and views in a context that respects and positively challenges diversity in opinion. CT&BT has taught me to be quiet and to actually listen to my pupils. Consequentially, I find that I am facilitating critical inquiry, talk and discussion that is more substantial and worthwhile than I could have ever imagined.* (Written evaluation from KW, June 2013)

Invitation not coercion

It is difficult not to coerce children into your way of thinking but such coercion can be resisted. By having a set of procedures planned for the CT&BT sessions, and a shared set of ground rules negotiated democratically, to which teacher and children alike must adhere, you will find that becoming a participant in the discussion rather than dominating it, will gradually become easier. For example, I felt really proud one day, when Alberto, a Spanish student who was on work experience in my class, wrote:

> I think that although the children had all the discussion responsibility, the teacher also had a very responsible role ...the teacher had to listen carefully without speaking for a very long time. This is a difficult skill for a teacher to learn, because normally the teacher is the one who does most of the talking in the classroom.
>
> (Roche 2007, Appendix H6)

Bear in mind, however, that this comment was made in 2004 and I had been teaching since 1973. It took me a long time to learn to sit back and let go of the urge to control. This does not entail a loss of power: it is a different use of power in the classroom. Ciara (aged 9) has recognised the inherent difficulty this presents for dominant children and teachers alike:

> ...[CT&BT] is really good for us. Sometimes it's a bit of a challenge, because there could be yappers in our class and they have to be quiet and think as well. But it's also good for the teachers because they sit down and listen to what the kids have to say.

Examining the relationships among language use, social practice and power

'What methods help develop students as critically thinking citizens who use language to question knowledge, experience, and power in society?' (Shor 1999 p 5 in Shor and Pari 1999).

Critical literacy involves examining the 'relationships among language use, social practice and power' (Stevens and Bean 2007 p vii). Picturebooks provide a perfect means for engaging children in dialogue and critical thinking while also fulfilling aspects of your language and literacy programme. Critical literacy also involves seeking out and examining the overt and covert ideology that each book contains. McLaren (2002) defines ideology as 'a way of viewing the world, a complex of ideas, and various types of social practices, rituals, and representations *that we tend to accept as natural and as common sense*' (p 205 italics in original).

As we are beginning to see, children who are exposed to the CT&BT approach are positioned as people who are meaning makers and knowers, capable of forming opinions and articulating them. They are being encouraged to think critically, to listen and evaluate the responses of others and to engage in co-constructing knowledge with their peers. There is an emphasis on respect, courtesy and care. The children are being encouraged to develop their tolerance, understanding and empathy towards others. The requirements for this work are a 'good' picturebook and at least 45 minutes, but this approach also demands a certain kind of teacher who is intellectually curious, and active in her learning.

Let's not forget pleasure

Then there is the very important area of pleasure. Picturebooks are immensely aesthetic objects. Listening to a story being read aloud, and being given time to examine the pictures, are both very pleasurable activities. Sharing in talk about a story and co-constructing knowledge together is also very pleasurable. For example, 12-year-old children – about to leave the primary school where I worked – were invited to present a display of memories of primary school. Most of the graduating group chose their Critical Thinking and Book Talk sessions as one of the highlights of their primary school life.

> The best picturebook authors/illustrators are in tune with human needs and desires…
> [they] illuminate places within the reader's experiences and cast light in those shadowy corners that lurk alongside the pathways to new understandings. The new understanding can be self-understanding or a greater awareness of one's place in the world. Young and older children … deserve the time to ponder and the opportunity to discover forms of representation and inquiry that will develop their capacity for poetic searching. … Contemporary picturebooks are filled with new forms, images, and intersections, and are vital spaces for collaborative imagination and inquiry…
> (Wolfenbarger and Sipe 2007 pp 279–80)

Although I am now working in a teacher education college, preparing students to be secondary teachers, I spent most of my career in primary education. I also worked in primary teacher education and on postgraduate programmes. During my career as a primary teacher I taught in several different kinds of primary schools: disadvantaged inner-city schools, single-sex schools and mainstream schools. I taught Infants for many years, and for many of those years I felt that education wasn't quite doing justice to how children learn. I was conscious that children needed more opportunities to think for themselves and to talk. As we are all well aware, small children are intensely intellectually curious and active in their learning, but many children seem to lose this quality as they progress through school. CT&BT is an approach that seeks to interrupt that trend. Along with encouraging children to dialogue and interact and think together, there are many other cognitive and affective benefits that derive from this kind of approach, and we will talk about these benefits a little later.

Summary

Literacy involves using and understanding spoken, written and digital language. Visual literacy involves the ability to deconstruct, interpret and analyse images. Children must be taught to make meaning not only of written words but also of multimedia and complex visual imagery. Critical thinking, at its simplest, is the act of actively thinking for oneself rather than passively receiving the ideas and thoughts of others. Throughout the rest of this book readers will be given an overview of many different models for developing critical thinking in children. They will begin exploring the huge potential of using picturebooks as a tool for literacy and critical literacy development at all levels of the school system.

Recommended reading

Cowhey, M. (2006) *Black Ants and Buddhists: thinking critically and teaching differently in the primary grades.* Portland, Maine: Stenhouse Publishers.

Marcus, L.S. (ed.) (2012) *Show Me a Story! Why Picture Books Matter: conversations with 21 of the world's most celebrated illustrators.* Somerville, MA: Candlewick Press.

Paul, L. (1998) *Reading Otherways.* Stroud, Glos: Thimble Press.

Vasquez, V. (2010) *Getting Beyond 'I like the book': creating space for critical literacy in K-6 classrooms.* Newark, DE. International Reading Association.

Chapter 2

Comprehension and meaning making

Different perspectives on literacy

There are several different lenses through which literacy may be viewed. Hall (2003) organises these lenses or theoretical underpinnings into four main groups: psycho-linguistic (reading as a problem-solving activity); cognitive-psychological (words matter); socio-cultural (reading and communities of practice); and socio-political (reading the word and the world). Jerome Harste (in Lewison *et al.* 2011 pp 104–7) lists the different perspectives as: linguistic, psycholinguistic, cognitive, reader response, sociolinguistic and critical. He issues some caveats about favouring any one approach over another and one such caveat is that we must ask ourselves 'Why do I hold this belief?' (See also Harste 2006.)

In light of Harste's caveat then, I will make my stance clear: in relation to teaching reading and writing, I take a multiple perspective approach. I appreciate the linguistic, cognitive and psycholinguistic approaches. I have used them in my teaching. But in read-ing picturebooks aloud and inviting discussion, I locate my values-base in the critical domain – in perspectives to do with the socio-cultural and socio-political. I ask questions like 'Why educate? What's education *for*?' and 'Why teach people to be literate? What's literacy *for*?' and when I pare back my values to the essence, my answers have something to do with 'living a fulfilling life in a just world'. Other approaches appear to be more neutral. Yet, unpacked, they have strong value-bases too – be they pragmatic or func-tional or political. Keep these ideas in the background as you read on.

Keep in mind also that, as well as identifying where I locate myself in the many com-peting discourses around literacy, when I read a picturebook aloud to a class and then invite them to discuss it, I am drawing on several different kinds of knowledge, skills and values – both my own and the children's. One of these sets of skills is to do with com-prehension and meaning-making.

Comprehension

Courtney and Gleeson (2009 p 5) define comprehension as intentional thinking during which meaning is constructed through interactions between reader and text. Courtney and Gleeson (op. cit.) focus on 'transaction' as a key aspect of reading comprehension: the transaction between the reader and the text.

The Rand Reading Study Group, led by Catherine Snow, (2002) state in the introduction to their report that their thinking about reading comprehension was informed by 'a vision of proficient readers who are capable of acquiring new knowledge and understanding new concepts, are capable of applying textual information appropriately, and are capable of being engaged in the reading process and reflecting on what is being read' (RRSG 2002 pxiii).

Comprehension is one of the pillars of literacy instruction. Without comprehension children who can decode or 'look at and say' words may be merely 'barking at print' (Rose 2006), without demonstrating very much understanding of what they are reading. Goodman (1980) explained this when he used his 'Barpie was proving his kump' argument. A child could answer the following questions: Who was proving his kump? What was Barpie proving? What was Barpie doing? etc. If the child answered correctly we could assume that the child has mastered skills of comprehension even though the sentence itself was nonsense. But do the child's answers show meaning-making? Not unless the child said: 'This is rubbish! It doesn't mean anything!' Others have used Lear's *Jabberwocky* to make the same argument. I remember a colleague describing to me some years ago, a discussion she'd had with her 11-year-old daughter, of a dramatisation of Roald Dahl's *James and the Giant Peach* that they had both just attended. Her daughter had read the book three years earlier but could not recall reading about any of the events that they had just seen dramatised. My colleague said 'I realised then that she had read the words in the book. She probably even understood most of the words she was reading. But she hadn't grasped the story or the meaning'. In other words, her daughter could have most likely told you 'what Barpie was doing'.

Like my colleague's child, some children may be able to decode or 'sound out' individual words and read each word in a text but have no idea what the text is about. Other children may be able to make use of the context to help them read words that are new or unfamiliar and we can see that they are trying to make sense of the text. When we say that a child 'is reading' we take it that the child understands what they are reading, can make meaning from it that is relevant, and that connects in some way with something the child already knows, and that it adds to their understanding of the world. We expect that the child could tell us about what they have read, explain their understanding of it and speculate about it. We will hope that the child may even be able to critique what they have read. But we go beyond what the RRSG (2002) outlined above, when we realise that, in participating in classroom discussion about a text, the child is also learning social skills and ways of sharing her thoughts and ideas with courtesy and consideration. She is learning about democracy and fairness through democratic ways of being in her classroom; she is creating and co-creating knowledge and is learning more about her peers' personalities and her teacher, through hearing what they say. She is engaging in what O'Donohue (2003) and Farren (2006) and Glenn (2006) call 'a web of betweenness'. She is participating sharing in meaning-making, in a 'spirit of dialogue' – 'a stream of meaning flowing among and through us and between us' (Bohm 1998 p 2).

> The picture or image that this derivation suggests is of a stream of meaning flowing among and through us and between us. This will make possible a flow of meaning in the whole group, out of which will emerge new understanding. It's something new, which may or may not have been the starting point at all. It's something creative. And this shared meaning is the 'glue' or 'cement' that holds people and societies together.
>
> (Ibid.)

Noddings (2002, 2006) argues the case for educating students to think critically about what is involved in living an ordinary life, creating a home, learning how to learn, and learning how to be happy. She emphasises (2006) that students should be provided with opportunities to ask critical questions concerning their own lives:

> The neglect of topics that call forth critical and reflective thinking pervades our system of education ... why do we not teach critical lessons ...? One answer to this question is ignorance. People who never explored these topics are unlikely to provide opportunities for others to do so: the notion never arises.
>
> (pp 2–3)

Comprehension is necessary then for meaning-making and for critical thinking. It is essential that children are able to comprehend what they are hearing, seeing, and reading so that they can critique. My worry is that, as teachers faithfully and industriously try to teach the skills of reading comprehension, they lose sight of *why* we need to be able to understand what we reading. If you ask teachers 'why teach comprehension' you may hear answers like: 'so the children will know what the text is about' or 'so they can understand the text' or 'so they can answer questions about the text'. Rarely will anyone say 'so they can question the assumptions made in the text; so they can challenge the ideology inherent in the text; so they can live an examined life; so they can have agency; so they can ask what Brookfield (2012 p 9) calls "the big questions of life"'.

These aspects of the transaction or interaction between reader and text are not often discussed when the teaching of discrete comprehension skills are considered. As we saw earlier, these aspects are, as Haynes (2002) said, located in critical theory and draw on socio-cultural and socio-political approaches. In a CT&BT session children are listening actively to the story, thinking actively and critically and creatively about it, discussing the text, explaining their points of view, listening to others, learning what others think, all of which adds to a sense of understanding and meaning-making.

The affective domain is a key aspect of all pedagogy but especially when we are seeking to engage children critically with literature. Mem Fox, says that, when doing literacy research we may need 'to readjust slightly the direction of our questioning, from cognitive to affective, away from the over-researched brain towards the unattended heart' (http://www.memfox.com). I believe that the success of any pedagogical approach lies in the relationship a teacher or caregiver has with her children. With the guidance and facilitation of a thoughtful teacher, who is passionate about reading and passionate about wanting her pupils to be able to think for themselves, children can easily begin the process of critical engagement. From my experiences in the classroom I saw that this kind of critical engagement can range from:

• 4 year olds being engaged with why Humpty was up on the wall in the first place; or explaining to each other why the Little Red Hen's friends failed to help her; or exploring together if Jack of beanstalk fame could be called a hero (Shermis 1999, Roche 2007);
• to an 8 year old wondering why (and then providing a very good reason why) the queen needed to choose a wife for her son in the Princess and the Pea story;

- to 7 year olds wondering why princes usually rescued princesses and not vice versa; and debating whether the prince would have danced with Cinderella had she been wearing her kitchen clothes;
- to a 9-year-old boy wondering whether McDonald's had links with Disney because 'the merchandise of the latest film usually ends up in Happy Meals' (Roche 2007);
- to 10 year olds asking 'what is freedom?' or questioning the 'woolly thinking' in some of their geography, history and RE texts;
- to 12 year olds unpacking the misogyny and fundamentalism in Van Allsburg's *The Widow's Broom* (see Roche 2007);
- to a first year undergraduate asking if the assumptions about traditional versus creative teaching constituted overt or covert ideology in McNaughton and Kitamura's *Once Upon an Ordinary School Day* (Roche 2013);
- to an experienced teacher marvelling at, and trying to unravel the complexity of Barbelet and Tanner's *The Wolf*.

The discussions from which these extracts are selected (and which we will revisit throughout this book) all involved oral language. Like Snow (2013), Wells (1986) and many others who have researched this field, I believe that oral language is developed and consolidated through discussions. However, oral language is not being taught in CT&BT discussions as a discrete set of skills. Comprehension is evident in the excerpts, and I believe that the excerpts also demonstrate that, in order to engage in such discussions, children also need interpersonal and intrapersonal knowledge, social and emotional intelligence and critical thinking, yet, in CT&BT discussions, we will not itemise any of these as discrete sets of skills to be taught or measured. I am not suggesting that the teaching of discrete skills should be ignored. I would advise, however, that such direct teaching would be separate from CT&BT discussions which should flow organically and naturally.

Now let's explore comprehension and meaning-making some more, because both are core to discussing picturebooks.

Comprehension and making meaning

Does 'comprehension' differ from 'making meaning'? I believe it does. I believe that comprehension is an essential *aspect* of meaning-making. Questions matter: questions asked by the teacher and questions asked by children. In an interview (August 1998), Catherine Snow said:

> The kinds of questions we ask make a big difference in terms of the language opportunities we offer children. For example, if you read a book and then ask children questions such as 'What is this?' or 'Where did he go?' you're asking for specific, closed answers. On the other hand, if you ask questions such as 'What do you think is going to happen next?' or 'What do you like best about the book?' then you're asking for what we term non-immediate talk inspired, but not totally determined, by the book. In the context of daily life, questions that ask children how or why clearly help them think about using language in ways they never would if they're asked only questions that require predetermined answers.
>
> (np)

A large body of literature about reading exists that lists 'the skills of comprehension'. You have probably seen any amount of workbooks that provide examples of, and tests in, inference, prediction, making connections, etc. Guppy and Hughes (1999), cited in Browne (2009 p 34), identified three levels of comprehension that are needed: *reading the lines, reading between the lines and reading beyond the lines*. However, the skills of comprehension in workbooks are often decontextualised and taught explicitly using excerpts of text from existing books or specially made up texts, or even using picturebooks (a search on the internet provides lots of examples of Lesson Plans based on picturebooks). And, because we live and work in a 'culture of performativity' (Ball 2003) and 'audit culture' (Shore and Wright 1999), it is considered necessary that the comprehension skills can be itemised so as to be considered to be teachable and measurable. I am not in any way trivialising such skills, because they are essential skills. I would be very supportive of the idea of teaching the skills and knowledge of reading comprehension such as is outlined in Courtney and Gleeson (2012). But more than extracting the literal meaning of a text is needed for meaning-making. As well as, not *instead of*, teaching knowledge and skills, we are trying to develop habits of mind and attitudes/values/dispositions. These are complex and abstract and personal and unique to each knower, and very difficult to define or itemise as box-tickable 'learning outcomes'. Hoffman (2010 p 11) explains this well when she talks about 'constrained and unconstrained skills'.

According to Hoffman (ibid.), constrained skills involve measurable skills that 'develop in a relatively short period of time because there is a concrete limit to the understanding needed for mastery'. Unconstrained skills, she says, 'continue to develop over the life span because there is no limit to the understandings encompassed by these skills'. Meaning-making belongs in this latter category, as does oral language development. 'Unconstrained skill instruction is embedded in authentic language and literacy practices' she says and 'we do not have a reliable method for measuring unconstrained skills. It is difficult and messy, and close examination of the issue calls into question the practical validity of existing measures' (p 12).

Hoffman (p 13) argues that, because unconstrained skills are inherently much more complex to teach, learn and assess, many researchers argue that it is precisely these types of skills that are just as, if not more, central to later literacy outcomes. You can see why templates just cannot be applied to unconstrained skills. Parents must be aware that they begin at birth: teachers and school staffs need to be mindful that work on these unconstrained skills must begin the day children enter the school and continue until the day they leave and then they must be taken up again in the next level of education. I believe that unconstrained skills are limitless and that I am still developing mine. What we can take from all this is that as well as the teaching of discrete skills of vocabulary building and extending, and the direct teaching of specific comprehension skills, we must *also* create lessons that involve authentic and holistic language – and literacy practices in which meaning-making and learning are integrated into real language and literacy practice. And the values, dispositions and attitudes that are part and parcel of such teaching may never be measured, yet may have an educative influence in lives long after the teacher's name and the texts are forgotten. Perhaps the saying 'what can be measured is what becomes valuable' means then, that these less assessable qualities of critically discussing texts with children quickly become 'devalued' in classrooms where efforts are concentrated on raising 'test scores'. In a later paper Hoffman (2011) says:

In addition, if the ultimate purpose of language and literacy development is to promote meaningful interactions among people, then such development requires not just discrete skills that can be mastered in a short period of time, but also learning that integrates a complex set of skills focused on meaning making that develops over the life span.

(p 13)

Decontextualising reading comprehension skills, then, is a risky business. Luke (1991) suggests that some of the problems that teachers and their pupils encounter are 'the result of the technologies we have made, of the social practices we have prescribed' (p 141). A common tendency that, Luke argues, is encouraged by teacher training institutions, is to attribute classroom problems to 'the failure of method'. Luke suggests that it may be the case, ironically, that some students' problems are the result of *successful* instruction; that as teachers we induce and cultivate particular social practices, and then complain when pupils don't demonstrate other kinds of social practices, or else that they uncritically or inappropriately repeat those emphasised. He goes on to give the following example:

> ...lack of comprehension of text meaning at the upper primary and secondary level may be induced by an overemphasis on lower order reading 'skills.' Or perhaps students' inability to read and write expository prose in secondary schools is induced by, inter alia, the near exclusive emphasis in literacy teaching on the non-critical reading of narrative (e.g., recall) and the writing of narrative. Or perhaps graduates often have trouble criticizing or contesting a distorted or biased text because of years of learning to be acquiescent to the text and to teachers' readings of texts.

(Ibid.)

Let's look again at definitions of reading comprehension. The RRSG (2002 p xiii and p 11) define it as: 'the process of simultaneously extracting and constructing meaning through interaction and involvement with written language'. The report documents a large range of factors that influence and impact on how reading comprehension is taught/learned. As well as all the other civil, social and emotional aspects outlined earlier, also missing from the report, in my opinion, is any discussion about how the *passion* of an enthusiastic and committed teacher can have a positive educative influence in the engagement of a group of learners. Teachers are mentioned, but not their passion and enthusiasm for critical thinking and their love of reading, unless it is included in the 'panoply of practices' mentioned below:

> Most people do not realize how complex teaching is. Effective teachers do more than teach specific strategies or make available to students a wide variety of texts. Indeed, effective teachers of reading engage in a diverse array of instructional practices (NRP, 2000; Pressley et al., 2001; Taylor, Pearson, Clark, & Walpole, 1999). This panoply of practices results in a complex environment in which comprehension can be fostered.

(RRSG 2002 p 42)

People who inspire readers and influence them to love reading – people like Donalyn Miller, author of *The Book Whisperer,* are often recognised for awards such as 'teacher of the year'. Miller's passion for reading and books is evident on every page of her book. I am certain this passion and enthusiasm influences her children far more than the books she recommends to them. Yet when research on literacy is cited as 'evidence-based', the stories of people like Donalyn rarely feature. Following his address to a Reading Conference by an eminent US-based researcher whose work has huge influence, I challenged the absence of references to teachers' subject knowledge and teachers' love of, and passion for, reading. I was told that such research belongs to the field of sociology or anthropology but not to literacy. It would appear that despite Harste's (2006) caveats, referred to earlier, certain 'theoretical underpinnings/perspectives/hypotheses' really do dominate. Dombey (2009) would appear to agree:

> Government bodies tend to place most value on quantitative research – experiments and surveys yielding apparently clear cut numerical data. But capturing learning in classrooms is a complex task, and very many educators see that, although experiments and surveys have much to tell us and are invaluable to certain kinds of decision-making, to do justice to the complex process of education often requires a qualitative approach.
>
> (p 1)

In the same document Dombey (op.cit. p 23) states that effective teachers of literacy need to be readers themselves; they need to have developed a coherent philosophy towards literacy, involving substantial attention to meaning; and they need to demonstrate that language and literacy are interesting, pleasurable and purposeful, adding that engagement is crucial to effective literacy learning.

What's the point of discussing picturebooks?

I would argue that what we are seeking to achieve when we introduce children to carefully selected picturebooks that do not yield up their meaning or their secrets too easily, has to do with 'promoting meaningful interactions among people' (Hoffman 2010 p 13) and 'learning to be curious, skeptical, engaged, and non-complacent' (Luke 1991 p 143). When a child is listening to a story being read and, when she has the luxury of having time to dwell on the pictures and talk about them, and has time to discuss the book and to co-construct knowledge with peers in a safe and interactive social setting, a whole new sense of making meaning comes into being. Let's look briefly at visual literacy and critical literacy.

Visual literacy

First of all we will take as an example some discussions based on the book: *Once Upon an Ordinary School Day* by Colin McNaughton and Satoshi Kitamura (2004) which, during the years 2004–8, I introduced to several whole class groups of 8 and 9 year olds. These were children who had been discussing picturebooks since they were in Junior Infant class (Reception class). They understood the conventions of courteous discussion and had no inhibitions about articulating their ideas and asking for clarification, or agreeing or disagreeing with each other and with me.

Endpapers (3rd class 2007)

Initially the children were shown both sets of endpapers and asked what they might be able to learn from them. The front endpapers show a pattern of white birds standing on a greyish background. The 'ordinary schoolboy' is shown wearing striped pyjamas, seated or crouching with his knees drawn up and exuding, thanks to Kitamura's genius as an illustrator, a downbeat demeanour. The back endpapers show a bright blue sky with a pattern of white birds flying with wings outstretched, and, arms outstretched, soaring happily among them is our pyjama clad 'ordinary schoolboy'.

I asked the children to look carefully at both sets of endpapers and then asked them to predict what the book might be about.

- *Andrew: That first one reminds me of ...what do you call it... the book about the boy and the concentration camp? (Interruptions: Oh yeah The Boy in the Striped Pyjamas!) so I think the book is about a boy who was in prison and who escaped some way, maybe by flying.*
- *Geraldine: I think it's going to be about something like a boy going from a sad time to a happy time.*
- *Rory: I think it could be about freedom – like the Yellow Bird book - cos I think, Teacher, that you like books like that. (Mmms of assent could be heard)*
- *Beth: the end bit makes me think it could be about learning to fly. And maybe at the start he's sad and lonely and the birds cheer him up.*

Many of the other children agreed broadly with these responses (and it is worth noting how Rory has observed that I seemed to have a particular taste in picturebooks). At this point I hadn't yet displayed the cover.

The children were then shown the cover of the book which was displayed on the whiteboard. Lauren immediately said 'Oh. Its Satoshi – this'll be good'. The children had already discussed *Angry Arthur* and *Lily Takes a Walk*, and were familiar with and liked Kitamura's work. They also knew that Kitamura, like all good picturebook artists, would have carefully constructed the picture and that nothing was in there by accident. I asked the children to discuss the cover of the book in pairs.

For about five minutes I walked around and joined in with some pairs as they noted different aspects of the illustration. Jamie and Sam argued about the plant.

- *It's probably for school. He's bringing it into school. Could be a project or something or the nature table.*
- *I dunno, it mightn't ... it's there for a reason. And there's probably a watering can in the school. So why would he need to bring the watering can?*

Lauren and Jane were carefully examining the 'ordinary' schoolboy. They were convinced he was either going to or coming from school but which was it?

- *Look at his mouth. He's definitely going to school and he doesn't like it.*
- *Yeah, well I dunno...he could be coming home as well after a bad day! He looks like he's got a shock.*

Alfie and Evan were scrutinising the setting.

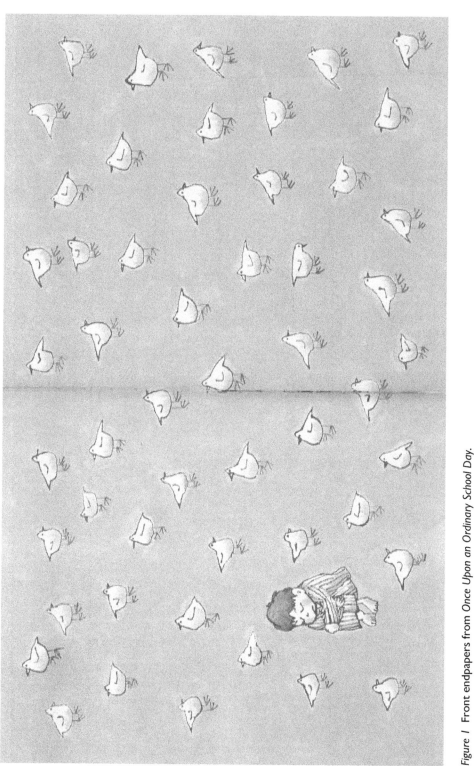

Figure I Front endpapers from *Once Upon an Ordinary School Day.*

Figure 2 Back endpapers from *Once Upon an Ordinary School Day.*

Figure 3 Front cover of *Once Upon an Ordinary School Day.*

- *There's a lot of buildings and a lot of people and a lot of bare ground and hardly any green trees so his school is in a town.*
- *Yeah and it's not a very nice place to live I'd say.*

Evie and Amy decided he was actually in a schoolyard rather than on the way to or from school.

- *No. It's the yard, he's in the yard they're the other kids and he's kind of alone.*
- *Yeah it's a yard cos it's so bare.*

Most pairs had commented on the cat – 'Satoshi loves cats!' – but after the five minutes were up and we got together for the plenary, Alison said '*I wonder why did he draw the cat facing backwards?*' Several explanations were offered:

- *He's looking at all the people in the background and maybe Satoshi wants us to look at them too.*
- *He's bored.*
- *Cats hardly ever look at you. My cat ignores us.*
- *Maybe he followed the boy and now he's looking back to check the way home.*
- *We'll need to see more of the story before we know for sure.*

I decided to probe a little and asked what might a cat symbolise (I was hoping someone would say 'curiosity' but no one did). They said that the boy might have a pet cat and maybe he followed the boy out of the house and maybe that's why the boy was worried-looking. Others speculated that perhaps it was just a stray cat.

Then I asked about the boy's expression. How might our feelings about the book change if the boy were smiling. (I drew a smile on his face with a whiteboard marker.)

- *Oh! Yes, it really would change your feelings. You'd be expecting a much different story!*
- *Yeah, I agree. It would make you imagine that he loves school.*
- *It makes me feel like this could be a bit of swindle, like he's saying 'Hey kids. School is FUN'.*
- *Yeah, that smile completely changes the book now.*

Here the children were beginning to realise that author and illustrator combine to pass on messages about something; that illustrations tweak our 'feelings'; that we can be manipulated by images and words. Later they examined 'smiles' and mouths in other Kitamura books – *Angry Arthur; Lily Takes a Walk; Sheep in Wolves' Clothing*; and *Comic Adventures of Boots*. The discussion ranged widely about how artists like Kitamura can depict feelings and emotions in characters and how, in turn, our feelings about the characters can be manipulated.

In all of these discussions there was real engagement, lots of argument and good-humoured disagreement and the children were eager to get into the story.

So what was going on during the 10–12 minute session (5 working in pairs and 7 in plenary) based just on the picturebook cover alone? Think about what the children did. They thought individually and in pairs. They thought for themselves and they scaffolded each other's thinking. They accepted that there could be more than one correct meaning. They looked at the picture but also at the symbolism of different elements of it and tried to figure out what 'Satoshi' intended them to think and feel. They were beginning the process of challenging normal interpretations of 'reality' and seeing if they could find alternatives. But they accepted that they needed to 'see more of the story' in order to understand that cover illustration. They were working together – involved in what Luke (1991) calls 'a social practice'. For Luke, 'literacy is not just a set of decontextualized skills, but is a demonstrably significant cultural practice. That is, it is about something, something valued by the community and culture, something vital for its participants…' (p 139). He goes on 'try as we might to avoid it, [literacy] historically has been tied to the constitution of ideology, of beliefs, of subjectivities'. This brings us on to a brief examination of ideology.

Ideology

Hollindale (2011) begins his essay on ideology by saying

> … there is no such thing as a simple story, or a simple reader or watcher or listener. Every story we hear, by whatever means, is full of hidden signals, transmitted consciously or unconsciously by the storyteller, whether the teller is Jesus of Nazareth narrating a parable or a neighbour gossiping in the street. Stories are full of values, beliefs and attitudes, whether knowingly or not. And so are we as readers and listeners, even as young children, because we are constantly forming our own values, beliefs and attitudes from our own life experience, and our response to stories is affected and conditioned by them whether or not we realise it.
>
> (p 9)

Bruner (2002) states that 'Stories are surely not innocent: they always have a message, most often so well concealed that even the teller knows not what ax he may be grinding' (p 5). Luke (1991) argues that teaching literacy is likewise an ideological-laden activity.

Stephens and Watson (1994) state that 'societies, or groups within societies, share bundles of ideas or assumptions about the world, about how it is or should be organised, and about the place or role of people in it'. Such a bundle of ideas, they suggest, is known as 'an ideology' (Stephens and Watson 1994 p 14).

Like Hollindale (op. cit.) Stephens and Watson argue that all texts embody an ideology and no text is innocent. An ideology may not be easy to spot – even for those aware of the political nature of texts. They repeat Hollindale's point that the teacher's task is to teach children how to read so that they will not be at the mercy of *what* they read.

So let's continue with the example of *Once Upon an Ordinary School Day*. What message might McNaughton and Kitamura want to convey about education? What ideology do *they* share and, perhaps, want us to share? What about *my* values-base or motives, my ideology or agenda? Why did *I* choose this story from the many picturebooks available? (Think again about Rory's observation that I 'like books like that'.) All of these various kinds of ideologies compete and combine to influence consumers of text.

Let's see what one group of 8 and 9 year olds said after they had heard the story and examined the pictures. We will look at their scrutiny of some of the illustrations. We will also examine the responses of a group of first year teacher education undergraduates, and then the responses of a group of experienced teachers who are au fait with the CT&BT approach.

The children had only a slight sense of the author 'passing on a message about education'. It could be that this was because they agree completely with what is being presented. They appeared to accept that the message was that 'ordinary' school is boring and 'freezes your imagination' unless you're lucky enough to meet an innovative teacher. One child seems to grasp that the illustrations/colour have an effect in how he responds when he says: *Everything was so ….ordinary, boring, grey, no changes…suddenly it's all colour and everything changes and brightens up. That teacher brightened up his life.* Others agree.

(The following is part of a transcript excerpt taken from my doctoral thesis, and I used abbreviations of children's names rather than pseudonyms: see Roche 2007 Appendix C7.)

- *Se: I find it very interesting. Everything was so ....ordinary, boring, grey, no changes...suddenly it's all colour and everything changes and brightens up. That teacher brightened up his life. I agree with Cr because his life might have gone on being so boring, go to school then work, work, work for all of his life. It would have been really ordinary and boring. But that teacher brightened it all up with imagination and music.*
- *Mre: Everybody should get the chance to let their imagination go free...get the thoughts out of your head instead of having them just stuck. When he did let go his thoughts – look what happened – all the whole thing looked different...all the colours, his life was brightened up. The teacher brightened up the boy's life by letting his thoughts go free...if you didn't ever let your thoughts out no-one would ever know what you had inside your head...*
- *Dn: I think I liked the way the story just changed in the middle all of a sudden. At the start I was like 'Aw! Come ON'...I didn't think it was very interesting with all those 'ordinaries' all the time...then suddenly it went from being black and white to really colourful. I suppose that was when he started using his imagination. He had to let it go sometime...he wouldn't have liked his life at all if he didn't let his imagination go.*
- *B: I think he did have an imagination all along. The teacher didn't give him an imagination, he just allowed him to use it by playing the exciting music...but like Dn said at first he wasn't good at it then... when he heard the music ...and he flew ...and he was cheerful and he wasn't bored any more.*
- *Cn: Well I'm glad...I'm very glad that that teacher came in when he did, cos with that teacher the boy was changed. He could only see things black and white until that day and then that teacher lightened up his life.*
- *Mn: I think that your imagination is like water. It's like water because it can be frozen and the only time it freezes up is when it's not running and being used. It freezes up if you don't use it.*

It is possible to see that the children were thinking for themselves, building on each other's ideas and trying to make sense of the story. With a different group of children, following a reading through of the story, we went back and looked closely at the illustrations. The children showed that close examination of the illustrations gave the story even more meaning. For example, in the opening where 'the ordinary boy' is walking to school, the children spotted two key pieces of information: a poster of a wolf on the gable-end of a building and a man feeding birds from a dormer window.

Several children spotted the wolf poster. I asked the children to think in pairs about this detail using the following question: What do wolves usually do in traditional stories? They came up with answers such as:

- *Amy: Wolves are usually bad news.*
- *Graham: They're evil in stories usually.*
- *Sean: They usually try to kill the good guy.*
- *Emily: They kind of have no mercy for kids or small animals.*

Then I asked them to get into pairs once more and think about the wolf poster again, using this question: Why would Satoshi Kitamura have put a wolf poster in this story? This really got them buzzing:

And as he walked through the ordinary streets, the ordinary boy thought his ordinary thoughts,
past the ordinary shops and across the ordinary roads,

Figure 4 Going to school in *Once Upon an Ordinary School Day*.

Figure 5 Detail from Figure 4: the wolf poster in *Once Upon an Ordinary School Day.*

- **Beth:** *Oh...oh...It's a warning sign – I betcha something bad is going to happen.*
- **Will:** *Going to school could be full of dangers for some kids.*
- **Jack:** *Yeah – school can be bad for some kids.*
- **Amy:** *He wants us to think that there's something dangerous coming.*

- *Emily:* *Go to the last picture where the boy's dreams are floating out of him – there's a poster on his bedroom wall of a little schoolchild happy pig. Look he has a school bag on his back! That kind of wipes out your feelings from the other poster of wolf on the wall.*

Children need time to examine pictures like this. As can be seen already, they made far more meaning from the book when they had opportunities for finding clues and cues in the illustrations. They were involved in 'close looking' (Doonan 1992) as the next examples show:

When they examined again the opening that shows the boy going to school, after seeing the illustration of Mr Gee striding into the classroom, Will shouted 'Go back to the part where he's going to school…yeah…look! That's definitely Mr Gee up there feeding the birds!' There was excitement as the others saw what he was pointing to. I must admit that this was the first time I had noticed this detail – and I had looked at these pictures many times. Then the children linked this image with the endpapers: they agreed that birds are important in this story and they began to see that, in picturebooks, cues and clues are provided by illustrators to help them fill what Iser (1988) called 'Gaps' in texts. The children also looked at the image of the children seated in their classroom and Sarah pointed out that 'they're all sort of square and he's [Mr Gee] all curvy'; 'they're all greyish and he's really yellow and colourful'. In short, they see things in the illustrations that were not in the text at all. They are using skills of *visual literacy* to make more meaning now from the text than they might have done if they had just listened to the words of the story. This aspect of text and images complementing each other is one of the hallmarks of a good picturebook and we will explore this in a later chapter.

Overall, without overtly stating it, the children all seem to have an embryonic awareness that the author and illustrator together have a belief (ideology) about education that they want to share.

What student teachers thought (2012)

When I introduced this picturebook to a group of Year 1 undergraduate education students in their first month in college, I did so in the context of a philosophy of education tutorial on 'the purposes of education', following an introductory session based on Woods (2011). After two readings of the book – beamed onto a screen using a projector so that the illustrations could be seen by all – I posed specific questions for the students to work on in groups. The questions included: *What do the authors appear to believe about education and what do you think they want us to believe?*

The answers, as summarised by the reporters from each group, included:

- *The author seems to think that teachers should be full of bells and whistles and fancy ideas otherwise kids will be bored.*
- *He (author) seems to be one of those people who swipe at schools, saying things like 'School should be interesting. All children should be having fun'. [There's] No mention that you might also have to do a bit of work.*
- *He (author) thinks that children need more from school than what they're getting.*
- *A good teacher can change a child's life for the better.*

"Good morning, everybody!"
said a quite extraordinary figure
bounding into the classroom.
"My name is Mister Gee
and I'm your new teacher.
Now, you don't know me and
I don't know you,
so, to help me get to know you,
I've had an idea . . ."

As Mister Gee handed out paper
he said, "For our first lesson together
I want you to listen to some music and
I want you to let the music make
pictures in your heads.
Is that clear?"

Figure 6   Mr Gee arrives in *Once Upon an Ordinary School Day*.

Figure 7 Detail from Figure 4: Mr Gee feeding the birds in *Once Upon an Ordinary School Day*.

- *School should have more creativity like Ken Robinson says on TED.*
- *Education should be for the whole person not just the brain.*
- *Education should be for every kind of child not just the swots.*

What experienced teachers said (2013)

I ran a series of workshops for teachers on using picturebooks in the classroom during 2012–13. When we examined *Once Upon an Ordinary School Day*, the teachers, unsurprisingly, displayed lots of professional insights. When we examined the cover, for example, they thought that the plant and watering can were metaphors for a child's mind needing nourishment just as a tender plant needs water. They felt that the repetition of the word 'ordinary' (which annoyed some of the children and some of the college students) was there to emphasise the hum–drum nature and drudgery and boredom some children experience at school. They noticed that the ordinary boy was never named – he was just 'a pupil' in a uniform – part of the herd. Then one teacher said 'But there were a few children named by the end of the story'. They thought that, had Mr Gee stayed with that class, he would have seen each child as an individual. After all when he introduced himself he spoke about how he wanted 'to get to *know* you' and then used his music activity for that purpose. This sense of a child being anonymous, the teachers thought, was part of the hidden message, the ideology – that in an 'ordinary school', children can be 'lost in the crowd', and that uniforms and seats organised in rows can serve to keep children anonymous. I believe it links with Benhabib's (1987) idea of the 'real and concrete other', referred to earlier. The teachers saw a strong contrast between the activity of the school yard and the passivity of the classroom prior to Mr Gee's arrival and thought that this was a clear example of 'the ideology at work'. They suggested that the cat was in every picture as a metaphor for curiosity and learning, and that birds were an important motif representing freedom, and that the scarcity of plants represented sterility and stagnancy. They agreed with the children's comments about 'the pupils being square and Mr Gee all curvy'. One teacher thought that, again, this was part of the ideology and said:

- *The children are all in 'little boxes' like in that song some years ago 'Little boxes on a hillside', whereas Mr Gee is anything but square: he is flamboyant and flouts convention. What schoolmaster wears a yellow suit to work – a very unconventional one!*

The reference to Pete Seeger's Little Boxes song sparked another connection: this time to Harry Chapin's 'So many colours in the rainbow' and some wondered if Colin McNaughton had been influenced by it. A few teachers surmised that Mr Gee was a substitute/supply teacher. One teacher, who was sceptical throughout, and who remained unconvinced by Mr Gee's innovative teaching methods, said:

- *There's a particular sub who often comes to our school. Like that Mr Gee fellow, he drives all the kids mental with all sorts of tomfoolery. Then the teacher has to come back and mop up while listening to whines from the kids about how much fun the sub was.*

When I pointed out the posters of the wolf and of the little schoolchild piggy, and the man feeding the birds, etc. and told them that the children had noticed these details, they were surprised. They hadn't spotted the clues. One teacher, who was nearly at retirement age said: 'Isn't it so interesting that the children noticed details in *pictures* whereas we're more focused on details in the *text*'. All agreed that hearing what the children had said helped them to see the story differently. They also said that having some understanding of picturebooks as a genre, and some knowledge about concepts like ideology and visual literacy meant they were now examining the books differently. This raises some interesting questions about professional development for teachers. At the end of our series of five workshops one teacher said:

- *It really is only since we've begun these workshops that I've come to realise how much I was missing by focusing on comprehension and prediction and retelling the story, etc. There's so much more to know…I have much greater insights and I think I'll be able to ask much better questions now and, probably, be better at 'hearing' answers also.*

What some education faculty thought (2012)

As we prepared the tutorial for the undergraduates, two Education Department colleagues and I studied the pictures and the story to see what else we might glean from it. One illustration detail, that seemed to have been overlooked by the other groups, caught our eye: the LP with the name Klaus Flugge on it. We 'googled' it and got a very pleasant surprise (I won't spoil it – try it for yourself). Once again we were reminded that no detail is accidental in a good picturebook. We agreed with the teachers that there was a lot of significance in the repetition of the word 'ordinary': we agreed with the children that the boy's facial expression, up until the point where he begins to think creatively, is one of apprehension and depression. We saw that in this book, the traditional classroom with uniforms and ordinariness and serried ranks of children is being critiqued. The original teacher is missing but the evidence is that this is a very strict classroom run on behavioural lines. The children 'whisper' when they talk at the beginning of Mr Gee's class. Then we hear them 'shouting out' answers when the music stops. We realise that the 'ordinary schoolchild' isn't expected to think, to be an individual, to be different. The opposite is true: conformity, silence and control seem to matter.

This classroom, and this education model, seems to be teacher-centred and subject-centred. It is premised on epistemological values that understand teaching as transmission and learning as passive reception of knowledge. Buber's (1965) *I-it* interpersonal theory comes to mind. Mr Gee comes in and talks about 'getting to know you ...' and immediately everything is changed: we are now thinking of the children as individuals who can also create their own knowledge. We begin to find out something of their individual personalities and we learn who some of them are. Later, after school is over, when Mr Gee inadvertently embarrasses the 'ordinary boy' by asking him if he still thinks he (Mr Gee) is barmy, he is immediately aware of the boy's discomfort and affirms him and restores his self-esteem by saying that he can't wait to read his story. It's a different epistemological framework; a more learner-centred approach to teaching and a different view of 'the other' – an ontological stance more like Buber's (1965) '*I-thou*'. We wondered too if, in choosing Mr Gee's name, McNaughton is making a sly reference to James Gee (1993) who wrote about postmodernism and literacies. Or is it merely Gee! as in Gee whizz! because he is so different to an 'ordinary teacher'.

We also recognised that McNaughton is not saying to us that every child will flourish in such a classroom. He leaves us with an awareness that, for some children, the traditional is 'safer' and more suited to their learning style – so long as it is informed by teaching for understanding. He is, perhaps, advocating that we examine the premises of an education system that still largely operates on a model dating back to the Industrial Revolution, where children are in large classes grouped by their age and perhaps – where streaming occurs – by their cognitive ability. It could be interpreted as a sterile and stagnant model. McNaughton is not offering innovative and creative teachers as a panacea – but he *is* raising questions.

Summary

Critical engagement with both text and illustrations incorporates several different levels of comprehension and meaning-making. For it to work well the teacher needs to be knowledgeable about the book she is using; critically aware, willing to listen to, and open to learning from, her pupils; enthusiastic and committed to creating a community of enquiry in her classroom: she needs to exhibit Dewey's (1910) three qualities of wholeheartedness, open-mindedness and intellectual responsibility. The questions she asks herself, and the questions she gives her pupils opportunities to ask, and to answer, really do matter.

Recommended reading

Alexander, R. (2006) *Towards Dialogic Teaching: rethinking classroom talk*. 3rd ed. UK: Dialogos Ltd.
Baddeley, P. and Eddershaw, C. (1994) *Not So Simple Picture Books: developing responses to literature with 4 to 12 year olds*. Stoke-on-Trent: Trentham Books.

Brandt, R. (1993) On teaching for understanding: a conversation with Howard Gardner. *Educational Leadership*, 50 (7): 4–7.

Dombey, H. (2009) Research with a focus on the teaching and learning of reading in the pre-school and primary years. NATE/UKLA Online, available at: http://www.ite.org.uk/ite_research/research_primary_focus/ (accessed Nov 2013).

Dombey, H. (2013) *Synthetic Phonics is Not Enough: teaching young children to read and write in English*. Paper presented at 18th European Conference on Reading, Jonkoping Sweden, August 2013.

Fisher, R. (2009) *Creative Dialogue: talk for thinking in the classroom*. Abingdon Oxon: Routledge.

Mackey, M. (2012) (ed.) *Picturebooks and Literary Understanding in Honour of Lawrence Sipe*. New York, London: Springer.

Chapter 3

Interactive, or dialogic, reading aloud

What does interactive (dialogic) reading mean?

Dialogue is an interactive process. It involves relationship, curiosity, thinking, speaking, listening, reflecting and responding and more. Dialogue is about far more than mere conversation or idle chat. It has within it an implicit assumption that there is a purpose to the talk; that meaning is being created and furthered. Care, courtesy, respect and attention are also implied. In an interactive read aloud of a picturebook, a teacher uses the reading of a book to engage children in authentic dialogue with her, and with each other, about the book. We saw an example of this process in Chapter 2 where the children and I discussed McNaughton and Kitamura's *Once Upon an Ordinary School Day*.

What does authentic dialogue involve?

Authentic dialogue means that there is real engagement and attentiveness in listening and responding to the other. It takes time, effort and preparation on the teacher's part. It demands, as we saw earlier, a certain kind of culture and atmosphere: one of trust and openness and caring and respect. In a classroom, it means negotiating an equitable and democratic structure for ensuring fairness, so that children feel they have access to opportunities to speak and listen in a safe and supportive environment: it does not mean a teacher asking a few random, closed questions to which children engage in a hands-up practice, bidding for the teacher's attention (Alexander 2006) as they seek to be chosen to answer.

   To revise what we have said already: dialogue about picturebooks can focus on all aspects of the book – the characters, events, setting, language, illustrations, or plot. It can lead to asking why the author and illustrator might have made this book in the first place. It can provide a link between the child's own life and the lives portrayed in the book. It is underpinned by a Vygotskian approach that allows the teacher, the text and articulate children to act as 'more knowledgeable others' who can support children in thinking aloud, elaborating on ideas and thus scaffolding each other's learning. Interactive read alouds then can provide opportunities for children to develop their literacy skills as well as create and foster a community of readers and literate enquirers. Reading followed by dialoguing is an extension of Bakhtin's (1981) idea that every act of reading involves dialogue, even if it is between just the reader and the book. Without this, Bahktin says, comprehension could not happen. I believe that interactive readalouds are genuine and authentic spaces for a real engagement with literature.

Three benefits of engaging with literature

'It enables us to go beyond our individual lived experience'

Gordon Wells (in McMahon *et al.* 1997 pp 109–10) states that engaging with literature has three benefits: first, he says, *'it enables us to go beyond our individual lived experience'*. This means that using our imaginations, we can begin to imagine other possible events, actions, or feelings that, as Wells says, 'deepen our understanding and extend our potential for responding sympathetically and intelligently to the situations that we actually encounter thus contributing significantly to our personal development'. Although from the womb she is absorbing sound and atmosphere, and beginning the process of building her language, values and knowledge, a child has a limited experience of his or her world. She may be exposed to other worlds through television and films but this experience is largely a passive one. Reading and discussing a picturebook together with a caring adult's participation, can widen her experience and allow her to see events though other's eyes.

For example, when a class of 5 year olds and I read Tomi Ungerer's *Three Robbers* together, we stopped after the first few pages because Jan asked: 'Why did they have to be robbers? Is that their job?' The children began to discuss what caused the three robbers to take up robbing as a career.

- **Jan:** *Well they mightn't of had any money and they needed some to buy stuff.*
- **Simon:** *Yeah, maybe they didn't want to do it but they had to.*
- **Anne:** *Yeah well that's not fair if you take someone else's stuff then. Like when I lost my pencil if …I took one from someone else …cos then they'd have to rob another one too.*

We continued with the story and we came to the part where the character, Tiffany, asked: 'What's all this (stolen loot) for?' The story continues: 'the robbers choked and spluttered: they had never thought of spending their wealth!' I asked:

- **Me:** *Wow! I wonder what they will answer!'*
- **Peter:** *Well maybe they'll say that they just wanted to get rich because they had an axe and the stingy stuff …pepper …and the …gun thingy.*
- **Greg:** *Yeah maybe they wanted to be really rich, cos if you're really rich you can do lots of stuff.*
- **Andrew:** *They shouldn't of been scaring people and they shouldn't of broken the wheels… and the horses were scared too. Why didn't they just do the lottery? They could get rich if they did the lottery.*
- **Me:** *What does rich mean?*
- **Will:** *It means you have loads of gold – and it's all shiny and goldy and you can count it at the night.*
- **Eve:** *Yeah, you could have golden treasure and you'd be so, so rich.*
- **Ian:** *Maybe they wanted all the money to build a big huge mansion for theirselves.*

We went on with the story. They were happier when the three robbers began to use their wealth to help orphans. At this age they weren't discerning enough to question the ethics of using stolen money to do 'good'. However, Eve did see a problem:

- **Eve:** *The robbers kept finding more and more children. Why didn't the parents come and take them back?*
- **Kate:** *Yeah, I agree with Eve, what's going on in that place? Where are all the Mammies and Daddies?*
- **Timmy:** *Yeah. I agree with Eve too and Kate: why didn't the robbers just give the money to the poor parents?*
- **Sarah:** *Maybe the robbers might of been poor children when they were small.*
- **Ger:** *Naw. I disagree cos they didn't even think of any of that stuff until they kidnapped Tiffany! And that was so lucky for her as well cos she was so scared of going over to her bad auntie's house.*
- **Mary:** *Doesn't she have any Nana? Don't any of the babies have a Nana? My Nana would mind me!*

The conversation about different aspects of the book lasted for around 50 minutes and at the end Peter said: 'Woo! Can we read that again tomorrow? It's really interesting!' When I agreed he said, 'Woo this is my lucky day!' I can't but think that the children who participated in this discussion had 'their horizons widened and their experience deepened' as Wells (op. cit.) stated, as they began to challenge some of the aspects of the story that may have gone over their heads had the story just been read in the usual way, without discussion.

My 3-year-old nephew George also loved this story and would ask me to read it with him each time he visited. When I asked why he said: 'I just love it … that's the why …' and then one day he said 'D'you know why I love that story? Cos they're good baddies!' When I discussed the same book with a class of 8 and 9 year olds they found much deeper meanings, but basically agreed with George's summary, that it presented a complex picture of what 'bad' means.

- **Jane:** *It's hard to say whether they're bad. I mean they're definitely not good…but I don't know if they're bad.*
- **Andrew:** *Threatening people, scaring horses, destroying property and robbing – that has to be bad, c'mon!*
- **Hannah:** *Yeah but, they are not really evil. I mean they don't seem to realise why they're robbing. When Tiffany asked them they were actually embarrassed that they hadn't thought about that at all.*
- **Jenny:** *I agree with Hannah, they're kind of stupid more than bad.*
- **Cathal:** *Well, they did good things eventually. I mean they sort of changed their lives and used the money for a good charity.*
- **Me:** *But was it their money?*
- **Cathal:** *Mmm good point. Pass – I'm still thinking.*
- **Kevin:** *I agree with Teacher that they should give back the money and then let the people decide if that's what they want to do.*
- **Ciara:** *Yes but that would mean they'd get put in jail! I mean, how could they do that without getting caught?*
- **Jack:** *Put an ad in the paper? (laughter)*
- **Beth:** *Yes well maybe it would have to be something like that. Teacher's right. It's not their money.*

- *Paul: Well I agree that it's not their money but I disagree with Kevin and Jack because maybe nothing would happen and by the time people got around to doing something those orphans would be dead.*
- *Sophie: I agree and look, someone had to mind those orphans. The town wasn't doing it; the good people weren't doing it – so it's just as well then that the robbers did it.*

To return to Wells' assertion however: the children discussing this story and other such picturebooks were going well beyond their lived experience and were responding sympathetically and intelligently to the situations encountered in the picturebooks they were sharing together. Meek (1988) reinforces Wells' assertion: she says 'When the structure of the story is familiar, readers are free to look at other possible lessons to be learned from events they may never encounter and kinds of people who may never cross their path'. She adds that, when this is the case, the reader can ask 'What would I do if I found myself in that situation? Do I or do I not care for people like that? Is there a part of me that understands them?' These lead to further explorations, she says: the value system that prevails in the world and the one revealed in the text (pp 28–9). We can clearly see how a value system about what 'rich' means, and how one might go about becoming rich (win the lottery), as well as values about caring for the young, influenced the younger children's responses. The older children show more mature responses that echo prevailing attitudes to crime and punishment, as well as some glimpses of their embryonic understanding of how morality is complex and of how maybe what's legal isn't always what's moral – or to be more exact – maybe what's illegal isn't always clearly immoral. The value system overtly revealed in the text seems to say that it is right to use stolen money to do good; it could also be about the power of one good person (Tiffany) to transform others.

'Literature helps us relate to our cultural and historical heritage'

The second of Wells' benefits is that, *'literature helps us relate to our cultural and historical heritage'* (in McMahon *et al.* 1997 pp 109–10). Reading picturebooks together about historic events helps children to understand events in a way that perhaps their history textbook would not allow. For example, children reading Marcia Williams' *Archie's War* can respond empathetically as the First World War is charted through the eyes of 10-year-old Archie Albright who assembles a detailed scrapbook of events; Michael Foreman's *War Game* allows them to see the complexity of the First World War as they watch the famous football game on Christmas Eve; Yukio Tsuchiya and Ted Lewin's harrowing account in *Faithful Elephants* depicts 'the grief, fear, and sadness' (from blurb) of war, and allows children to see that war affects not only innocent human beings but also innocent animals; Amy Hest and P.J. Lynch's *When Jessie Came Across the Sea*; Shaun Tan's *The Arrival*; Armin Greder's *The Island*; David McKee's *Tusk Tusk* and *The Conquerors*; Paul Fleischman and Bagram Ibatoulline's *The Matchbox Diary;* Dyan Sheldon and Gary Blythe's *The Whales' Song;* Mary Hoffman and Karin Littleton's *The Colour of Home;* and many other books by authors such as Eve Bunting and Patricia Palacco, Anthony Browne and Chris van Allsburg, allow children to experience and relate to their own or other's cultural history. A book like C.M. Millen and Andrea Wisnewski's *The Ink Garden of Brother Theophane,* uses a unique story and brilliant illustrations to show children how early manuscripts like 'The Book of Kells' were made. It is based on actual practices of copying books during medieval times and allows children to realise that thinking 'outside the box' can lead to very beneficial and interesting outcomes even in places like an ancient monastery. Mordicai Gerstein's *The First Drawing* is an excellent book for encouraging children to ask questions such as 'How and when and why did people first get the idea to make pictures of things they saw or imagined.' It is possible to find rich picturebooks that may offer children from diverse cultural backgrounds an eye into their shared cultural past. However, we don't always have to go back into a distant or a violent past: stories that examine our shared cultural understanding of what family means; or what difference, separation, illness, disability, or death mean; or what friendship means; or what courage, loyalty and justice mean, are all to be found in picturebooks. Interactive reading in the social setting of our homes, or classroom groups allows children and teacher alike to explore with interested others the significance of what is read.

'Literature can add to our aesthetic sense'

Wells' third benefit (in McMahon *et al*. 1997 pp 109–10) – '*literature can add to our aesthetic sense*' – is especially true of picturebooks. A book like Tine Mortier and Kaatje Vermeire's *Maia and What Matters* deals with the subject matter of old age, illness and death in a remarkably non-maudlin and sensitive way. A lot of the credit for the success of this book must go to the artist. In a review I wrote for *Inis*, the magazine of Children's Books Ireland (Roche 2013a), I said:

> Kaatje Vermeire's illustrations are superb. They capture the exuberance of a life lived fully and the stillness of illness, sadness and death. Her artwork is subtle and delicate and she manages to portray the difficult subject matter deftly and gracefully. Her illustrations make reading the story an intense yet gentle experience and will help children to make meaning of the subject matter while forming a close connection with Maia and her Grandma.
>
> (Roche in *Inis*, Dec 2013)

When children are allowed to discuss diverse artwork – by artists such as Jon Klassen, Chris Judge, Niamh Sharkey, Emily Gravett, Shaun Tan, Tomie de Paola, P.J. Lynch, Dick Bruna, Maurice Sendak, Satoshi Kitamura, Julie Vivas, Oliver Jeffers, Helen Oxenbury or Jane Ray (I've been less than objective here and listed just a few of my favourites) – they are exposed to feelings and language and experience that words alone could not offer. In Chapter 2 we saw, for example, how close examination of *Once Upon an Ordinary School Day* led to much richer interpretations of the meaning of the story.

Other benefits of dialogic reading

Meek (1988) provides an excellent example of dialogic reading with a child who was making slow progress with the phonic checklist and sent for what was called at the time 'remedial intervention'. I completely agree with Meek's explanations. In almost three decades of doing interactive or dialogic readalouds, it has never failed to surprise me how children who were deemed as 'failures' by standardised texts scores often 'shone' in dialogic situations (Roche 2000, 2007, 2011). Zucker *et al*. (2013) also suggest that all children appeared to benefit from frequent shared reading that included rich, extratextual conversations. They state that educators and researchers must continue to strive to understand *what* occurs during shared book reading and *how* what is done impacts long-term literacy outcomes (p 1437). Research, like that of Zucker *et al.* (op. cit.) shows that, while many teachers read aloud, not all provide authentic interactive opportunities for rich vocabulary development, meaning-making, or critical engagement.

In the next section we will look at how reading aloud can be an important starting point for dialogic reading.

Reading aloud

Mem Fox begins her 2008 edition of *Reading Magic* with the words 'I'm excited!' She is excited, she says, because she feels that 'rather than being viewed as a mildly pleasant educational activity, it feels now as if the entire world is in a frenzy about reading aloud, for a variety of reasons' (p xi). Mem dedicates her book to Jim Trelease 'King of the Read-Alouds'. Since 1979 Jim Trelease has been advocating readalouds, for encouraging children who *can read* to become people who *love to read,* with his publication *The Read-aloud Handbook* (1980) which, since it was first published in 1980, has never been out of print. Straub and Dell'Antonia (2006) state that:

> ...we all want to raise readers – kids with empathy for other characters (and people), kids with big vocabularies, kids with big imaginations, and kids who can always slide into another world with a book. But raising a child who reads doesn't start with teaching a child to read – in fact, it doesn't start with a child at all. It starts with a baby.
>
> (p x)

Likewise, the 'Reading Rockets' website is littered with good advice for reading aloud, as are many early learning and parenting websites.

All seem to agree that reading aloud is essential to giving children an early start in literacy success. The 'PISA in Focus' report (OECD 2011) showed that:

- Fifteen-year-old students whose parents often read books with them during their first year of primary school show markedly higher scores in PISA 2009 than students whose parents read with them infrequently or not at all.
- The performance advantage among students whose parents read to them in their early school years is evident, regardless of the family's socio-economic background. (OECD 2011)

> ...students whose parents reported that they had read a book with their child 'every day or almost every day' or 'once or twice a week' during the first year of primary school have markedly higher scores in PISA 2009 than students whose parents reported that they had read a book with their child 'never or almost never' or only 'once or twice a month'. On average across the 14 countries for which data are available, the difference is 25 score points, the equivalent of well over half a school year;
>
> (OECD 2011 p 2)

If reading aloud is so essential for literacy development, it begs the question 'why then are so many schools and parents not doing it?'

Several anecdotal reports suggest that classroom reading aloud is infrequent, especially in senior primary classes. For example, an Ofsted (2012) report on literacy suggests that too few schools instil their children with a lifelong love of reading, and suggested that this may in part stem from the lost art of reading stories to children. Wells (1997, in McMahon *et al.* 1997) tries to establish reasons for the failure of so many schools 'to create classroom communities that support the development of fully literate individuals' (p 108). He speaks about 'the politicizing of some of the issues involved' and 'the absence of a coherent theoretical base' for that politicizing (op. cit.). The current argument about teaching phonics might be a good example: or the scramble to look good in PISA rankings.

This 'lost art' of reading aloud is not limited to schools: for example, a news report for RTE (26 July 2012) suggests that 18 per cent of Irish parents never read to their children. A report in the *Guardian* (30 April 2010) shows a similar startling finding in the UK: 'Many children are starting school having never been read a story' the *Guardian* report states. It continues: 'more than half of primary teachers have seen at least one child begin formal education with no experience of being told stories at home. Teachers said the stories pupils did know often seemed to come from watching Disney cartoons'. Pie Corbett, educational adviser to the government, when interviewed for that *Guardian* article, described the findings as a 'national disaster', warning that 'such children were at risk of being left behind at school and failing to develop the creative talents needed to lead happy and productive lives'. Stating that too many children were left to watch TV instead of being read a bedtime story, often by busy middle-class parents, Corbett said:

> This isn't just an economic thing – it's not just people who come from poor back-grounds, it's across the whole of society. You get a lot of children coming from very privileged backgrounds who've spent a lot of time in front of the TV and not enough time snuggled up with a good book. The TV does the imagining for you – and it doesn't care whether you're listening or not.
>
> (*Guardian* 2010)

Haven (2007) argues that research from the fields of cognitive science and developmental psychology shows us that human minds rely on story and 'story architecture' as the 'primary roadmap for understanding, making sense of, remembering and planning our lives – as well as the countless experiences and narratives we encounter along the way' (p vii). Egan (1989) argues that storytelling is crucial because 'children's imaginations are the most powerful and energetic learning tools' (p 2). Bruner (2002) suggests that 'we like to say that literary fiction does not refer to anything in the world but only provides the sense of things. Yet it is the sense of things often derived from narrative that makes later real-life reference possible' (p 8). Robin Campbell (2001) provides a compelling case based in research of the literacy benefits of interactive reading aloud to young children. Leland *et al.* (2013) have a whole chapter devoted to reading aloud entitled 'Why Reading Aloud is Crucial' (pp 17–34).

In an interview for the *Guardian* (23 August 2013), author Philip Pullman, speaking about the importance of the bedtime book said: 'The book is just so important, an impor-tant thing, a valuable thing. Just the sharing time, with the child and the book; and letting the book absorb the attention of the child, getting a bit scuffed, the pages being a bit ripped, scribbled on perhaps'. He continues: 'When you read a storybook to a child: Don't skip the pictures. I've seen some parents race through a book, just reading the words, one eye on their watch. The way to do it is to talk about the pictures as well – ask questions.' When asked why exactly he thinks that the storybook, and the story, are so crucially important, Pullman replies that he's convinced that storybooks and nursery rhymes are 'the foundations of all subsequent language skills. These are the fundamental things, the real basics. Our politicians talk about "the basics" all the time, but what they mean are things that you can correct at the last minute on your word processor: spelling, punctuation, that kind of thing. But the most basic thing of all is your attitude to language'. He adds:

> If your attitude to language has been generated by a parent who enjoys it with you, who sits you on their lap and reads with you and tells stories to you and sings songs with you and talks about the story with you and asks you questions and answers your questions, then you will grow up with a basic sense that language is fun. Language is for talking and sharing things and enjoying rhymes and songs and riddles and things like that. That's so important. I can't begin to express how important that is; the most important thing of all. A sense that language belongs to us, and we belong in it, and that it's fun to be there and we can take risks with it and say silly things in it and it doesn't matter and it's funny.
>
> (*Guardian,* 23 August 2013)

As Pullman and so many others have said, there has to be more involved than just reading aloud. There has to be **interaction**.

Interactive reading

A large body of literature exists that deals with 'interactive reading', 'shared reading' and 'dialogic reading'. Many of these literatures refer to Gordon Wells' (1986) Bristol Study of Language Development. Wells himself (2003) says:

> Being read to is probably most children's introduction to written language. ... The value of this practice in preparing children to succeed in their formal education is now well attested. For example, one of the most striking findings from the Bristol Study of Language Development (Wells 1986) was that the frequency with which children were read to during the pre-school years strongly predicted not only their knowledge of literacy on entry to school but also their overall academic attainment five years later, at age ten.
>
> (p 56)

Wells (ibid.) suggests, when children have experience of listening to stories being read aloud, they 'become familiar with the cadences of written language and with the generic structure of stories and other types of text' (ibid.). He goes on to say that children's vocabularies increase 'in domains that are rarely the subject of everyday talk'. Also, Wells argues, 'children learn that books are a source of interest and enjoyment that can introduce them to real as well as imaginary objects, and places and events that they do not encounter in their immediate environment'. In all these ways, he says, 'the practice of reading to children in the early years enlarges their experience in ways that prepare them to make the most of the instruction they will receive in school' (p 56). Wells then goes on to explain why reading aloud in itself is not enough when he says:

> Listening to a story or non-fiction book is only part of this valuable practice, however. Much of the benefit – as well as of the child's enjoyment – comes from *the talk that accompanies the sharing of the book*. Discussing the characters and their actions, predicting what is likely to happen next, clarifying the meaning of particular words and phrases – all these kinds of talk help the child to make connections between the meanings and language forms of the text and his or her actual experiences, including the use of language in other familiar contexts.
>
> (Ibid. my emphasis)

The OECD (2011) report 'Focus on PISA' has another interesting finding for us which resonates with Wells above:

> Interestingly, different types of parent-child activities have different relationships with reading performance. For example, on average, the score point difference in reading that is associated with parental involvement is largest when parents read a book with their child, when they **talk** about things they have done during the day, and when they tell stories to their children. The score point difference is smallest when parental involvement takes the form of parents playing with alphabet toys with their children.
>
> (p 3)

It would appear that trying to teach a very young child to read by focusing on skills like alphabet learning or whole word 'look and say' is a counterproductive endeavour. The research suggests that it is the interactive nature of reading aloud in the context of a warm interpersonal relationship that makes the difference. Let's look at an example.

Reading aloud with George aged 3

My nephew George (5 at time of writing) was read to almost daily for the first five years of his life. He was and is a precocious speaker and often surprises his family with his literacy abilities. It was always easy to read aloud to George. Even as a very young baby he would sit or lie calmly, listening attentively and examining the pictures closely. When he was almost 3 years old, I read him John Burningham's *The Magic Bed*. We spoke about the cover and the characters as we went along. George was delighted to find that the main character was called Georgie. In Burningham's delightful story, Georgie needs a new bed and Frank, who seems to be his mum's partner, buys him a second-hand one. The bed turns out to be magic and each night Georgie embarks on a new adventure.

One night the magic bed lands on a deserted beach. In a cave, Georgie finds an open treasure chest with some jewellery spilling from it onto the sand. Beside it are a cutlass and a pistol. Thinking George might make the connection between sea, sand, treasure, pistol and cutlass I said: 'Wow! I wonder who owns that treasure chest?' and without hesitating George said, 'Hmm. Maybe a knight in shining armour? It *could* be.' (Up to this, the only other 'treasure chest' he'd seen was in a poem about a spider who sat 'on top of the box with the rusty locks that holds the key to the castle' in the book *Twinkle, Twinkle Chocolate Bar* (Foster 1991).

When we turned the page over and we saw the pirates, whose treasure chest it was, George said, 'Well it *could be* some knights in shining armour … it could be knights in shining armour who say "Yo Ho Ho and a bottle of rum!"' He was peeved that he had been mistaken and quick to recover. I was amazed at the speed with which he had made that connection, and also with the fact that neither of us had mentioned pirates by name at this stage. He'd seen the picture and made the connection with the 'Yo Ho Ho' almost instantly. It was a very good example of intertextuality, because another of George's favourite books was Julia Donaldson's *The Troll* which features pirates. Also the film series 'Pirates of the Caribbean' had remained popular enough for a lot of merchandising to be still available and possibly advertised on TV. George had enough intertextual knowledge to be able to link this new 'pirate' information in Burningham's illustration with his previous encounters with pirates. He was also annoyed at being caught off guard with his 'knight in shining armour' answer.

Intertextuality

Parkes (1998, in Evans 1998 p 53) defines intertextuality as 'the process of interpreting current books by making connections between them and previously read texts' and she suggests that, for young children engaged in interactive reading where they are given opportunities to stop and talk about the text, 'the combination of story language and oral language is also a form of intertextuality that carries meaning for [the child]'. Citing research by Harste *et al.* (1984), Parkes (op. cit.) states that :

> the evidence from the data suggests that emergent literacy learners not only make connections between past and current texts in the search for meaning but also use the process of intertextuality for the generation of meaning through other communication systems.

> Intertextuality is then a powerful potential for meaning making, supporting and sustaining the informant's engagement by providing a network of possible interpretations.
> (Parkes op.cit.)

Without early interactive and interpersonal dialogic reading children miss out on major opportunities for meaning-making, vocabulary extension and an understanding that reading books is a normal, natural and very pleasurable part of life. Children develop 'readerly' behaviours quite early when these are modelled to them as tiny infants: behaviours such as page turning, reading from left to right, holding a book, pointing to interesting things. They will mimic reading even before they have speech: children have been filmed copying expressive intonation even though what they are actually saying is meaningless to others, as any search on YouTube will demonstrate.

George's experience of books has always been in the context of dialogic or interactive reading. Illustrations are examined in detail and discussed. There is always time for 'I wonder why-ing' and 'do you think-ing'. As well as such cognitive activities, there has also been ample time for developing emotional and aesthetic responses to texts. Mem Fox writes on her website http://memfox.com/ about the dangers of ignoring the fact that children *have hearts as well as brains,* and she critiques 'the current (if changing) climate, in which quantitative educational research rates more highly than qualitative research'. Fox argues that it's not surprising that the affective is virtually forgotten:

> Matters affecting the heart are far more elusive than those affecting the mind. There's no simple way to measure the role of the affective in teaching children to read. It can't be recorded in numbers. It can't be caught in a statistical net. It can't be pre-tested or post-tested. Its subjects can't be divided into control groups because the affective aspects of any given situation are unique to the situation at the moment of its happening and cannot be replicated. Measuring such indefinables as the effects of expectations, happiness, eagerness, fondness, laughter, admiration, hope, humiliation, abuse, tiredness, racism, hunger, loneliness and love on the development of literacy is so difficult, even within ethnographic research, that to my knowledge it is attempted rarely. But the affective won't go away. It's always there, whether researchers admit it or not. The plain fact of the matter is that teachers and children have hearts, and those hearts play an enormous part in the teaching/learning process.
>
> (Mem Fox's website np)

An example of the emotional response came when George and I reread *Time for Bed* (Mem Fox and Jane Dyer 1997), a board book that has remained a firm favourite as George's 'very last bedtime story' (he usually stockpiles two or three picturebooks at bedtime – or more, if indulgent Auntie Mary is involved). There is a lovely gentle rhythm and pace to this book – with, on each opening, a mother animal telling her baby that it is time for bed, or time to sleep. The book is perfect for lulling a small child off to sleep and George's eyes were usually closing, until the last opening when he would perk up and say 'Look! It's me!' and sure enough there is a child with a mop of bright curls. 'I so love that book. That's me and my beautiful Mum. It's my favourite sleepy book.' And he would snuggle down again smiling. I feel sure that ending his busy day with this calm little book was beneficial – comforting and reassuring in the little ritual that had evolved, and calming in the rhythm and rhyme of the text.

During read alouds with George there have been many opportunities for prediction, synthesis, clarifying, questioning and inference as well as making connections. In fact all of the comprehension skills are covered in an organic and authentic way as the reading takes place. New words, phrases and similes were also acquired, as we saw with 'Yo Ho Ho'. A book that created opportunities for inventing new similes was *I'm as Quick as a Cricket* (Wood 1990). George added 'I'm as sleepy as a pillow'; 'I'm as tickly as a laugh'; 'I'm as smelly as a pogel' at which he roared laughing. (Pogels were his word for what he fished now and then from his nose.)

When he was three and a half, George and I read Osborne and Potter's (2000) *Kate and the Beanstalk*. I was researching the process of doing CT&BT with preschoolers for the (Irish) National Council for Curriculum and Assessment (NCCA). The podcast and videos – including a few with George – can be accessed on their 'Aistear Toolkit' website. As I read the story we encountered the word 'despair' in the sentence 'Kate's mother was in despair'. I asked George if he knew what 'despair' meant. I saw him mouthing the word silently as he pondered. He then said 'I don't know that word. What is it?' I explained that Kate's mother felt so sad and so worried that she couldn't think of a single happy thought. As we continued through the book we came across another image of

Kate's mother looking glum. I asked: 'Look at her face – what do you think she's feeling?' George answered immediately 'Catter… kitter … do you know what that means? It means worried'. I was puzzled at the time but later, as I reflected on this, I realised that perhaps he remembered that despair had two syllables and ended with an 'r'. The nearest he could come to it was catter or kitter. I'm not a linguist so this is a very tentative guess, but I wondered if this is one of the ways in which a child learns a new word – memorising the 'sound/rhythm of it' (phonemic and syllabic awareness) –des-pair/catt-er/ kitt-er and making a connection to another better known word – worried.

It would be very unlikely that George would come across the word 'despair' without experiencing the real and authentic context for learning new words such as is provided by reading a story aloud. It is also important that when we meet a word like 'despair' in a picturebook we have the illustration to scaffold the learning. There are many more instances of opportunities for vocabulary building in the story alone. At the very beginning of the book we read that Kate and her mother lived in a 'humble' cottage. I asked George what kind of a cottage this might be. 'Tumbling down?' was his reply. I expect that he recognised the rime 'umble' and put two and two together. I explained that in this case it meant 'not very big or fancy, just sort of poor and ordinary'. When we came across the beanstalk for the first time George said, 'It's a big plint … plint'. I replaced the word for him – 'plant?' 'Yes', he said, 'plant'. I asked 'How do you think it grew?' George replied immediately – 'remember when she threw the beans out the window?' And as he spoke, he mimed exactly the backward throwing action of Kate's mother, even though we had barely looked at that picture earlier. 'Well' he continued 'that must of been what made it grow'. George's grandfather, Pop, is a keen gardener and George has often pottered about the garden 'helping Pop'. Pop's probable frequent references to plants; as well as, perhaps, seeing Pop planting seeds, meant that all these words and phrases were assimilated by George and added to the same schema.

In the reading and rereading of *Kate and the Beanstalk* George learned about crystal streams, rolling sheep meadows and flocks. He learned again about keyholes and castles which he linked immediately to 'The rusty box that holds the key to the castle' and to Ruth Brown's (1981) 'A dark, dark tale'. He learned words like forlorn, despair, grieving, and plucky and 'avenging treachery'. But along with access to texts that expand and reinforce vocabulary and syntax, George has also been exposed to ideas that are challenging and require a different kind of cognitive engagement. For example I asked him if he thought Kate should have climbed the beanstalk, when climbing a beanstalk was dangerous. 'Yeah but she had to cos no way could her Mum climb up that thing!' I probed further 'Shouldn't she have asked her Mum for permission?' 'Naw…she'd just prob'ly say that's wayyyy too dangerous.' He seemed to have an understanding of Kate's sense of justice, duty and responsibility as well as a mother's prioritising of care over possible wealth. George thought Kate was perfectly right in everything she did. Why? 'Because she's really good at doing all that stuff you know!' He also had opportunities for speculating and pondering: for example, he wondered about the mighty castle in the sky. 'How did that castle get up there?' 'That giant is a baddie and he didn't have any nice friends like smart George' (a reference to Donaldson and Scheffler's *The Smartest Giant in Town*); and he wondered 'Hey Mary d'ya think are there more houses up there, I wonder?'

Kate and the Beanstalk is a sophisticated rendering of the traditional Jack story where all of the main characters, except 'the baddie' giant, are 'good' females, but even though

I probed gently about gender, George was nonplussed by Kate being a girl. For example, when I asked him if he thought this could be the same story as Jack and the Beanstalk, he decided it wasn't. 'No. It's another different beanstalk.' I commented that so many of his stories were about boys, and he said 'Yeah, course. That's cos *I'm* a boy'. George hadn't yet realised that many stories feature male protagonists.

Interactive readalouds in preschool and early years

When I carried out some research in his playschool, it was easy to see that George belonged to a small group who were used to hearing stories being read and discussed. Other children seemed to be unable or unwilling to participate. This may have been due to shyness too, of course. George knew me, obviously, and felt safe in contributing frequently to the discussion of *Penguin* and *Rosie's Walk,* including his insightful comment about the latter: 'Guess what? I think Rosie knew all the time that that bad fox was behind her and she's setting loads of traps to catch him' (traps were one of George's fascinations at that stage). Because a child like George – who had the twin benefits of good language skills and a relaxed attitude – could easily dominate in a small group it was really important that I negotiated some ground rules with the children. Before we began any readalouds we spent one session on learning how to 'pass the tip' (Donnelly 1994) from child one to another, to support the learning of 'communicative and social behaviours' (Fisher 2009; Leland *et al.* 2013; Lewison *et al.* 2011; McCall 2009; McMahon *et al.* 1997; Wells 1986; Roche 2007, 2011). This will be examined more fully in Chapters 6 and 7 of this book.

Interactive read alouds are often deemed to be of importance only in early years' settings. I have experimented with them and found them beneficial for developing comprehension oral language, critical and visual literacy at all levels of the primary school as well as with undergraduates and experienced teachers, as we will see below. We will begin with children in middle primary classes.

In middle school

In middle school, children who had experience of doing classroom discussion about picturebooks from Infants onwards demonstrated amazing insights and empathy when reading. An 8 year old, J, explained that Cave and Riddell's *Something Else* nearly made her cry 'because it is just so sad that any creature would be living all alone'. She demonstrated a very definite sense of empathy and said 'I think that story is about stereotyping people really'. Her parents were quite amazed at her participation and responses to the story when, as part of my validation process for my doctoral work, parents were invited to view videos of classroom discussions. J's parents were amazed, because up to this J was considered to be in need of help with literacy. Until now they had been unaware that, not only did she know words like 'stereotype', but that she could use them naturally in discussion. They were also amazed at the way in which, despite a camera and a microphone pointing at her, she spoke clearly, confidently and assertively, because they knew her to be a very shy little girl. K (9) responded to the same book by saying 'That book makes me think of what we were doing in History about Mahatma Ghandi, and the part where he wasn't allowed to travel in the first class carriage even though he had paid for his ticket'. K's parents were amazed, not because of his ability to make an intertextual link, but because, although he had high cognitive ability, he was considered to have social difficulties. Yet the video showed him agreeing and disagreeing with equanimity and calmly accepting classmates disagreeing with him. E (8) found the book to be about a much larger issue when she asked 'Why do people treat each other so badly when we all know what we should do to live right?' 'Even in babies' class (infants)' she said passionately, 'there are mean people who bully the small people and the shy people. What makes that happen? Why?' E is another child who struggled with shyness and, possibly, had real life experience of being intimidated. C (9) who was often 'in the sin bin' during yard time, spoke about how 'Some kids just get used to being bad: they don't even mean it after a while'.

Discussions, such as this one about *Something Else*, often continued into and influenced other lessons, for example SPHE (friendship): 'Remember when we were doing *Something Else*? Well that story is like this lesson'; History (Anne Frank): 'That's like when Something Else said "Go away you are not like me!" That's what people were really saying to the Jews: ye are not like us. Go away! Except they never said "Come back" like Something Else did before he hurt someone's feelings'. Colleagues, to whom I passed on my classes, told me anecdotally that children often referred to stories I had discussed with them. The discussions would appear, then, to have been relevant to the children's experience and to have had an influence in their lives (see also Roche 2007).

Interactive reading aloud with teachers

From 2010 to the present I have faciliatated a series of workshops for teachers where we read at least three picturebooks aloud at each session and then discuss them. One experienced teacher remarked that listening to a story being read aloud was a very different experience for her, compared with reading it silently herself or reading it aloud to children. It seems to 'demand a different set of comprehension skills or a different part of your brain', she said. The picturebook in question was *The Black Book of Colours* (Cottin and Faria 2010). I asked her to write her thoughts about the experience: This is what she wrote:

> *The Black Book of Colours* is an extraordinary picturebook. It defies the definition of a picturebook. How could it be a picturebook? It has no pictures. However the raised line drawings are beautiful. Initially I had a very conflicted relationship with the book. When I saw it first I browsed through it, but I didn't read it. I wanted to read it but I felt slightly intimidated by it. I found the appearance of the book daunting. It seemed a bit intellectual, like a famous painting that challenges the viewer to interpret it. Eventually I read the book. It is very beautifully written and like most picturebooks is not just for children. It has incredible depth. In my opinion, however, it is necessary to listen to *The Black Book of Colours* in order to explore it fully.

> I don't think that *The Black Book of Colours* is about imagining blindness. I think that it's about experiencing colour. The black appearance of the book belies the depth of colour and emotion in the content. Listening to the book being read aloud, as opposed to reading it myself, gave me a deeper appreciation of the content. I could actually visualise the colours. I could see the pictures. It took me to a different place. Perhaps it provides sighted people with the opportunity to experience colour and

the emotion of colour at a deeper level. For me this could only be achieved by listening to the book being read aloud.

(Email from M McG, 6 July 2013)

Another experienced teacher, who was a recent convert to using picturebooks in his class, also spoke about the experience, in a workshop, of hearing a story as well as seeing a story. After we had done an interactive readaloud of *Once Upon an Ordinary School Day*, he spoke about how the experiences added to his own understandings about the illustrations. 'Beaming the illustrations onto the whiteboard as you read aloud is a really good idea. It was when I looked at the pictures as you read the text, and then afterwards I listened to what children had said, and then listening to what my peers were saying, that I began to see so many possibilities for making new meaning and interpretation.' D teaches middle-school classes. He has been using picturebooks now for over a year and loves the opportunities they provide for authentic and meaningful discussion. In an email following the workshop, he wrote:

> This approach to using picture books has given me the opportunity to engage children in meaningful discussions about critical issues in their development: gender, power, identity and citizenship. Significantly, I believe that high quality picture books are central to children questioning their own thinking through a medium that doesn't bore or intimidate them and the children themselves seem to appreciate this alternative to closed questions regularly completed as an accompaniment to traditional school texts.

(Email from D McC, 7 August 2013)

Summary

Interactive reading aloud demands a high level of engagement from both the teacher and the children. It demands choosing, as D McC says, 'high quality' picture books, reading them carefully and preparing questions to get the dialogue started. It also involves careful planning and timetabling to get the most from the session. For a parent in a one-to-one setting it makes fewer demands: it still means choosing books carefully (while then allowing the child to choose within the selection). It also demands time. But for both teachers and parents alike it demands, most of all, reflection, critical thinking, open-mindedness and a willingness to listen carefully to children.

Recommended reading

Bohm, D. (2004) *On Dialogue*. London and New York: Routledge Classics.
Evans, J. (2009) *Talking Beyond the Page: reading and responding to picturebooks*. London: Routledge.
Fox, M. (2008) *Reading Magic: why reading aloud to our children will change their lives forever*. Orlando, New York and London: Harcourt.
Greene, M. (1978) *Landscapes of Learning*. New York: Teachers College Press.
Hoffman, J.L. (2011) Coconstructing meaning: interactive literary discussions in kindergarten read-alouds. *The Reading Teacher*, 65 (3): 183–94.
Sipe, L. (2008) *Storytime: young children's literary understanding in the classroom*. New York and London: Teacher's College, Columbia University.
Trelease, J. (2013) *The Read-Aloud Handbook*. 6th ed. New York: Penguin Books.

Wells, G. (1986) *The Meaning Makers: children learning language and using language to learn*. Portsmouth, NH: Heinemann.

Zevenbergen, A. and Whitehurst, G. (2003) 'Dialogic reading: a shared picture book reading intervention for preschoolers', in A. Van Kleeck, S.A. Stahl, and E.B. Bauer (eds) *On Reading Books to Children: Parents and teachers*. Mahwah, NJ: Lawrence Erlbaum.

Chapter 4

A focus on oral language development

Introduction

'Language is the essential condition of knowing, the process by which experience becomes knowledge' (Halliday 1993 p 94).

In previous chapters we have made references to the potential that reading and discussing picturebooks holds for the development of oral language. We will now examine this aspect in some more detail.

> Reading books is a fantastic activity for expanding vocabulary, partly because books bring in topics and thus words that wouldn't normally occur in everyday conversation. So they support parents and teachers to use those words, and most importantly, they introduce the words in ways that children can get access to them, and then can use them themselves – if the opportunity is offered to discuss the books with the children. *It's the conversation around the books that really makes the difference,* not just reading aloud.
>
> (Snow 2011 np on http://www.pbs.org/parents/martha/experts/ my emphasis)

As I said earlier, I have been discussing picturebooks with all age groups of primary schoolchildren since the 1990s. Before that I read and discussed books with my own children every night, and long after they could read for themselves. At that time I really did not appreciate the huge significance this would have for their language and comprehension. I did it because I loved it and they loved it, and because my parents had read aloud to me and my siblings. It was what all parents did, I thought. I now know differently. Honig (2007) makes the point that:

> Despite our innate propensity at birth to be able to learn any language, the loving caregivers who socialize babies and young children are crucial for ensuring the power to use language as a rich symbol system that permits humans to share meaning with one another and to advance learning. Language learning depends on genetic potential and on social interactions.
>
> (p 582)

The awareness of the link between potential cognitive development and language is well illustrated in the following startling fact from Honig:

...long years ago in Tsarist Russia, if usurpers staged a coup to overthrow the emperor, the infant heir in line to the throne would be put in a tower with a deaf-mute caregiver, to ensure that the baby would never grow up normally or ever become a threat to the usurpers.

(Ibid.)

Language deficits entering school

I know that there are many children entering primary school who have a serious language deficit. I know that by around 10 years of age (Primary 2, grade 4 or 4th class) there could well be an even wider gap between those who can read fluently and those who can't. Research by Chall *et al.*(1990) noted that that particular stage represents a critical transition period in children's literacy ability. At around this time children are moving from 'learning to read' to 'reading to learn'. Chall *et al.* (op. cit.) suggested that, what they termed 'the 4th grade slump', might be related to students struggling to progress from reading fairly unchallenging, or familiar words and passages, to trying to read and comprehend increasingly difficult words and texts. Another cause appears to be related to the amount of vocabulary that the children have. Chall *et al.* found that the vocabularies of children from low-income backgrounds, in 2nd and 3rd classes/grades, were generally equal to the rest of the student population. However, at this level, vocabulary *tests* tend to be based on fairly basic and familiar words. They suggested that this could serve to conceal the fact that low-income students often only know about 50 per cent of the words that students from higher socio-economic groups know.

Stanovitch (1986) coined the phrase 'the Matthew Effect' (the rich get richer and the poor get poorer) to describe what happens as such a gap widens: children with strong vocabularies find reading easier and more enjoyable; thus, they read more and develop ever larger vocabularies. Children with weak vocabularies, on the other hand, find less enjoyment in reading. This means that they read less, and thus fail to develop the vocabularies that they need to become strong readers and learners.

From my experience and research I know now that children involved in good quality discussions on a picturebook with their teacher and peers are listening and improving their receptive language skills. They are participating, thinking critically, getting ideas from each other, agreeing and building on these ideas, or disagreeing and justifying their decision to do so and improving their expressive language. They are part of a collaborative culture, a democratic space, actively learning how to be democratic. And of course they are learning new vocabulary, new forms of syntax and using these to further their comprehension and their expressive language.

Alexander (2006) states that children construct meaning not only from the interplay of what they newly encounter and what they already know, but also from interaction with others. Alexander continues by saying that, in turn, this interaction is critical not just for children's understanding of the kind of knowledge with which schools deal, but also for their very identity – their sense of self and worth (p 11).

In Dawes and Sams (2004 p viii) Mercer says that unfortunately the practice of having good discussions is not something that many children experience. From my own experience of teaching for nearly 40 years, and as I act as tutor to student teachers on school placement, I saw how so many teachers feel that time is being wasted in dialogue; how it takes 'from getting things done'. This resonates with what Alexander (2006) has found internationally. He says that 'In most classrooms those kinds of discussions are unfortunately rare'. He advocates that teachers take time to reflect on this phenomenon. It may be, he suggests, that as teachers, we assume that most pupils probably know how to talk and work together and so, we rarely give children explicit guidance or training in how to generate good discussions nor any experience in having reasoned discussions (see also Honig 2007). Without this, children may not understand or value or know how to use language appropriately. However, with practice and experience children can learn how to think and reason and talk together and achieve far more than they would alone.

Lindfors (1999) talks about how in a 'dialogue of enquiry' children have to learn to deal with and adapt to what she calls 'positive and negative politeness' – the way in which true dialogue includes disagreements and challenges as well as agreement and consensus. Learning to accept being disagreed with is as important as learning to disagree politely and will only come about with practice. This point is also well made in Dawes and Sams (2004) when they talk about 'exploratory talk'. Exploratory talk is what happens, they say, when 'people engage critically but constructively with each other's ideas', when 'everyone shares relevant knowledge; when contributions are actively sought from each participant; and when challenges and proposals are accepted, but must be justified by reasons' (p 3).

> When children are using language in this way, their reasoning becomes visible in the talk – for example, in their frequent use of words like 'I think…' 'because….' And 'why…?' This kind of rational discussion is of great value in education. Through engaging in exploratory talk children learn to develop their own ideas and learn from those of others. They also learn skills in talking and thinking which enable them to work more effectively in teams and to take an active role in society. Exploratory talk is a very intimate way to talk to other people, in that it allows access to what other people really think; it is also quite impersonal in that it can take place in any group of people, even complete strangers. *However, research has shown that in most primary classrooms – anywhere in the world – hardly any exploratory talk normally takes place…*
>
> (Ibid. my emphasis) (I would add from my own experience that the same is true in most post-primary classrooms.)

In my early attempts at writing about providing children with opportunities to think, reason and talk together (Roche 2000) I described how steady practice in discussions had quite profound effects on children's ability to express themselves. The children with whom I was working at the time were in an all boys' school, and were mostly very disadvantaged children. Many of them had poor vocabulary and often used phrases like 'the whassisname' when they didn't know a word. And yet other teachers, as well as parents, began to recount to me how, out in the yard or at home they began to use phrases like 'I really agree' or 'I disagree' (see also Roche 2000). From initially asking me 'when can we do that poshy-talk stuff again' they began to refer to our CT&BT sessions as 'our classroom discussions'. The weekly discussions, or at least the versions of them that the children had related to their parents, began to feature in almost every interaction I had with parents. Children began to request to take home the books we had discussed in class. These were boys who, up to this, had strongly resisted any invitations to take books home for reading for pleasure. They read in school. That was more than enough, they seemed to feel. Now, however, they were clearly demonstrating discernment as they expressed their preferences for the books they wished to take home. This in itself shows that they were engaging with pleasure in the reading process.

A study by Sullivan and Brown for the Institute of Education (2013) says that children who read for pleasure are likely to do significantly better at school than their peers. Believed to be the first research to examine the effect of reading for pleasure on cognitive development over time, the study found that children who read for pleasure made more progress in maths, vocabulary and spelling between the ages of 10 and 16 than those who rarely read. The study also says that children who were read to regularly by their parents at age 5 performed better in all three tests at age 16 than those who were not helped in this way.

Vocabulary

So far we have established that talk is good, interaction is good, and reading for pleasure is good. But for all of these we need vocabulary.

Biemiller (1999) argues that to succeed at reading, a child must be able to identify or 'read' printed words and to understand the story or text composed of those words. Both identifying words and understanding text, he says, are critical to reading success. For many children, increasing reading and school success will largely depend on increasing oral language competence in the elementary years. He also states that current school practices typically have little effect on oral language development during the primary years. Because the level of language used is often limited to what the children can read and write, he says, there are few opportunities for language development in primary classes. He recommends introducing the teaching of vocabulary through both direct and indirect means. He argues that listening comprehension continues to grow during the elementary years and that the typical 3rd-grader can comprehend more complex oral stories, expositions, etc., than the typical 1st-grader. Broadly speaking, language can only 'grow' through interaction with people and texts that introduce new vocabulary, concepts, and language structures. Like Snow, whose work was mentioned earlier, Biemiller and Boote (2006) realise that reading alone will not necessarily improve vocabulary. Neither will reading aloud, on its own, achieve any noticeable improvement in vocabulary. As we have seen earlier, it is the *interactive* element – the conversations, discussions, chats, and questions about the story and the pictures – the to and fro of dialogue about the book – that will make a difference to the consolidation.

> Three studies showed great success with year-long interventions. Many people have shown that word meanings can be learned when taught in conjunction with repeated reading of stories. This will mainly involve oral sources of language, and directly teaching meaning in context. Several studies have shown that when books are repeatedly read with word explanations, around 25% of meanings are learned.... In a recent study, adding reviews to explanations of words in stories read to students resulted in learning 40% of meanings taught. In kindergarten, grade one, and grade two, students learned an average of 8 to 12 meanings each week, mainly depending on the actual number of meanings taught in that grade.
>
> (Biemiller and Boote, 2006)

Bromley (2007) suggests, as one of her nine strategies for improving vocabulary, that we read literature aloud to students, stopping to explain and talk about words they may not know. She argues for sharing Trelease's (2006) notion with students 'that the best SAT preparation course in the world is to hear literature read aloud because the richer the words student hear, the richer the words will be that they can read and give back when they speak and write' (p 529). In Chapter 3 we saw how, when George and I were discussing the word 'despair', we were also consolidating that word in his repertoire. Re-readings of *Kate and the Beanstalk* reinforced the word and he used it effortlessly, in correct contexts.

Wells (2001 p 174) says that each classroom must find its own way of working as they seek to improve dialogically. Likewise, it is up to each parent to find comfortable ways of reading with pleasure to their children and making time for interaction about the book and pictures. For many this may be limited to weekends when the pressure of work and home life ease somewhat. It would be detrimental to the process if a parent is hurried and hassled as she reads, because a child would quickly absorb the message that reading is not fun.

Likewise it is up to each teacher to exercise their 'pedagogical content knowledge' (Shulman 1986) to extend and transform talk into 'educationally productive discussions' (Boyd and Galda 2011 p 2).

Some examples from practice

- **George age 3:** *(Discussing* Rosie's Walk): *Mary, do you think Rosie knows the fox is behind her? I think she knows. She's thinking 'A-ha! Take that, sneaky foxy fellow. You better be gone when I turn around'.*
- **Amy age 3:** *I know what a mill is for: making corn for bread!*
- **Charlie age 4:** *I know what the most beautiful sound in the world is. If you were all alone in a deep dark forest and there were all shadows and scary things and then you heard 'Cam, I'm over here: it's Mummy. THAT would be the most beautiful sound in the world!*
- **Jim age 5:** *Teacher, do you know that some spiders actually eat their own web? ....Apparently it's got some nutritional benefit.*
- **Me:** *No. I didn't know that.*
- **Me:** *That's very interesting! Wow I've learned something new today. Did you?*
- **Jim:** *Not really.*
- **Ashley age 7:** *(discussing 'A Swim' from* Frog and Toad are Friends *(Lobel 1970): I think there's two kinds of laughing. It's an instinct to laugh at something that's funny and they couldn't help themselves. But it was mean to* **want** *to do it – to come along just to laugh.*

I think you will agree that each of these children exhibits an impressive facility with language and thought. They are not exceptional children: over the years that I spent teaching young children I came across many children whose ability to reason and articulate their thoughts was significant. Interestingly many of these articulate and critically engaged children did not perform well in written standardised tests (Roche 2000, 2007, 2011, 2012).

For example, look at this excerpt from a conversation with Sarah age 5 (name has been changed). It occurred during her second year in school.

- **Sarah:** *Teacher, will I tell you a very, very sad story that my auntie told me?*
- **Me:** *Sure!*
- **Sarah:** *D'you know down in West Cork … there's a big sort of house … and a kind of white stone on the side of the road?*

- *Me: Er, yes…kind of…*
- *Sarah: Well that's where the sad thing happened: See there was this really rich man and he had one beautiful daughter and guess what? She fell in love with a commoner and her Dad didn't want her to marry a commoner so he said No and he locked her up and she died. Of a broken heart. That's what my auntie said. Teacher, isn't that just so, so sad?*
- *Me: Yes it really is very sad; but what's a commoner?*
- *Sarah: I'm not totally sure; I'd say he's a kind of servant.*
- *Me: I wonder why her Dad would not want his daughter to marry a commoner?*
- *Sarah: Maybe he only had one or two and he needed them … to do the work.*

Sarah's face, as she told me this story was bright and animated. She loved being able to 'explain' something to me – 'commoners' was not a word I expected to hear from a 5 year old (Roche 2007 pp 208-9; see also McDonagh *et al.* 2012).

Children like Sarah have been read to from infancy. They are included in conversations with parents, aunties, grandparents and neighbours. In the chat Sarah had with me above, she used all the elements of a narrative – a setting, a plot, characters, a beginning, middle and end – as well as an impressive facility with spoken language. Sarah was a pupil in a school that encouraged teachers to do my early version of what I later developed as CT&BT. The children were exposed to frequent classroom discussion about picturebooks from their first weeks in school. It showed. The annual standardised reading tests showed that quite a high number of children were above average and inspectors commented on the high standard of dialogic practice. However, I knew that some of the 'average' and 'below average' results completely concealed the high intelligence and the oral language prowess of several children for whom pen and pencil tests proved to be a challenge. Sarah was one of these children.

International research (e.g. http://www.sapere.org.uk/) has been conducted into the 'benefits' of providing children with opportunities to do philosophical enquiry through discussion. All the studies showed some positive outcomes in the following areas:

- Developments in critical reasoning skills and dialogue in the classroom.
- Emotional and social developments.

Among the findings from research carried out in the UK by Trickey and Topping (2004, 2007) were some of the following:

- Pupils increased their level of participation in classroom discussion by half as much again following 6 months of weekly enquiry.
- Pupils doubled their occurrence of supporting their views with reasons over a 6-month period.
- Pupils and teachers perceived significant gains in communication, confidence, concentration, participation and social behaviour following 6 months of enquiry.

In Ireland, there have been several postgraduate studies done that have enquired into various outcomes of doing 'philosophy *with* children' as per Donnelly's (1994) model. Anecdotally, there are many teachers all over the world who have engaged in similar programmes that involve regular discussion and critical thinking with their students, and who will testify that 'it works' (see, for example, http://www.philosophyforchildren.co.uk)

Evidence for the benefits of doing dialogic enquiry with children can emerge for other kinds of research also: one of my colleagues from my primary teaching days, who was working towards his MA in Ed, carried out interviews with focus groups as part of his data gathering. He interviewed several children from my class. This is an excerpt from what he later wrote about these interviews:

> As part of my research methodology while undertaking research for a Master's dissertation, I facilitated two separate Focus Group interview sessions. Each focus group consisted of six, nine-year-old pupils from the two 3rd classes in our school. Both interview sessions were of one hour duration (approx). Our topic for discussion was the pupils' experience with a digital media resource in the computer lab over five sessions.

> I was very impressed with a number of factors during the focus group undertakings... The manner in which the 'cut and thrust' of argument and of dialogue was handled within the focus groups was most impressive in the context of the participants' ages (9 years old) ...I attribute the uncommon skill with which the children handled the demands of a focus group setting to their experience of the dialogic process of their weekly [CT&BT] sessions in our school.

> (See Roche 2007 appendix B)

If pupils are demonstrating increased levels of participation, and increased communication skills and increased occurrences of supporting views with reasons, then they are all showing that they have a sophisticated oral language ability that has led to a sophisticated cognitive ability. Thinking out loud in a discussion depends on oral language – listening and speaking. Enquiring and wondering are largely dependent on language too, I believe.

Over the years I have accumulated a large database of deeply philosophical questions from having conversations with small children about picturebooks and all sorts of other topics. These questions were expressed using quite sophisticated oral language as well as keen intellectual curiosity. For example:

- *Do cats know that they're cats and that we're people or do they think we're kind of different cats?*
- *Teacher, you know green? Well, who gave green that name? Who gave all the colours names? Who gave everything in the world names?*
- *Is a million billion zillion the biggest number?*
- *When there were no people, did God know that he was called God?*
- *Is every single person in the world really different? Are there a few the same anywhere?* (Roche 2007 p 194)

I firmly believe that none of these children could have articulated these questions, however, without having been exposed to rich language and to conversation with adults or more articulate others since birth, or even before birth. The much cited study published by Hart and Risley (1995) showed a remarkable correlation between the amount of talking between parents and their children in the first 3 years and the child's academic success at 9 years of age. Notably, the more talking that occurs during infancy, the more likely the child will do well in school later in life, which as we have seen has been borne out by other studies such as those carried out by Wells.

Learning language

The ability to learn spoken language is one of the most amazing accomplishments of human beings. And, unless we are born with a condition that affects our ability to do so, we learn spoken language very naturally in our first few years. Crystal (2005) tells us that

> children learning the sounds of speech have quite a mountain to climb. In English, for example, they have over forty vowels and consonants to learn, some 300 ways in which these produce syllables, and several patterns of stress and tones of voice. But by three, the basic pronunciation system is established and by five there is very little left to learn.
>
> (p 79)

Later on he says: 'By the time their first words appear, babies have learned a great deal, both from observation and from practice, about what a conversation is and how to participate within it' (p 81).

Halliday (1993 p 101) speaking about how infants develop language, says that 'it is the combination of the *experiential and the interpersonal* that constitutes an act of meaning. All meaning – and hence all learning – is at once both action and reflection'. He goes on to speak about 'the dialectic of system and process' – 'the principle whereby (a) from acts of meaning children construe the system of language, while at the same time, (b) from the system they engender acts of meaning. When children learn language, they are simultaneously processing text into language and activating language into text' (p 104). In other words, as children are learning language, they are learning *about* language and learning *through* language. And they are learning to make meaning of themselves and others and the world through language.

> ...language development is learning how to mean; and because human beings are quintessentially creatures who mean (i.e., who engage in semiotic processes, with natural language as prototypical), all human learning is essentially semiotic in nature. We might, therefore, seek to model learning processes in general in terms of the way children construe their resources for meaning – how they simultaneously engage in 'learning language' and 'learning through language'.
>
> (Halliday 1993 p 93)

Authentic and meaningful experiences during the early years at home and in school, can provide language opportunities that will develop, enhance and sustain language growth (Fillmore and Snow, 2000). Early childhood teachers can provide opportunities for young children to play with language, and at the same time, gain an appreciation of the sounds and meaning of words (Rubin and Wilson, 1995). Berk and Winsler, (1995, p 12), cited in Pantaleo (2007 p 439) state that:

> language plays a crucial role in a socially formed mind because it is our primary avenue of communication and mental contact with others, serves as the major means by which social experience is represented psychologically and is an indispensable tool for thought.

Pantaleo (op. cit.) suggests that 'talk (oral or sign language) affects our construction of knowledge and understanding'. Drawing on Vygotskian theory she says that, as well as writing about the self-regulatory role of private speech or self-talk in guiding an *individual's* thought processes and actions, 'Vygotsky (1978) wrote about the fundamental role of language in *social* contexts in developing human cognition' (my emphases).

While also arguing that that oral language is crucial to literacy development and is a key indicator of children's reading abilities, Kirkland and Patterson (2005 p 391), citing Hall (1987), and linking with what Pantaleo (op. cit.) has to say, outline the conditions that allow oral language to emerge in children. The conditions are as follows:

> (a) children are the major constructors of language; (b) parent, teachers, and caregivers serve as facilitators, not transmitters, of language development; (c) language is embedded in the context of the daily life of the child; (d) children construct language in their pursuit of meaning and comprehension related to their world and print; (e) the conditions for developing language are identical to those for learning about the world; (f) social interaction is foundational to language development; (g) children understand the functions of language as they use it to clarify information about themselves and others; and (h) language is learned in a child-initiated, holistic manner.
>
> (Hall 1987 in Kirkland and Patterson 2005 p 391)

Suggesting that a classroom can serve as a hub of language events that help children to construct new understandings about receptive and expressive language, they cite Clay (1991) who states that children who have been offered few opportunities to hold conversations can have difficulties with comprehending oral and written language. 'Such children', Clay adds, 'may not have control of some of the most common sentence structures used in storybook English, and therefore are unable to anticipate what may happen next in the sentences of their reading texts'(p 38). Like many other commentators and researchers of early years education, Kirkland and Patterson (2005 p 397) argue that, as schools become more pressured to cover test content, opportunities for oral language in classrooms can very easily be sidetracked or even disappear. They suggest that teachers must ensure that they plan for and provide opportunities for children to engage in authentic language exploration in non-threatening contexts – in ways that allow every child to participate.

Storybook reading is acknowledged by researchers of literacy as a significant approach for increasing language learning in children. Studies, such as those carried out by Isbell *et al.* 2004; Kaderavek and Justice 2002; Lever and Sénéchal 2011; and Snow 2001, have shown that children make significant gains in a variety of different areas of development – both cognitive and social – through sharing in storybook experiences. Story reading offers children opportunities for developing their language and literacy, as well as allowing them to experience new vocabulary, and acquire readerly behaviours such as handling books, and reading from left to right. Story reading also fosters communication experiences for young children, when they have opportunities to discuss the text and illustrations (Kaderavek and Justice, 2002). Isbell *et al.* (2004 p 158) suggest that there are important connections between reading aloud to preschoolers and their later literacy success. Isbell *et al.* (op. cit.) also suggest that children who are frequently exposed to storybook reading are more likely to use complex sentences, have increased literal and inferential comprehension skills, gain greater story concept development, increase letter and symbol recognition, and develop positive attitudes about reading. Significantly, impressive improvement on measures of literacy have been found, when basic teacher training was combined with book readings in childcare centres serving low-income children (Isbell *et al.* 2004 p 158).

Halliday (1993 p 112) suggests that all learning – whether learning language, learning through language, or learning about language – involves learning to understand things in more than one way. He says that teachers often have 'a powerful intuitive understanding that their pupils need to learn multimodally, using a wide variety of linguistic registers'.

Picturebooks provide just such a multimodal language learning opportunity. Teachers who take time when reading aloud; who allow children to look at and engage with the pictures as well as the words; and who scaffold the children's learning by asking questions and inviting interaction, are supporting their pupils in learning not just about the story or the images, but about language itself. Jalongo and Sobolak (2011), writing about vocabulary development, state that, although it has been argued that children under the age of six months 'are not ready to attend to a story being read to them, research indicates that when infants are read to by parents and caregivers important literacy skills such as book awareness, print awareness, vocabulary development, fluency, and comprehension are developing' (pp 424–5). Kindergartners who had been identified as 'at risk', they say, were able to learn vocabulary effectively while sharing books. Moreover, the most effective way of accelerating vocabulary was for the adult to elaborate on the words in the story. In fact, the children with the lowest vocabulary made the greatest gains when the adult talked about the new words the children encountered in the book. All this would seem to point to children's active participation being essential for literacy growth. It would seem that reading aloud on its own is not enough. Jalongo and Sobolak (ibid.) suggest that repeated readings of children's books, as well as using literacy props and toys to extend the interaction, offer ways to enrich and extend young children's understandings of picture books. Others suggest encouraging children to draw their responses to stories (Evans 1998; Pantaleo 2005).

Reading picturebooks aloud and discussing them

Reading picturebooks aloud and discussing them offers a huge range of language experiences. Let's use three picturebooks as examples: one is a fiction story aimed at a readership of 0–3 years, one is a non-fiction book aimed at readers aged 4–8, and the final one is a fiction book aimed at readers of 8 years or older.

Time for Bed (0–3 years)

The first three openings in *Time for Bed* by Mem Fox and Jane Dyer (0–3) say: *It's time for bed, little mouse, little mouse, darkness is falling all over the house. It's time for bed little goose, little goose, the stars are out and on the loose. It's time for bed little cat little cat so snuggle in tight that's right like that'.*

Look at the language there. Small children are being gently introduced to baby animals and their mothers, with possibly new words, such as *calf, foal and pup,* being introduced for those who already know cow, horse and dog. They hear words like snuggle and phrases like 'darkness is falling', 'snuggle in tight', 'on the loose' and so on. If such words and phrases are repeated in rereads of the story and discussed and chatted about, the child is learning quite a lot about language and about the world.

My nephew George loved this book and could recite it from memory. He loved the phrase 'on the loose' and was able, at 3 years of age, to use it in varying contexts. 'Clean up those toys, Sophie: Mum's on the loose!' He made a 'spaceship' with some blankets and a play mat and told me he was collecting all the stars that were 'on the loose'. He also learned the phrase ' *hold your breath and make a wish*' from this story and would use it regularly. The ability to remember these phrases and use them correctly in appropriate contexts demonstrates a high level of comprehension.

Think of an Eel (4–8 years)

Karen Wallace and Mike Bostock's *Think of an Eel* is one of the most beautiful picture-books that I have in my collection, in terms of its language and illustrations. Aimed at readers aged 4–8 it is suitable for a much wider readership. The text has two different 'voices': the main 'story' is lyrical and poetic. The other voice is crisp and factual. The rich language is full of alliteration, onomatopoeia, and compound words. For example:

There's a warm weedy sea to the south of Bermuda. It's called the Sargasso. No wind ever blows there, no sailing ships sail there. For thousands of years there a secret lay hidden: this salt soupy sea is where eels are born. Deep down where it's blackest, eel egg becomes eel. He looks like a willow leaf, clear as crystal... The factual language accompanying those pages says: Baby eels are born in early spring. A real one is only this big (and there is a picture of a small leaf-like creature).

The lyrical text continues ...Imagine *this eel-leaf and millions just like him swimming on waves across the wide sea. Some are unlucky. The seagulls are waiting. Beaks snap like scissors through wriggling water.* The factual language says: *Young eels from the Sargasso travel to either Europe or to America – whichever their parents did before them.*

Snow (2013) suggests that 'we can teach children lists of words without expanding their knowledge, but we can't expand their knowledge without teaching words' (p 5). Books like *Think of an Eel* provide a rich range of vocabulary and help children hear and use new words, to develop what Snow (ibid.) says are 'webs of meaning around those words that give purchase on the meaning of the text'. Watery words flow through the text: ocean, sea, waves, flooded, seashore, stream, river, mudhole, pond, ooze, rapids, waterfalls, river banks, salt soupy sea, warm weedy sea. Words that characterise eels abound: 'swimming', 'navigating', 'slips through the ooze', slides from the mudhole', 'wriggling through the water', 'sinking through the sea'. Bostock's illustrations are sublime (see Mallett 2006 for a particularly good review).

When I introduced this book to children in first class (aged 6–7) they demanded repeated readings. The discussions were wide-ranging around the eels' intricate life cycle and the hazardous journey from egg to elver to eel to egg. They asked questions, demanded rereads, extra opportunities to re-examine the pictures again and again. They were fascinated by the seagulls' beaks 'snapping like scissors' and often repeated that line when using scissors. They wanted to find the Sargasso Sea on the globe to see if it really existed 'because it sounds like a fake place made up for this eel story'. They looked up eels on the computer in school and at home and parents reported that they were 'obsessed with eels'. They were aghast that a local smokehouse had smoked eel as a delicacy: 'after all those poor eels have to go through just to get born!' The book 'spawned' an interest in several other picturebooks in the same series but none of them held the children's attention quite like *Think of an Eel* had. In different classrooms with varying age groups the book sparked creative writing, oral language, artwork, science, geography, nature study and even music to accompany the eels' journey. The children decided that it needed a lot of different kinds of music because there were so many different parts to the journey. It opened up a discussion in SPHE about feelings and whether animals could feel emotions such as happiness, sadness or fear. There was talk about predators (those seagulls again), and about enemies and friends, and one child decided that survival was 'a war about staying alive that goes on all the time in nature'. Reading a book like this aloud and discussing it is only the merest tip of a vocabulary iceberg. Used as a cross-curricular thematic approach, it could constitute a whole term's work that would enhance several different kinds of language and literacy.

The Island *(8 years upwards)*

The third book: Armin Greder's (2007) *The Island* offers opportunities for expanding both vocabulary and awareness of issues around belonging, outsiders, inclusion and exclusion. It is a serious book and could be disturbing for some children. The 11- and 12-year-old children with whom I discussed this book had already discussed other serious books such as Van Allsburg's *The Widow's Broom*; McEwan and Innocenti's *Rose Blanche*; Skarmata and Ruano's *The Composition*; Bunting and Himler's *Fly Away Home;* Tsuchiya and Lewin's *Faithful Elephants* and Poole and Barrett's *Anne Frank*.

In *The Island*, a harmless stranger or outsider, naked and vulnerable, is washed ashore on an island and the island community react. The Island is populated by insular people. The cover of the book shows us a looming and gloomy, great, dark rampart and is quite off-putting, which is of course an intended effect. The illustrations help children to realise that words can sometimes obstruct truth. For example, on opening 1, the stranger stands helplessly near his raft as the villagers approach and the text says *'he wasn't like them'*. The children reacted strongly to this saying 'That's so not true! He's human, he's white, and he's a man. He is exactly the same as them!' On opening 3 we read 'So they took him in'. The illustration however shows a bunch of hefty male villagers with grim faces and armed with pitchforks, rakes, hoes and brooms herding the small naked, bewildered outsider in front of them. His nakedness serves to emphasise his fragility in the face of their clothed, robust and burly strength. They suggest that *'it would be best to put the man straight back on his raft and send him away without delay. I am sure he wouldn't like it here, so far away from his own kind'*. The children were amazed at this: 'Why did no one give him clothes? He must be freezing!' They slowly arrived at the idea that 'perhaps the people had more power if the man was left naked'. The islanders lock him up: *'they made him understand that he was to stay there and showed him where he could sleep on some straw'* says the text. And *'life on the island returned to what it had always been'* (opening 4).

When we examined the illustrations and looked at 'normal life' on the island one child said it was a bit like Anthony Browne's *Piggybook* 'because the mothers do everything and the dads just wait for their food and everything. The dads go out drinking with men and the mums stay at home washing up'. The children also commented on a detail on the bottom of the opening where the children are depicted playing a game that appears to imitate the behaviour of the adult males on opening 3. 'That's how the whole ... thing ...the ... hatred gets passed on. The kids learn it from the grownups.'

No one in the community, not even the teacher or the priest, helps the shipwrecked man. In fact they all find an excuse not to help him. The children saw this as being like the parable of The Good Samaritan in the RE syllabus. 'Except the good fisherman who wants to help the stranger never actually does anything really. He's too scared of them, and he's right, cos at the end they destroy his boat and he can't earn any money now. So they punish him for trying to help the stranger.'

As we worked our way through the uncomfortable text and the almost unbearable images, they felt at first that no people would really act like this if they came across a shipwrecked stranger, but gradually began to think about other stories where 'man's inhumanity to man' was all too evident. They surmised that every act of exclusion and every demonstration of hatred of others diminishes us. They made connections between this book and others such as Gandhi's story and were reminded of discussions we had had about Cave and Riddell's *Something Else*; Anne Frank's story in their history syllabus, McKee's *Tusk Tusk*, Foreman's *War and Peas*; Dosh and Mike Archer's *Yellow Bird, Black Spider* and Skarmata and Ruano's *The Composition*. They learned vocabulary such as racism, prejudice, zenophobia and misanthropy. They learned about how dictatorships exist through dehumanising others. These are serious topics and there are those who might frown at introducing them in a primary school. But if Viking invasions, Norman invasions, colonisation, and the genocide of the holocaust are included in the primary school history syllabus, then, we are already dealing with issues of cross-cultural hostility – unless we have become immune and desensitised to the realities of what *really* happens in war, colonisation, ethnic cleansing and invasion. The point I am making, however, in relation to language learning is, that merely creating a word wall or word bank of the words 'racism', 'stereotyping', 'prejudice', 'zenophobia' and 'misanthropy' would not lead to anything like the understanding and empathy that discussions about books like *The Island* can engender.

Rich language experiences

The three books explored above are just a tiny example of the kinds of rich language experiences that can be achieved when there is a symbiosis between a good picturebook, an enthusiastic teacher and a willing class of children. It is almost impossible to separate out language learning from the panoply of other kinds of learning going on – the democratic practices and social learning, the expansion of horizons, the development of emotional intelligence and the burgeoning critical literacy.

Summary

Oral language is central to learning. This chapter began with Halliday's (1993) statement that 'Language is the essential condition of knowing, the process by which experience becomes knowledge'. Research points to vocabulary building as being one of the most important aspects of developing children's language. We have seen that one authentic way of building vocabulary in a meaningful context is by reading aloud and discussing picturebooks with children. It is important to note that CT&BT should not replace existing specific oral language teaching; it should be seen as an opportunity for meaningful and authentic consolidation of oral language work.

Recommended reading

Biemiller, A. (1999) *Language and Reading Success*. Cambridge, MA: Brookline.
Boyd, M. and Galda, L. (2011) *Real Talk in Elementary Classrooms: effective oral language practice*. New York: The Guildford Press.
Crystal, D. (2005) *How Language Works*. London and New York: Penguin.

Dawes, L. (2005) *Teaching Speaking and Listening in the Primary School*. London: Taylor and Francis: David Fulton Publishers.

Evans, J. (2009) *Talking Beyond the Page: reading and responding to Picturebooks*. London: Routledge.

Fisher, R. (2009) *Creative Dialogue: talk for thinking in the classroom*. Abingdon, Oxon: Routledge.

Lindfors, J. (1999) *Children's Inquiry: using language to make sense of the world*. New York: Teachers College Press.

Mercer, N. (2000) *Words and Minds*. London and New York: Routledge.

Mercer, N. and Littleton, K. (2007) *Dialogue and the Development of Children's Thinking: a sociocultural approach*. Abingdon, Oxon: Routledge.

Chapter 5

Some picturebook theory

Introduction

As we have seen so far, my experience with picturebooks has been that they are immense sources of pleasure as well as a means of sparking off an interest in reading for children who are just beginning that process. We have seen how, by sharing them and discussing them together, children of all ages have developed thinking and dialogue skills. They are an excellent means of encouraging the development of critical literacy and visual literacy in people of all ages.

Discussing picturebooks has contributed hugely to my classroom becoming an open democratic space for collaborative enquiry and exploration. Picturebooks have provided my students and me with opportunities for creating knowledge and for expanding our understanding of and empathy towards others. Most of all picturebooks became a super resource for keeping engaged children who were in danger of losing the gift of loving to read. I know that picturebooks develop children's aesthetic interest and critical engagement and that they can spark lively discussions with people of all ages from preschool children to fully qualified teachers. As Nodelman (1988 p 284) says: 'The combination of words and pictures is an ideal way to learn a lot in a relatively painless way'.

Classroom practice

As I mentioned earlier, I have often used the same story in very different educational settings, as we saw with *Once Upon an Ordinary School Day*. Another example of this approach was when I read and discussed Dosh and Mike Archer's *Yellow Bird, Black Spider* with several different age groups. The story concerns an anarchic bird who flaunts convention and worries a spider who challenges this behaviour. Let's begin with what happened when I introduced it to a group of preschool children. They listened attentively to the story and when we began to talk about it, Amy led the discussion in a certain rather pragmatic direction – almost acting as a little surrogate black spider:

- **Amy:** *Birds shouldn't wear socks because their toes…their claws are kind of pointy and they would get stuck going in.*
- **Molly:** *It's the same for the ice-cream – he has wings and he doesn't have any hands.*
- **Jon:** *He couldn't live in a hotel cos you have to pay money and …he just couldn't.*
- **Lee:** *Yeah, I agree with Molly. How could he play the guitar? He don't have no fingers.*
- **Jenny:** *I don't like that spider.*
- **Niall:** *That bird is crazy!*

A group of 5 and 6 year olds however, focused on justifying the spider's demise. Led by Ian, they were glad the spider got his comeuppance:

- **Ian:** *Yeah I'm glad he got ate 'cause he was too bossy.*
- **Ber:** *He shouldn't of been telling the bird all them things in the first place.*
- **Laura:** *Birds are the boss of themselves and spiders are the boss of themselves, and say a mouse was bossing a cat? Well the cat would just eat it too.*
- **Cian:** *Yeah. He was a nerd. I was glad he got killed.*
- **Rob:** *Spiders don't know everything! He was just showing off.*

A group of 8 and 9 year olds saw the story as being about rights and felt the Yellow Bird's right to be himself was paramount.

- **Rory:** *That spider got what was coming to him. He was, like, sooo annoying.*
- **Essie:** *Yeah. I was really glad when he got eaten. He was nagging, nagging, nagging. Someone had to shut him up.*
- **Sarah:** *The bird needed to feel free to be himself and that spider was just bugging him. He was asking for it.*

In another class, Alice, aged 10, suggested that yes, the yellow bird had a right to be himself. Then she added:

- *But…I dunno…doesn't that mean that the spider has the right to be himself too? Yellow Bird took away the spider's rights when he ate him. We can't just give rights to one side and not the other!*

Suddenly I saw the story in a whole new light and it led us to new discussions about issues that are difficult to resolve because they involve a conflict of two or more rights. Pat (10) agreed:

- *Yeah that's probably why the North took so long to solve! Each side has to see that the other crowd has rights too!*

Other children amazed me by demonstrating knowledge of politics with which I would never have credited them – despite having long ago read Coles (1986) who wrote *about The Political Life of Children.*
    Greg (10) agreed with Pat:

- *Look at Israel and Palestine. And, like, everyplace where there's wars going on …well … that's just like being a bully. If you bully people they're going to fight back sometime. But if you think about people always having rights …well then, you could maybe talk to them about stuff.*

Third-level education students felt the story was about social acceptance, control, difference, freedom, individuality and civic rights, and felt it could be also be used to prompt discussion about inclusion and tolerance with second-level pupils as part of RE, SPHE, SESE, Civics or Social Studies. A group of qualified primary teachers felt the story was about identity, about conforming versus being creatively individual, and about the associated rights and responsibilities that being true to oneself can involve.

As you can see once again, one 'simple' picturebook can generate discussions that expose a wide diversity of perspectives and assumptions about the world. Picturebooks have huge potential for exploratory dialogues between adult and adult readers, as well as between adult and child and child and child readers. Picturebooks invite speculative and imaginative responses because of the indeterminacies, or gaps (Iser 1988), the filling of which makes the potential for meaning-making rich enough that the reader becomes a coauthor of the text (op. cit.).

It is possible, however, to use picturebooks in this way and never examine them other than for the quality of the text, illustrations and the potential they hold for classroom discussion. I did this for years. Then in the early 2000s I began to study the subject of 'picturebooks' and discovered some of the enormous volume of books and papers that have been written about them – not to mention the thousands and thousands of picturebooks that have been created since the early 2000s with advances in digital printing. Picturebooks have been examined as visual artefacts and narrative devices; they have been explored for their literacy and literary elements, their psychological import, their feminist stances, their criticality and their subversiveness and more. And, as I researched the genre, I became aware of new aspects of which I had been hitherto unaware: the 'intertextual', 'metafictive', 'semiotic', 'polysemic', and 'multimodal' elements of picturebooks. I read about irony and post-modernity and I discovered that the phenomenon of what constitutes 'picturebooks' represents an amazing diversity of perspectives in a very rich field of study.

So what are picturebooks?

We will now taste a sample from a smorgasbord of the many theoretical frameworks that surround picturebooks.

'A picture book has to have that incredible seamless look to it when it's finished. One stitch showing and you've lost the game' (Maurice Sendak, cited in Gollapudi 2004 p 112).

First of all we need to decide what exactly we are talking about when we say the word 'picturebook' and even this is complex. For example, there are several different ways to spell or to present the word – each of which carries a slightly different emphasis: picturebook, picture book, picture-book. Larry Sipe's posthumous paper refers to 'picture storybook' as well as 'picturebook' (in Mackey 2012 p 4). I also prefer to use the single word 'picturebook' because it seems to me to have within it the intricacy of the relationship between words and pictures and also allows for the 'wordless' form and the non-fiction form.

Somewhat in agreement, Perry Nodelman who, in 1988, wrote what is considered to be one of the first serious analyses of picturebooks, begins his book by saying simply 'Most picture books tell stories' (p 1) and that 'they are a successful and interesting way of telling stories and that they 'give pleasure to 'viewers and readers, both children and adults' (p 3). Because picturebooks are largely works of fiction, Nodelman (who, incidentally refers throughout to them using two words – 'picture books') suggests that they are intended largely for children and that those who want to study them should first of all study fiction in general. The word 'largely' is important to bear in mind as many exceptions occur. Non-fiction picturebooks like *Think of an Eel* are a genre all in themselves, as are picturebooks for older readers – think of Raymond Briggs' *Gentleman Jim, When the Wind Blows, The Tin-pot Foreign General and the Iron Lady, Ethel and Ernest,* as well as many other books like Morimoto's *My Hiroshima,* Skarmeta and Ruano's *The Composition* and Armin Greder's *The Island.*

Nikki Gamble (2013 pp 208–33) has devoted a whole chapter to examining 'picture books'. Her book is aimed at teachers and she too, emphasises the 'ways in which picture books provide a unique reading experience for readers of all ages, not only the very young' (p 208). Shaun Tan (2010) captures something of the complex nature of the intended readership of picturebooks in an essay entitled *'Pictures and Words: an Intimate Distance'*:

> If I happen to mention to someone that I write and illustrate picture books, they will often tell me about a child they know who loves reading, assuming that I am a children's author – which is neither correct nor incorrect. If I show an example of my published work, the question I am often asked is 'who did you do this for?', because the target age group is unclear. It's a difficult question to answer, as it would be for anyone who paints or writes according to their own personal interests. Not unsurprisingly, my books are simultaneously treated as children's, young adult and adult titles, depending on reader, bookseller, publisher and country of publication – it really seems more of a cultural question than an aesthetic one. As a creator, my main concern is simply to explore a form of visual and written expression which seems ideally suited for certain subjects.
>
> (np)

Two distinct modes of representation

Picturebooks combine 'two distinct modes of representation' (pictures and words) 'into a composite text' according to Lewis (2001 p xiii). Lewis introduces us to several of the puzzles that present themselves as we try to define what exactly constitutes a picturebook.

> Are picturebooks first and foremost books – that is, stories that just happen to be 'told' in pictures as well as words – or are they better thought of as a kind of narrative visual art that happens to be annotated or captioned with words? Is it really the pictures that lie at the heart of picturebooks, or do we need to look for ways in which the pictures and the words interact and work upon each other?
>
> (Ibid.)

Let's try to find out by examining more definitions.

Some of the many definitions of picturebooks/picture-books/ picture books

I have tried to find as many definitions as possible that simultaneously will show us the complexity of the term while also, perhaps, helping us to get closer to understanding the form.

Salisbury and Styles (2012 p 7) spoke about 'the role of the image in the narrative' and suggest that: 'The picturebook as it is today is a relatively new form. We may debate its true origins but it is only 130 years since Randolph Caldecott began to elevate the role of the image in the narrative'. Johnston and Frazee (2011) said:

> In the most basic, classic, and very best sense, you could say [a picture book is] a story for young children told in both words and pictures that unfolds over thirty-two or so printed pages that are sewn together at the spine and housed within hard card-board covers. And this story, when read aloud, will cast a spell over all who are present to hear it and look at it; and, with luck, it will go straight into their hearts and never be forgotten.
>
> (np)

Barbara Bader provided a different kind of definition back in 1976. Her definition is the most frequently used and, to my knowledge it has not been surpassed for its comprehensiveness:

> A picturebook is text, illustrations, total design; an item of manufacture and a com-mercial product; a social, cultural, historic document; and foremost, an experience for a child. As an art form it hinges on the interdependence of pictures and words, on the simultaneous display of two facing pages, and on the drama of the turning page. On its own terms its possibilities are limitless.
>
> (Bader 1976 p 1)

Margaret Meek (1991 p 116) refers to the rich potential of picturebooks for developing imaginative responses, when she says: 'Picture books are not simply privileged reading for or with children. They make reading for all a distinctive kind of imaginative looking'. David Lewis (2001) elaborates on the developmental or evolutionary aspect of the form and talks about the fact that reading picturebooks occurs at the intersection or at 'the point where adult, child and the wider culture meet', when he says that ' the charm and the challenge of the picturebook arise directly out of its variety and versatility, its capacity for endless metamorphosis' (p 136). Anticipating the future he said:

> We never quite know how the next generation of picturebooks will look. The capacity for genre incorporation will always ensure new words, new images and new combinations of word and image. The picturebook is thus ideally suited to the task of absorbing, reinterpreting and re-presenting the world to an audience for whom negotiating newness is a daily task.
>
> (Lewis op. cit. pp 136–7)

Lewis adds that:

> it is not an insignificant fact that the reading of picturebooks commonly takes place at the point where adult, child and the wider culture meet. The image of parent and child sharing a favourite picturebook is a key one, and it should remind us that in order to understand the book we need to understand its role in the complex inter-change of gesture, language, ideas and images that go to make up the picturebook reading event. Formal accounts of the picturebook will, in the end, never be enough.
>
> (Ibid.)

This is one of the real complexities: no one formal account will suffice because picturebooks are so diverse and because they are still in a process of evolution.

Michaels and Walsh (1990) wrote: 'Once upon a time picture books were considered to be merely children's books. ...they told tales that appeared to be simple and were constructed so that the story was enlivened by pictures ...for many years picture books have been confined to the menu for younger children' (p 3). Referring to the 'dual symbolic systems' of picture and book they go on:

> Pictures and picture books are an important part of the meaning making process. Reading pictures is just as complex, perhaps more complex, than reading print: it can also be just as rewarding as reading print. When the two symbolic systems work together the satisfaction, enjoyment and stimulation is more than doubled. ...In a world that relies increasingly on visual means of communication, picturebooks have established themselves as a complex literary genre in which both verbal and visual cues structure meaning.
>
> (op. cit.)

Perry Nodelman (1988) suggests that 'Good picture books offer us what all good art offers us: greater consciousness – the opportunity, in other words, to be more human' (p 285). Shaun Tan (2002) focuses on meaning-making and critical literacy when he writes: ' For me, a successful picture book is one in which everything is presented to the reader as a speculative proposition, wrapped in invisible quotation marks, as if to say "what do you make of this?"'

> What makes art and literature so interesting is that it presents us with unusual things that encourage us to ask questions about what we already know. It's about returning us, especially we older readers, to a state of unfamiliarity, offering an opportunity to rediscover some new insight through things we don't quite recognise ... The lessons we learn from studying pictures and stories are best applied to a similar study of life in general – people, places, objects, emotions, ideas and the relationships between them all. At its most successful, fiction offers us devices for interpreting reality, and imagining how many such interpretations might be possible. ... we go on being children, regardless of age, because in life we are always encountering new things that challenge us to understand them, instances where a practised imagination is actually more useful than all laboriously acquired knowledge.
>
> (Tan 2002 np)

In 2010 he wrote:

> 'Picture books' ... tend to feature a concise narrative, handfuls of words and pictures held between cardboard covers. There is an appealing simplicity in the form, which is not to say that it is necessarily simple: the restrained coupling of text and image can contain any level of poetic sophistication or complexity. ... Picture books are usually intended for children which, again, is not to say that they need to be: many contemporary picture books are not created with young readers in mind, including my own. If it is thought that picture books are for children, this is merely an observation of

conventional publishing culture in most English-speaking countries, not an intrinsic quality of the medium itself.

(Tan 2010 np)

Tan's differentiation between the 'appealing simplicity of the form' and the fact that picturebooks are far from simple is important. Some commentators focus on the 'appealing simplicity' aspect. Kate Edwards, Seven Stories UK, says that 'Picture Books are for everybody... Long before we can read words we can "read" pictures, developing a sophisticated enjoyment of story, empathy with others and understanding of the world – all vital skills for life today' (http://www.booktrust.org.uk/, np.) On the same website, Anthony Browne, talking about the reading of both pictures and words, refers to the idea of simplicity but also notes the 'tantalising gap' to be filled by the reader. He says 'the best picture books leave a tantalising gap between the pictures and the words, a gap that is filled by the reader's imagination, adding so much to the excitement of reading a book'.

Others see picturebooks as tools for encouraging thinking: Maagerø and Østbye (2012) are among many who write about using picturebooks for encouraging philosophising. Referring to the potential that picturebooks have for engendering rich, philosophical engagement, and also emphasising the 'gaps to be filled', Maagerø and Østbye (2012) suggest that 'gaps in the iconotext ...may encourage the readers to go into dialogues concerning philosophical wonderings and puzzles'.

The dialogue may involve efforts to define and agree upon what might be found within the gaps. Consequently, the adults' traditional position as the authority who knows the single right answer to questions within the iconotext is disturbed. Instead, both readers enter into an inter-dependent reading process there and then. This might make the dialogue turn into a more democratic one, as the co-reading is no longer a situation where the child reader constantly tries to 'prove' to have understood what the experienced adult reader already knows.

(p 324)

Baddeley and Eddershaw (1994) suggest that even the apparently simplest form of picture book (one without text) can be much more complex than it appears. They state that such 'textless' picture books are often regarded as straightforward enough for children to look at on their own 'because they have no print and anyone can follow pictures!' (p 2). This appears ludicrous, they say, because, in textless picture books the task of telling the story is passed to the reader. 'Unless children can understand the conventions in all their variations that illustrators employ, they will have difficulty understanding the story' (ibid.). This is especially true of highly sophisticated or 'postmodern' picturebooks, which flout conventions such as sequence and linearity of narrative, as we will see later.

Sanders (2013 p 79) states that research on children reading picture books has consistently revealed that there is one task in the process of interpreting them at which children are much better than are adults and that is noticing details. I have described how this frequently happens when I read books with children. They see minutiae and details that many adults miss. A class of 8 and 9 year olds noticed the wolf poster, the happy pig poster and Mr Gee feeding the birds in *Once Upon an Ordinary School Day*. My 9 and 10 year olds saw repeated motifs in David Wiesner's books, and spotted that Chris Van Allsburg's books always include the same white dog somewhere among the illustrations.

Sanders (op. cit.) notes that Arizpe and Styles discovered that children frequently noticed and drew meaning from formal aspects of images, such as illustrators' chosen media and technique as well as 'the use of shadows, line and, perhaps most frequently, colour' (Arizpe and Styles 2003 p 199). Citing Nikolajeva (2010) Sanders (op. cit.) argues that the more complex the illustrations on a double-page spread of a picture book are, the better children are at reading them, especially as compared with adults: 'Here, young children show extreme competence, studying the images carefully, while adults, focusing on verbal codes, feel an urge to go further onto the next doublespread' (Nicolajeva 2010 p 31). This was certainly the case in my experience. The children often wanted extra time to study one picture or asked to return to it where they saw details that I had missed. I described this process in Chapter 2.

Moebius (2011) noted: 'we read images and text together as the mutually complementary story of a consciousness', a metaphor that implies a harmony of related but different parts. However, he also comments on what he calls the '"plate tectonics" of the picturebook' so that sometimes, 'Between text and picture . . . we may experience a sort of semic slippage, where word and image seem to send conflicting, perhaps contradictory messages'(pp 142–43).

The idea of the complexity of picturebooks is very well developed in Nicolajeva and Scott (2006). They suggest that picturebooks made by single author/illustrators – who are 'completely free to choose either of the two aspects of the iconotext to carry the main load of the narrative' – provide the 'most exciting counterpoint between text and picture' (p 17).

The aesthetic relationship between pictures and text

Sipe (2012) examines the relationship between pictures and text and makes special reference to the 'highly sophisticated aesthetic' nature of picturebooks. And, if we are honest, isn't it that aesthetic quality that attracts us? Isn't that what leads us to pick up a book in a bookshop? It's that aesthetic quality, as well as the quality of the narrative, that hooks us into wanting to read the book. We already spoke about the beauty of images and language in books like *The Black Book of Colours, Think of an Eel* and *Time for Bed*. There are books like Mem Fox and Nicholas Wilton's *Feathers and Fools*, Shaun Tan's *The Red Tree*, Paul Fleischman and Bagram Ibatoulline's *The Matchbox Diary*, Margaret Wild and Ron Brooks' *Fox* or Jon Klassen's *This is Not My Hat* that struck an aesthetic chord with me. There are 'silent or wordless' books like Jerry Pinkney's *The Lion and The Mouse* and David Wiesner's *Flotsam*, Bob Staacke's *Bluebird* or Aaron Becker's *Journey* – all very beautiful books, where the illustrations tell the story and I just *had* to buy them. In each of these cases, and many, many more I chose the book simply because of their attractiveness as aesthetic objects.

Tastes differ

Interestingly, children do not always agree with my interpretation of beauty. *Looking and Responding to Art* is a strand of the Visual Art Curriculum in Ireland, so each year I spread out all our picturebooks on tables and invited the children (mixed boys and girls aged 8–9) to choose two or three picturebooks whose illustrative style appealed to them. They were then invited to discuss why they chose particular books. On several occasions, there appeared to be an immediate divide between those who liked representational art: books like Margaret Barbelet and Jane Tanner's *The Wolf*; Amy Hest and P.J. Lynch's *When Jessie Came Across the Sea;* and Dyan Sheldon and Gary Blythe's *The Whales' Song,* for example, and those who preferred books that had more cartoon-like art or had native or folk tale art. The reasons varied: Jeff and Beth both said they 'hated arty pictures that were like photographs':

- **Beth:** *When they're sad stories it's, like, nearly too much to take…it's kind of too real.*

On the other hand, Jeff thought they were 'a bit girly.. a bit soft, like…'. There were children who agreed with both, but despite Jeff's comment, there was no clear gender divide. Those who liked cartoon style or less realistic pictures spoke about individual artists:

- **Robin:** *Satoshi Kitamura makes me laugh. He's …like … able to make it look real even when it's not… he makes me laugh the way he does mouths and eyes!*

Several children liked humour. Many liked Anthony Browne's illustrations:

- **Anna:** *He's brilliant at doing fur and hair like in* Zoo *and* Gorilla… *and he does all these like, complicated sort of details in wallpaper that give you loads of clues and all like in* Gorilla *and* The Tunnel.
- **Jenny:** *He can make things look real but still you know it's only a story. Except for* Hansel *and* Gretel *– that's so scary. I can't look at that at all!*

Other children liked illustration that made them think. Carla and Peter led a group that loved Shaun Tan's work and David Wiesner's work:

- **Carla:** *You think you understand it, then you talk to someone else about what you think and they say 'that's not what I think' and they tell you theirs and then you go back and then you, like, see even more …different, sort of.*

Other children chose artists because they wanted 'to draw like them'. Evelyn and Shane both loved copying the style of art in Paul Fleischman and Kevin Hawkes' *Weslandia;* Aimée loved David McKee; Claudia led a group who loved 'the way Julie Vivas' people are so roundy and sort of cosy!'; several of the girls liked Jane Ray's work because of 'the gold and the swirly details'; some enjoyed the silhouettes of *The First Christmas* by Jan Pienkowski and Ciara said she had 'loved him ever since *Meg and Mog*' because she could 'draw the witch so easily by copying him'. Others agreed to varying degrees and cited 'The two Tomis' among their preferences: Tomie de Paola's 'Irish' stories and Tomi Ungerer's *The Three Robbers.*

This 'Looking and Responding' exercise was generally repeated at the end of each school year and the children's views usually remained largely unchanged. When children had studied an artist's work specifically, or an art technique like cross-hatching, they often grew in appreciation of the work. This happened after we looked at Sendak's different styles in *Where the Wild Things Are* and *In the Night Kitchen.* After a series of lessons on collage and Matisse, they appreciated Eric Carle's work all the more. The 'Looking and Responding to Picturebook Illustration' exercise is worth doing, I think, because learning about visual styles and identifying the styles of particular artists can lead to aesthetic development and active thinking about artistic styles and genres, and instigates what Jane Doonan (1993) calls 'close looking' when new picturebooks are presented for discussion. Teachers wishing to develop professionally in the area of visual literacy should read Doonan's and Perry Nodelman's work. They both provide an excellent starting point for examining pictures in picturebooks. But picturebooks have much more than artwork to offer. Let's look now at some of the other qualities of picturebooks starting with the metafictive element.

Metafiction

Mo Willems' *Piggy and Elephant* series features a book called *We are in a Book*. This is a good example of metafiction: characters that are aware of their existence in a book and, thus, make us aware of it too. Lane Smith's *Its a Book!* is a very metafictive book in that it constantly tells us that 'Its' a Book!' I read this book to my nephew George when he was four and he begged constant rereads from his mum. Throughout each reading he would laugh uproariously. This was somewhat to do with the deadpan humour and the fact that Gorilla is trying to convince Jackass that a book is not a digital device. (George thought that 'jackass' was a rude word, which added to the hilarity). But his delight also had a lot to do with his mum's ability to read aloud very dramatically.

Books that feature characters using crayons or pencils to sketch or draw themselves out of trouble, such as Crockett Johnson's classic *Harold and the Purple Crayon*, and more recently Anthony Browne's *Bear Hunt* are good examples of metafictive texts. Ahlberg and Ingman's *The Pencil* and Louise Yates' *Dog Loves Drawing* both show how characters subvert the normal course of narrative by seeming to be autonomous. Van Allsburg's *Bad Day at Riverbend* is slightly different because someone other than a character in the book – and not, it appears, the author/illustrator – is 'drawing'. Then there are books like Klausmeier and Lee's *Open This Little Book* where instead of characters in the book, you find more books; or McKinlay and Rudge's *No Bears,* a book that states 'there are no bears in this book', yet there is a bear on every page who helps solve 'the problem'. Emily Gravett's *Wolves* plays with alternative endings and Lehrhaupt and Forsythe's *Warning: Do Not Open This Book!* has the author speaking directly to the reader.

According to Cashore (2003) metafiction is 'self-conscious fiction, fiction that draws attention to its nature as a construction and as non reality'. She adds that metafiction is 'generally opposed to realistic fiction, which attempts to hide its representational nature by appearing as realistic as possible' (p 147). Beatrix Potter did it when she addresses the reader in *The Tale of Benjamin Bunny*; Charlotte Bronte did it when she says 'Reader I married him'. Contemporary picturebooks that speak directly to the reader in this way include the work of writers like Emily Gravett, David Macaulay, David Wiesner, John Scieszka and many more. Speaking about *The Stinky Cheese Man* Nikola-Lisa (1994) says that 'Scieszka and Lane Smith have produced the epitome of the postmodern book; not only do they turn upside down every popular tale related, but they bring into question the very nature of what a book is – this is deconstruction at its best!' (p 39).

Likewise, David Macaulay's *Black and White* is an incredibly complex metafictive picturebook. The author, in his Caldecott acceptance speech (1991), said that the subject of *Black and White* 'is the book. It is designed to be viewed in its entirety, having its surface "read all over." It is a book of and about connections – between pictures and between words and pictures'. In a humorous and yet serious speech, Macaulay criticises modern parenting and passive children trained not to look or see. Speaking of *Black and White*, he says enigmatically that it is 'four stories or maybe not, four journeys or maybe one. Black and White in full color. From utter confusion and disorder comes the illusion of utter confusion and disorder. Subversive publishing' (Macaulay 1991).

One of my teaching friends DMcC said that his class of 9 and 10 year olds 'were fascinated by *Black and White*. They thought it was very slippery and elusive: just when you think you have it figured out something else pops into your reasoning. They kept on going back to it and taking it to read in small groups and then arguing about it. They wanted me to return to it, read it again with them and have more classroom discussions about it. They had never experienced a book like it before' (extract from conversation with DMcC Nov 2013).

The word 'experience' is key here. You don't just 'read' *Black and White*: it is a complete literacy experience demanding very complex skills of comprehension, analysis and interpretation. It completely subverts the convention of linear, sequential narrative. Sanders (2009 p 350) suggests that most metafiction is inherently subversive and that it can encourage the development of critical literacy skills. In her foreword to *Don't Tell the Grownups*, Alison Lurie (1990) argues that 'we should take children's literature seriously because it is sometimes subversive: because its values are not always those of the conventional world'. Then she adds ' of course, in a sense, much great literature is subversive, since its very existence implies that what matters is art, imagination, and truth in what we call the real world, on the other hand, what usually counts is money, power and public success' (Lurie 1990 p xi). I think Lurie would enjoy many of the picturebooks listed here.

Pantaleo (2002) offers us a detailed discussion of the metafictive devices used in Wiesner's *The Three Pigs* and shows how children engaged with them.

> Wiesner's text demands that readers take an active role in the construction of meaning and participate in co-authoring the story. Writerly texts (Barthes, 1970) such as The Three Pigs require readers to make interpretations, generate hypotheses, draw inferences, fill in gaps, and make connections. Thus, these texts strongly encourage readers to develop their abilities in comprehending text both inferentially and critically.
>
> (p 81)

Pantaleo (op. cit.) also argues that the trajectory of these stories requires readers to engage in different ways of reading. A teacher needs to think carefully and pose thoughtful and intelligent questions when discussing these types of books, in order for them to construct meaning from 'the nonlinear, multilayered and non-sequential' texts, she says. Young readers need the scaffolding and support of interactive classroom discussions to help them make sense of non-linear and metafictive texts such as Wiesner's *The Three Pigs*. Bearing out what I have said in previous chapters about classroom culture, social interaction and community of enquiry, it is interesting to see that Pantaleo also draws attention to such aspects:

> The nature of the classroom interpretive community …will influence the interactions that occur during read-aloud sessions, and these interactions will subsequently affect children's responses to and understanding of literature ..the children and I were partners in creating and negotiating meaning. The peer exchanges afforded the

children collaborative opportunities for scaffolding interpretations, extending under-standings, exploring significance, and constructing storylines.

(Ibid.)

Like Pantaleo and Sipe and others who have carried out interactive readalouds, I have found that children draw inferences, make interpretations and connections, generate hypotheses, and create several possibilities of meaning when reading picturebooks (see for example Pantaleo 2002, 2007; Sipe 2000; Sipe and Brightman 2009; Wolfenbarger and Sipe 2007). They frequently make *intra*textual connections where they create con-nections and links to earlier episodes, phrases, actions, illustrations, and characters within the *same* text like Browne's *Voices in the Park* for example. Then there were the children with whom I discussed McNaughton and Kitamura's *Once Upon an Ordinary School Day* one of whom *intra*textually referred back to Mr Gee as 'that guy who was feeding the birds!' and who made *inter*textual connections (where they see connections between other texts or illustrations as well as cultural knowledge and artefacts) when he said – 'I bet Satoshi Kitamura has a cat like that – he often has cats in his books!' Picturebooks such as those listed throughout this book, require a great degree of what Pantaleo calls 'reader participation in the creation of meaning' (Pantaleo 2004 p 186). Over the course of the past four chapters we have seen that reader participation is crucial to meaning-making. There is no space here for passive listening.

Semiotic

Anything that stands for something else is considered a semiotic: words, images, sounds, gestures and objects can all be termed semiotic, according to Peirce (1931–58). Picturebooks incorporate two main semiotic systems – text (lexical) and images (visual). Both systems carry meaning that the reader must extract. Each system can have multiple meanings and so, can be considered *polysemic*. Ambrose and Harris (2008) suggest that 'semiotics is the study of signs that offers an explanation of how people extract meaning from words, sounds and pictures. An understanding of semiotics helps a designer to instil work with references that enable them to communicate multiple layers of information to a reader' (p 66). Speaking of how we interpret pictures, they say:

> The way in which an image is presented dramatically affects how information is interpreted. Images are powerful communication devices because people can extract many different values from them as they often have cognitive meanings far beyond their denotative elements. Cognition refers to things that we have perceived, learned or reasoned. …A denotative meaning is the explicit literal meaning that we take from an image, essentially, taking what we see at its face value.
>
> (Ibid.)

Picturebooks convey both temporal and spatial information (Nodelman 1988 p 198). Wolfenbarger and Sipe (2007) suggest that this is one of the most significant features of picturebooks. 'Scholars of children's literature concur that in many ways it would be pos-sible to call the object a picturebook text (Lewis 2001 p xiv) because the images and text work so tightly together to convey temporal and spatial information' (Wolfenbarger and Sipe 2007 p 273).

Trifonas (2002) suggests that 'the picture-book is essentially an open form, a fluid textual entity, incorporating lexical as well as visual signs variably codified in an unceasing interaction of word, image, and reader'. He adds 'moreover, because the picture-book genre, by definition, is dependent upon the interaction of two separate yet integrated systems of signification (lexical and visual), it is a unique combination of literary and pictorial elements exhibiting high semantic or semiotic capacity' and he argues that 'it is this obvious semantic-semiotic endowment of the picture-book – the formal properties of its construction and structure making it ideal for the purpose of teaching young children by establishing "contexts for literary and real world understandings"' (np). Booker (2012 p ii) states that 'this notion of how the text and images work together or against each other can be useful to teachers who are engaging children in picturebooks and wish to extend, challenge or focus their thinking'.

Semiotics and advertising

Kress and Van Leeuwen (1996) suggest that from birth children are bombarded with a multiplicity of visual signs and symbols from which they must learn to make sense. Think of logos, brands, advertising symbols, sports team colours, etc. Wolfenbarger and Sipe (op. cit.) state that these images signal meaning and interpretation without the need for accompanying text because children have become accustomed to them from a host of interconnecting sources like television and other visual media, and from other contextualised sources such as eating places and sports events, and, as we will see below, from toys. Children become adept at visual meaning building through early exposure to such semiotic systems – a fact not lost on advertisers and brand promoters. Research by McAlister and Cornwell (2010), for example, shows that 'preschool children are capable of recognizing brands, and it has been suggested that 3- and 4-year-olds can readily name brands such as McDonald's, M&M's, and Oreos' (p 206). McAlister's and Cornwell then tested 3–4 year olds on several other kinds of products and their findings suggest that 'children aged 3 to 5 years have an emerging capacity to understand the symbols of brands for which they form part of the target segment. Preschoolers can and do judge others on the basis of brand use' (p 224). Teaching them to begin to deconstruct the meaning of images in the safe atmosphere of a discussion on picturebooks could be seen as a very powerful way to counteract some of the risks associated with being targeted by producers of commodities as outlined by McAlister and Cornwell (2010).

Teachers cannot hope to be able to teach children how to examine all kinds of media messages. However, by discussing the different semiotic systems of the picturebook, children may learn transferrable skills and knowledge that can be used to think critically about texts that are not readily available for discussion in the classroom. A similar point is made by Carrington 2003 when she says that being 'literate' is about 'having the skills and knowledge with which to participate in and transform one's social and cultural context'. The literacies with which our young children must engage to achieve this are 'increasingly multi-modal, complex and intertextual' she says (p 85). Here Carrington was examining the text phenomenon of what she calls 'glocalized' toys, in this case a brand of doll called Diva Starz. She says:

> It is incumbent upon us, then, to examine the kinds of messages these dolls send to our girl-children as they interact with them. They are clearly not printed texts. Instead, the Divas are powerful markers of the necessary expansion of the notion of

'text' in contemporary post-industrial societies and, more specifically, in discussions around literacy. …print literacy, in and of itself, is no longer sufficient to ensure successful participation in civic and social life.

(op.cit. p 84)

To be literate in relation to these texts requires different sets of skills and knowledge argues Carrington. This broader notion of text does not in any way negate print, she says, but 'goes beyond this one mode of message transference. Carrington (op. cit. p 95) argues that the emergence of consumer culture and 'the dominance of information technologies in the workplace and as a cultural icon have resulted in a change in the nature of 'text'. Messages can now be transported across time and place in an increasing number of media and modes' she says. She continues:

As we know, our understandings of literacy are always embedded in broader social and economic landscapes. … Children in contemporary western societies operate in new and different social and economic landscapes, characterized by new texts and technologies of production and dissemination. Undeniably, they require new and different literacies. Toys are one such text – that is, one such medium for transporting a message across time and place.

(p 94)

Children who have experience at discussing and examining picturebooks for their hidden messages or ideology may be able to begin to critique the consumerist ideology that is inherent in messages such as those implied by the utterances of Diva Starz. Carrington provides the following example of the Diva Starz dolls' utterances:

- *I just love to go shopping with my friends. It makes me so happy. Do you like shopping for birthday presents? Let's invite a friend to go shopping. Who should we invite? Fabulous. Let's go to the mall with our friends and find something we can wear to parties. Do you like shopping? What's your favourite store?*
- *Do you like shopping? What's your favourite store? That's a good one. Let's go to the mall with our friends and buy something we can wear to school.*
- *I'm so sad. I so need a new school outfit. Wanna go to the mall? Let's invite a friend to go shopping! Who should we invite? Fabulous, let's go to the mall with our friends and buy something we can wear to parties. Wanna go to the mall?* (cited in Carrington 2003 p 89)

In the same way as I asked children what they thought the authors of *Yellow Bird, Black Spider* wanted us to believe, or what they thought McNaughton and Kitamura felt about schools, we could ask what the makers of toys that talk about shopping and fashion want us to believe. It might provide us with valuable insights. Unfortunately I did not read Carrington's paper until 2013, and so I never facilitated a discussion about specific toys like Diva Starz with my primary school classes. However, we will see in Chapter 6 how children referred to Bratz dolls when asserting that princesses are hampered by the clothes they wear and are usually in need of rescue by a male prince. I did, however, discuss Carrington's paper with teachers during a workshop. They were horrified by the messages being transmitted by toys and admitted not to have given much thought to this aspect of ideology:

- *I had no idea. I just never thought about toys like this. I mean, I was aware about how the makers of ads about drink and cigarette and fashion and that, try to make us buy them and buy into a particular mindset etc... but not about toys!*
- *Its no harm at all to know this. Just the fact of even having our awareness raised is beneficial. It will inform how we address issues to do with advertising, as well as maybe ask children to examine what messages are being transmitted by digital and online games, etc.*

In 2006 I videotaped a discussion with 8 and 9 year olds based on reading Lobel's Frog and Toad story about *Dragons and Giants,* which examines the concept of bravery and whether courage or bravery can be visible in a person's appearance. In Lobel's story, Frog and Toad look in the mirror to see if they looked brave. This led to a lively discussion that quickly focused on gender.

CY, arguing that courage was not something that showed in a person's appearance and was not synonymous with size or physical strength, illustrated his point by suggesting that:

- *you could see this big strong guy and think he looks brave, but then something bigger comes along and then he's really scared and runs away screaming like a girl.*

In the video clip, one can hear a shocked intake of breath, followed by slightly embarrassed laughter from the other children, who were beginning to recognise gendered comments when they heard them. Subsequently, the dialogue turned towards discussing whether girls are as courageous as boys.

- **CM:** *Well men probably have a teeny bit more courage than women but only because they can get them to do things. Girls are treated like things – they stick them in their underwear [in ads] and throw them on the bonnet of a car – just to sell the car!* (Roche 2007 p 111)

Examining the lexical and visual semiotics of picturebooks and challenging their overt and covert ideologies, can become part of a practice that gradually extends children's awareness of self and identity of what it means to be a girl a girl or a boy: or of what it means to be human. They can begin to examine texts for bias and discrimination and, this may lead them to challenging covert consumerist messages as Carrington suggests needs to be done:

> A critical literacy capable of contributing positively to the life pathways of children in new economies must provide skills and knowledge to mediate 'self' in relation to global mass media and economic flows because, in the end, literacy is about who you are allowed to become in a given society.
>
> (op. cit.)

Intertextuality

This refers to the way in which links and connection are made between books and other texts. References can be direct or indirect, and work at both the visual and the verbal level. Books for younger children are frequently intertextual. Sipe (2000) states that when adults read they continually make connections between what they are currently reading and other texts they know in that they make links between their history as readers and what is currently in front of them whether it is an academic paper or a piece of fiction. Stories always 'lean on other stories' he says, and 'we understand stories partly in relationship to other narratives we have we have read or heard' (ibid.).

Think of the Ahlbergs' *Each Peach Pear Plum*, or McNaughton and Chichester Clark's *Not Last Night but the Night Before*: each of these depends on a child's knowledge of nursery rhyme characters in order to increase enjoyment as familiar characters are recognised and to extend interpretation and meaning-making. More elaborate and metafictive books such as Scieszka and Smith's The *Stinky Cheese Man* or Wiesner's *The Three Pigs* do the same thing, but at a more complex level, because they poke fun at conventional narratives. Other books subvert the well-known stories in other ways: some change the gender of the protagonist such as Osborne and Potter's *Kate and the Beanstalk* but maintain the narrative in a fairly traditional way; others subvert the traditional narrative such as in Babette Cole's *Princess Smartypants* or *Prince Cinders*. To enjoy Cole's stories best, however, we need to 'know' the original or traditional version. Books like Trivizas and Oxenbury's *The Three Little Wolves and the Big Bad Pig* take the traditional story and bring it into a contemporary setting, while also reversing the roles of goodies and baddies. Scieszka and Johnson's *The Frog Prince, Continued* parodies the 'happy ever after' element of the traditional story by imagining what happens after the Princess and her Frog Prince fall in love and marry. Mini Grey's *The Very Smart Pea and the Princess-to-be* tells that tale from the perspective of the pea, while Scieszka's *The True Story of the Three Little Pigs* invites readers to consider the wolf's point of view. Emily Gravett's *Little Mouse's Big Book of Fears* refers to characters like the Three Blind Mice who lost their tails. Nadia Shareen's *Good Little Wolf* depends on our understanding of what 'a big, bad wolf' is, in order to make complete sense. Again, a knowledge of the original story or rhyme enriches the meaning-making and interpretation opportunities, and of course, the enjoyment.

Other kinds of prior knowledge also extend the pleasure and the interpretation possibilities of picturebooks. If you know *Spinal Tap*, then the illustration in the Archers' *Yellow Bird, Black Spider,* depicting the eponymous bird holding a red electric guitar, has a little hidden meaning about which you can feel smug – that is if you 'get' the fact that the amplifier dial is turned to 11. As we mentioned before there are lots of similar clues in McNaughton and Kitamura's *Once Upon an Ordinary School Day*. Remember the wolf poster and the schoolboy pig poster? Have you looked up the Klauss Flugge reference yet?

In 2005 my daughter illustrated a children's book called *Billy Where Have All Your Friends Gone?* (Carville and Roche 2005). When Sarah created Billy's bedroom, she included references to a family photo; a poster about reading that she had made in the 1990s for my classroom (now featuring on the cover of this book); and some of her favourite toys and books. These references were subtle and would only be understood by close friends and family. Nevertheless, it made me wonder how much of each artist's personal life is included in the books they illustrate. In an interview, Anthony Browne spoke about his father's sudden death and how he used *My Dad* to remind himself of happier times. Each illustration has the orangey-brown tones of his Father's dressing-gown. 'It smelt like him and, hanging on a hanger, it looked like him. It just reminded me of how he was. I'd been wanting to do a positive book about fathers for some time but hadn't found the right way. The dressing gown was my starting point.' (Eccleshare, *Guardian*, 29 July 2000). Patricia Polacco's *Thank You Mr Falker*; Junko Moromoto's *My Hiroshima*; Raymond

Briggs' *Ethel and Ernest;* and Michael Rosen's *The Sad Book* are also examples of the inclusion of autobiographical elements in picturebooks. I have found that children engage differently when they are made aware of personal connections between books and their authors or illustrators. They often seek out these books for private reading or request to take them home after the more public classroom discussion ends.

Anthony Browne's books: *Gorilla; Voices in the Park;* and *The Tunnel,* for example, are full of both overt and subtle visual intertextual clues. We see Hannah and the Gorilla at the cinema watching Superman (or Supergorilla) and we see a reference to King Kong. Hanging in Hannah's room is a map of Africa. *Voices in the Park* is full of references also: to Mary Poppins and King Kong, to Magritte's art (bowler hats), da Vinci's *Mona Lisa,* Frans Hals' *The Laughing Cavalier,* Munch's *The Scream.* It is a complex book in that as well as all those intertextual references there are intratextual references within the story: the dogs chasing each other throughout, the changes in the various art pieces to reflect the mood of the viewer, etc.

Children who know the story of *The Snow Queen* might see a connection with that story and *The Tunnel.* However, *The Tunnel* is also highly intertextual in relation to the art of René Magritte (as are several of Browne's other books like *Voices in the Park, Changes,* and of course, *Through the Magic Mirror.* Those who are familiar with Magritte will enjoy the book at a different level to those who don't. According to Hateley (2009) Browne's references to Magritte are more prevalent in *The Tunnel* than in his earlier picturebooks and would seem to perform 'a kind of productive induction into cultural knowledge' (p 330). For those children who, independently or guided by adults, learn about Magritte's paintings, she says, 'a rich, intertextual reading experience will be available to them, and for those who do not the picturebooks still offer valuable opportunities to experience stories of childhood agency' (ibid.).

Wilkie-Stibbs (2005) however, describes 'the challenges and possibilities opened up for producers and decoders of intertextualities' and warns:

> Literature for children has to tread a careful path between a need to be sufficiently overreferential in its intertextual gap-filling so as not to lose its readers, and the need to leave enough intertextual space and to be sufficiently challenging to allow readers free intertextual interplay. It is on the one hand formally conservative, yet it is charged with the awesome responsibility of initiating young readers into the dominant literary, linguistic and cultural codes of the home culture.
>
> (pp 176–7)

Irony

Irony can be interpreted as saying the opposite of what we mean. Picturebooks present real opportunities for ironic representation. Nodelman (1998) devotes a whole chapter to irony. For example, he speaks about Pat Hutchin's *Rosie's Walk,* in which the text, one single and simplistic sentence describing where Rosie the Hen went for her walk, ignores the threat posed by the fox who is even depicted on the cover, shown again on the title page and on every single opening. This dialogue between the image and the word is the root of the 'irony' that Nodelman finds at the heart of the best picturebooks. Margaret Meek describes how small children immediately spot the fox, thus entering into a little conspiracy with the author – against the adult reading the book – so that the child listening to the story and looking at the pictures shifts perspective and 'becomes both the teller and the told' (Meek 1988 p 10). Dombey (2009 p24) says:

> What is not said may be as or more significant as the words on the page. In picture-books, such as Burningham's *Come Away from the Water, Shirley,* an apparently banal verbal text may be given enormous significance by the visual images. Through engagement with (not mere exposure to) such rich texts, children learn to shift perspectives … They learn that reading is an elaborate game with rules, that the printed word can offer satisfying complexities of meaning making through which they may explore other possibilities and other relationships with the world than those provided by first-hand experience alone.

Nodelman (op. cit. p 227) says that 'the irony inherent in the different natures of pictures and words is often subtle – easy to experience but hard to notice and comment upon'. He draws our attention to the irony presented in Sendak's *Where the Wild Things Are* where the story presents nightmarish ideas about monsters threatening a small child but where, in fact, the illustrations depict these monsters as soft and cuddly. 'Pictures are always different from words', he says 'and pictures and words together are always different from either on their own' (p 228). Nodelman also talks about 'two specific sorts of irony which develop when words and pictures come together in narratives'. He suggests that the first is 'the distance between the relative objectivity of pictures and the relative subjectivity of words; the second is the distance between the temporal movement of stories and the fixed timelessness usual in pictures' and he adds that 'all picture books are ironic in the extent to which they express these qualities' (p 229).

Many of the characteristics and qualities of picturebooks described so far can all come under an umbrella term called 'Postmodernism'.

Postmodern picturebooks

McNulty (2003) argues that children's texts both old and new are now scrutinised through the lenses of contemporary literary theory. Contemporary literary theory, she says, also has a role in the creation of these texts as well as in the criticism of them and, as a result, the books themselves demand much more sophistication in readers. She argues that many books written for children since 2000 bear the influence of postmodernism. Some of the influence, she says is visual as well as textual.

> Experimental forms, the play with words and forms, self-referential irony, and the questioning of ultimate meaning are not limited to adult work. In Black and White, the narrative, as well as the illustration, is divided into four strands. The author states at the beginning of the book that the four strands may combine into one story, or they may not. …Indeed, adult readers often complain because this does not fit their preconceived notion of what a picture book should be.
>
> (p 34)

McNulty (op. cit.) describes Sciezka and Smith's *The Stinky Cheese Man and Other Fairly Stupid Tales* as 'the best known of postmodern picture books'. In this book, she says:

one can view postmodern play at its best. It has a self-conscious play with the conventions of the picture book format, as well as the overturn of the expected story line. The title page, the endpapers, and the table of contents are all altered to show a self-conscious awareness of the conventions, which, in turn, call the reader's attention to that which we take for granted. The dedication page is printed upside down.

(p 34)

Citing Stevenson (1994) who says the book 'alters book elements that kids do not even know, or do not know they know; often the book teaches convention by subverting it' (p 33). McNulty continues by saying that children know from observing many other texts that the

convention of the printed page is a consistency in font size but Jack's story is a repetition of the same text in decreasingly smaller font. The book is postmodern not in text alone. The final endpaper is placed earlier in the book by Jack the Giant killer in order to fool the giant into thinking that the book is finished.

(Ibid.)

Sutton (1992 p 34) refers to the technique of Scieszka's book as 'bibliometricks–meta-tricks?' which calls attention to the fact of writing and book making (cited in Stevenson 1994 p 34).

I would rate Nadia Shareen's *Good Little Wolf* as another example of postmodernism. In a review (Sept 2011) published in *Inis* (the magazine of Children's Books Ireland) I wrote:

Straightaway an adult will sense that there is a bit more going on in 'Good Little Wolf' than meets the eye. Where's the copyright information? And the dedication? They should be at the front, shouldn't they? …why does South Park come to mind as we look at the innocent characters waiting for Mrs Boggins to begin the story? Shireen's tongue-in-cheek handling of the clever intertextual referencing is superb.

(Extract from Roche 2011a, *Inis*, Sept 2011)

According to Pantaleo (2005a p 19) several critics believe that the changes in contemporary children's and young adult literature reflect the broader historical, social, and cultural movement referred to as postmodernism. Pantaleo (2007 p 49) suggests that postmodern texts are self-conscious and self-referential, offering a plurality of meaning and a playfulness that invite the reader or viewer into a co-construction of meaning. Playful picturebooks, she says, such as those that 'adopt game-like disguises, break rules, and subvert conventions' are postmodern according to Lewis (2001 p 81).

Postmodern picturebooks then are books by authors and illustrators 'who deliberately work against a linear story pattern' (Wolfenbarger and Sipe 2007). Postmodernism, according to Booker (2012), is characterised by 'the mocking of traditional art forms'. Citing Goldstone's work (2002), Booker identifies four characteristics of postmodern books' designs and characteristics that distinguish them from more traditional books. They are: nonlinearity, self-referential, a sarcastic or mocking tone and an anti-authoritarian stance. These characteristics may not all be present in any one book however.

McNulty seemed to think that postmodernism is a feature of children's books since 2000 or so, and chose Wiesner's *The Three Pigs* as the ultimate in postmodernism because, she says, Wiesner has embedded characters and scenes from his previous picture books.

> The dragon comes from his 1988 *Free Fall*, and one of the scenes that the pigs pass through in their travels is a variation of page from his 1991 *Tuesday*, also a Caldecott Award winner. The boy dreamer from *Free Fall* also makes a cameo appearance in the *Three Pigs*, and the pigs themselves bear close resemblance to the pigs found briefly in both *Free Fall* and *Tuesday*.
>
> (McNulty 2003 p 35)

Interestingly the 9 and 10 year olds in my class had discovered some of this for themselves.

Pantaleo (2007 p 48) chooses *Black and White* as *her* ultimate example of postmodernism. She states that several researchers and theorists have written about *Black and White* and that:

> All acknowledge and respect Macaulay's genius and several write about the influential nature of his picturebook in the field of children's literature. For example, Dresang and McClelland (1995) describe *Black and White* as a 'masterpiece' (p 707), 'a journey that changes the very essence of literature itself' (p 704), and a book that provides a 'hypertext experience' (p 707).

Recently as I read Mo Willems' *That is Not a Good Idea* to two 4 year olds, Ian turned to Amy at the point where the wolf introduces his soup pot and said 'Uh-oh...I bet it's all a trick!' When I asked why he thought that, he said 'well it's a movie, right ...like a ... cartoon? and they *always* play a trick on the wolf'. At the end he said 'See? I knew it: I just *knew* it!' Interestingly, the ending had come as a surprise to his grandparents who said they had expected a typical traditional story ending, like Red Riding Hood. They thought at first, they said, that maybe a 'saviour' like the woodcutter would arrive and then Ian's grandfather said 'or maybe not because kids nowadays are used to violence and so I kind of half-expected it to be gory'. The opposite happened when I read Nadia Shireen's *Good Little Wolf*: the grandparents 'got' the ending, but the 4 year olds were oblivious of the reasons for the wolf's big tummy.

McClay (2000) has a different take on what 'kids nowadays are used to': She says that children encounter the postmodern 'at every turn in their fictional worlds'. While many adults see the postmodern as a departure from or a comment on 'tradition' in literature, she says, it *is* the tradition that children meet on television and in movies' (p 91). She suggests that even familiar shows such as *Sesame Street* use 'doubling, intertextuality and other metafictive devices' that children readily 'get'. She argues that the tacit knowledge that children gain through visual media can then enhance their reading of print literature – an enhancement that adults may 'undervalue or miss entirely' (p 91) – and she concludes her paper with the advice that 'We do well to take a lesson from [children's] use of computers—children install the program and start to play; they don't read the manual' (p 105).

In print media, picturebooks provide a means of exploring children's abilities to understand the postmodern. They are full of ambiguities, are playful and parodic and often take visual and textual licence. Meek (1988 p 30) notes that a reader's move into newer, harder books depends on a tolerance for ambiguity; an understanding that patience is needed; and a sense of confidence that the author will eventually resolve the puzzles. McClay (op. cit.) suggests that a tolerance for ambiguity marks the difference between readers who only read the same kinds of reading material and those who move on to more varied and difficult reading (p 105). This would seem to me to be a plea to teachers to introduce children to postmodern picturebooks as a means of developing sophisticated comprehension and meaning-making skills. It would appear, from my reading of many commentators, that research shows that most children are able to cope with postmodern ambiguities.

Lewis (2001) writes that, 'one can see why metafictive devices are essential to the post-modernist enterprise, with its sustained attack on all manifestations of authoritative order and unity' (p 94). Egoff (1981 p 248) argues that the current state of picture books exemplifies a 'double paradox'. She goes on to suggest that the seemingly cosy and simple picture book actually produces the greatest social and aesthetic tensions in the whole field of children's literature, and also, that the genre which seems to be the simplest actually is the most complex, employing two art forms, the pictorial and the literary, to engage the interest of two audiences (child and adult) (see also Evans 1998).

Sipe (2000) warns about ignoring the power of complex children's literature. Speaking about the life-informing and life-transforming power of such literature, and its ability to 'defamiliarise life' so as to help us imagine the possibilities of social change and a more just social order, Sipe (op. cit.) cites Hunter (1992) and says that 'literature should allow children to have [their] imagination carried soaring on the wings of another's imagination, to insert the texts they hear and read into the texts of their own lives, and to broaden their view of what is possible'. According to Sipe (op. cit.), 'every child – and each of us – stitches together a view of reality made of many texts, and stories may figure largely in the bricolage that each of us produces'. And this, he says, 'is the real work of life' (p 89).

Summary

We have seen that, far from being simple children's stories, picturebooks are complex structures, full of interpretative potential for play and fun. They are polysemic and multimodal and ironic and intertextual and metafictive and postmodern, and ultimately children will either like them or not. Understanding some of the theory is useful and may help us to choose picturebooks for discussion and interpretation with children. However, while having our awareness raised about the many underlying traits and characteristics of this genre will prove very beneficial when choosing picturebooks and analysing them in advance of introducing children to them, it is quite possible to have wonderful discussions with children about picturebooks without knowing their many theoretical frameworks.

Recommended reading

Arizpe, E. and Styles, M. (2003) *Children Reading Pictures: interpreting visual texts*. London: RoutledgeFalmer.

Doonan, J. (1992) *Looking at Pictures in Picturebooks*. Stroud, Glos: Thimble Press.

Evans, J. (ed.) (1998) *What's in the Picture: responding to illustrations in picture books*. London: Paul Chapman.

Gamble, N. (2013) *Exploring Children's Literature*. 3rd ed. London and Thousand Oaks, CA: Sage.

Graham, J. (1990) *Pictures on the Page*. Sheffield: NACE.

Lewis, D. (2001) *Reading Contemporary Picturebooks: picturing text*. Abingdon, Oxon: Routledge.

Nicolajeva, M. and Scott, C. (2006) *How Picturebooks Work*. New York and London: Garland.

Nodelman, P. (1988) *Words about Pictures: the narrative art of children's picture books*. Athens, GA: University of Georgia Press.

Stewig, John W. (1995) *Looking at Picture Books*. Fort Atkinson, WI: Highsmith Press.

Chapter 6

CT&BT in the classroom

Reading is necessary to an open mind. It makes us think. Even if we disagree with what we read, we are weighing that information against what we already believe or know. That act alone can bring about a deeper understanding, or a desire to read more. I believe that not only should all children be taught how to read, but they need to be exposed to great literature and provided time for thoughtful conversations.

(Schaefer 2013 np)

In Chapter 5 we looked at picturebooks and briefly examined the many literatures around some of the characteristics and complexities of picturebooks. Now we will quickly recap on what I mean by a 'good' picturebook and then examine how I used them with different age-groups beginning with the junior classes in primary school.

A good picturebook

As we said in Chapter 5, picturebooks occupy a very special place in children's literature. We have learned that picturebooks vary from being very basic to very complex. We have looked at some of the ways in which such books can 'capture and hold children's attention' (Stewig 1995 p xv) and we agree that a 'good' picturebook should not just be an 'illustrated story'. The pictures and text in a good picturebooks should complement each other in a special way, each leaving gaps for the reader to fill, perhaps even telling different narratives, and demanding different types of analyses and comprehension. For example, *Harry Potter* (J.K. Rowling) with Jim Kay's illustrations (in press) or *Charlotte's Web* (E.B. White) with Garth Williams' illustrations will each contain the same story and meaning even if the pictures are removed, although both might be much the poorer in terms of enjoyment. Pat Hutchins' *Rosie's Walk*, on the other hand, would just not be the same story without the pictures (see also Meek 1988). In *Rosie's Walk* there is no mention in the text of the fox that is stalking Rosie on every page. Rosie manages to outwit the fox, but we are left to ponder if this was intentional or accidental. The text without the pictures would provide a very different reading experience.

Before I asked my 8- and 9-year-old pupils to discuss what might be a good way to describe the difference between an illustrated book and a picturebook, I provided them with some examples of both. The illustrated books I chose were: Lynne Reid Banks' *Indian in the Cupboard*, illustrated by Brock Cole; Roald Dahl's *The Witches* illustrated by Quentin Blake; and E.B. White's *Charlotte's Web* illustrated by Garth Williams. The picturebooks were: Pat Hutchins' *Rosie's Walk*; Chris Van Allsburg's *The Stranger*; and David

Wiesner's *The Three Pigs*. The children took the exercise seriously: they worked in groups, and each group had a *rapporteur* who summarised their thoughts. Here are some examples:

- **Jane's group:** *Well the novels are very long and if you're reading one by yourself the pictures could kind of help you to keep going …and as well, you already know what a cowboy and an Indian look like or a pig and a spider and a witch …and they're small and in black and white. But even though the picturebooks are shorter you might take longer to look at the pictures…and they're doing a kind of different job to the ones in the novels …they make you feel more.*
- **Sarah's group:** *You need to be in a different mood for each of them. Sometimes you just need a long peaceful read and other times you want faster ..excitement.*
- **Katy's group:** *We think that the biggest difference is that you could read the novels to a blind person no problem and they could enjoy them fine, but you couldn't really read the picturebooks to them. Well, you could, but they wouldn't get all of the …message. You have to be able to look at the pictures. Like, you'd be really exhausted trying to explain how The Three Pigs book works to someone who couldn't see the pictures… and it could end up being boring for them.*
- **Paul's group:** *We kind of said the same, sort of, as Katy's group. …And d'you know the ones with only pictures like Flotsam? …well if you were reading to a blind person like Katy said, you'd have to try to talk about the whole thing and it would end up being probably really, really boring for someone listening to you who couldn't see the pictures for themselves …and the real book isn't boring at all…*

The children demonstrated that they thought about the differences between the two genres in different ways, but to me, Katy's group's comments seem to sum up how 'good' picturebooks work. It's a pity that at this stage they hadn't yet experienced Menena Cottin's and Rosana Faria's *The Black Book of Colours*. It might have made the discussion even more interesting.

It is important for children to realise that in good quality 'picture and text picturebooks' the text has been pared down to its essence and the pictures have been very carefully constructed. Nothing is there by accident. In 'wordless' or 'pictures only' picturebooks the illustrations carry the whole meaning, and again, making meaning from these books is rarely linear or straightforward. Wordless picturebooks are usually very complex and multilayered. Think of David Wiesner's *Mr Wuffles* or *Sector 7*; Shaun Tan's *The Arrival* or Aaron Becker's *Journey* for example.

In a recent workshop a group of teachers agreed that a very high level of comprehension was needed for making meaning from wordless picturebooks. The teachers worked in pairs with each pair sharing a wordless picturebook between them. I asked them to note the strategies they employed to make sense and meaning of the story.

- **CL:** *(Sector 7) We found that with each opening we had to continually go back to check details in previous pictures. It was great to have another person … to sort of bounce ideas off them. So you need to keep on rechecking within the book itself and also rechecking your ideas with your partner.*
- **DMC:** *(Mr Wuffles) Yes. It was amazing how often we had to interrupt what we were doing to go back. Before we began we decided we'd look through the whole book slowly and silently first but we couldn't! We just got to the second opening and I said 'Hang on a minute: I need to check something'.*

- **SMC:** *(The Red Book) I don't think very small children could do this without a LOT of support and talk. And I wonder if it would be a story as such: would they think they were just seeing a lot of lovely pictures. It would be a really interesting research project.*
- **AW:** *(The Arrival) I have a background in art and I found it nearly a hindrance because I was being distracted from the narrative, by the artwork techniques.*
- **NL:** *(Why?) I think what SM said is right — infants would need a lot of scaffolding in order to make sense of these stories. But I wouldn't dismiss it on that basis: these kinds of books provide a whole different reading experience. But yes, a high level of intelligence as well and the support of a partner or a small group. I mean without there being two of us working together here, we wouldn't have succeeded in interpreting some of the books as well as we did.*

We all agreed that a spiral curriculum, in relation to developing visual literacy and visual comprehension, probably needs to be put in place in schools with every bit as much assiduity as, say, phonics is. Bruner (1960) first introduced the idea of a spiral curriculum. He argued that 'any subject can be taught effectively in some intellectually honest form to any child at any stage of development' (p 33) and that 'a curriculum as it develops should revisit this basic ideas repeatedly, building upon them until the student has grasped the full formal apparatus that goes with them' (p 13).

The teachers then said that they would welcome continuing professional development (CPD) in visual literacy so as to give children the best possible start.

- **DL:** *I mean look at all we're discovering since we started these workshops. Definitely, we need CPD. Intense CPD on 'visual literacy for teachers'. Even a little bit of knowledge about images makes the reading experience so much more exciting and enriching.*
- **DMC:** *Yes and it would be good if the teachers could give support to the parents as well. Maybe hold a parents' evening and devote one session to visual images. That would really be great, to think that children were being scaffolded at home as well.*

Consensus was reached that teachers trying to vary the reading experiences of their pupils must ensure that a good supply of wordless picturebooks has a place in the classroom library. A variety of approaches could be used for reading these: a whole class 'reading' where the images are projected for all to see; small group or pair work or individual work but followed by a plenary so that ideas could be shared.

In an interview with Booktrust.org, (nd) Oliver Jeffers said: 'the best illustrators take their work for children just as seriously as they would anything else that they produce. The painting references that go into any and all of my books are immense'.

> For example, there are huge Edward Hopper or Constable references in *How to Catch a Star* and *Lost and Found* — even just the way the light is used, the way the houses are done. In *The Incredible Book Eating Boy,* that collage aspect is quite similar to Robert Rauschenberg, so it's rifled with reference and with heavy artistic influence, and if that's a doorway for young children into a world of art where they can look at it on their own terms, that's a huge thing.
>
> (Nd on Booktrust.org)

On the same website, Nicolette Jones, Children's Books Editor with *The Sunday Times*, says that she believes that picturebooks are undervalued in Britain.

Few recognise that the best not only instil a love of books in small children, and nurture crucial visual skills as well as literacy, empathy and imagination, but are also enduring works of art.

Being practiced at reading images gives very young children a huge advantage when they are learning to read texts. But even very sophisticated readers need never grow out of pictures. The creations of our best contemporary illustrators are both aesthetically and intellectually stimulating: they are works of art.

Nicolette Jones (nd leaflet on Booktrust.org.uk)

Beginning CT&BT in junior classrooms

'Sharing picture books with children leads to amazing conversations.' (Anthony Browne on Booktrust.org)

Now let's examine some case studies from my own practice in relation to reading and discussing picturebooks. The first case studies deal with my learning from the attempts I made to create a classroom culture where discussion and conversation are encouraged.

How discussing picturebooks can help us get to know a class

In November 2001, I began teaching a class of 4- and 5-year-old boys and girls who were very upset by having a change of teacher so soon in their school career. Because I believed that one of the fastest ways of getting to know a group of children is to hear what they think, during the first few weeks I read several stories aloud and gently invited comments and questions. As the children began to get used to me and to the idea of discussion, I then began to hold more formal classroom discussions where the children sat in a circle. I would introduce a topic through a story or a poem and they learned to contribute one at a time, if they wished. This is important: children should not feel coerced into speaking. They can learn a lot by listening too. For instance, during an in-service course on classroom discussion, I watched videos of my nephew John taking part in classroom discussions. The discussions had been filmed when he was in Infants. In the video it was obvious that he participated but never spoke. Each time his turn came around, he hesitated and then passed. He was 10 by the time I saw the videos: I asked him if he had enjoyed those discussions and I reminded him that he had passed in all of them. He explained:

> ...I loved doing the discussion when I was in Infants. I was very shy so I didn't really want to talk. But you'd learn loads when you listen. I often only had one idea starting off and then after – at the end –I'd have about thirty and you'd be thinking out in the yard and in bed and everything.

To return to what happened in my class: we read the picturebook *My Many Coloured Days* (Seuss, Johnson and Fancher). The children offered their ideas:

- **Brian:** *I have a red power ranger suit that my brother gave me and I have superpowers when I put it on.*
- **Me:** *Like what?*
- **Brian:** *They're secret.*

- *Paul: The best colour to be is the colour you are supposed to be.*
- *Me: What colour is that?*
- *Paul: The one what you get when you're born.*
- *Ruth: That book says that you can have a colour on the outside of you and then a different colour in your mind. And then you can change your mind colour whenever you feel different.*
- *Me: Can you explain that a little bit more? What do you mean about changing your mind?*
- *Ruth: Well … say you have a white face, you could be green or blue or red in your mind. If you were angry or mad you could be red or purple and then if you got sweets or a new toy you could be yellow or soft in your mind. But your face would still be white.*
- *Me: That's interesting. And what if you have a brown face?*
- *Ruth: Same. You'd still be a different mind colour.*

A few days later I introduced a poem about colours from Fisher's (2000) *First Poems for Thinking*. One line in the poem spoke about colours 'dancing'. I said: 'the poet says that colours dance: in what way might colours dance?' Some children's answers were very lyrical. But for others this poem did not have any great impact.

- *Kayleen: I don't really get that. They're not alive. The things they're on are alive … well some are, like orange tigers.*
- *Fred: Maybe they dance with paintbrushes – when you paint.*
- *Sam: They could flop around when someone makes things out of Márla (plasticine).*
- *Kavanagh: They dance at night. No one knows because they sing really quietly at the same time. They have little legs – they grow little legs and in the morning they fall off.*
- *Jenny: They might do it upstairs when no one's watching.*
- *Brian: Colours are in pages. Then when children move the coloured pages they can dance.*

Dan was unresponsive so I probed gently:

- *Me: Do you agree with the others, D? Do you think colours dance?*
- *Dan: I don't agree. I don't think they can dance – they're just colours.*

I began to see that I had poets and philosophers and scientists and dreamers and pragmatists in my class. During the week that followed this discussion a few children mentioned the picturebook. One child said 'Today in the yard I felt like a million different colours. It was because I had so much fun'. Some children mentioned the poem saying things like 'I'm still thinking about the colours dancing and …', which demonstrated to me that they were still actively thinking and engaged with ideas, long after the book was closed.

We discussed Molly Bang's *When Sophie Gets Angry – Really, Really Angry*. The children looked carefully at the pictures and we listed the different stages of Sophie's anger: screaming and roaring, shaking, stomping and kicking, wanting to smash the world to smithereens, running until she was worn out, crying, climbing a tree and letting the 'wide world comfort her'.

- *Ben: I wouldn't do all of that – just some of it. I might shout a bit…and cry very loud.*
- *Diane: I would get in so much trouble if I did any of that stuff. Anyway I always let my sister have turns of my toys.*
- *Me: But Sophie isn't a big girl like you – she's only 2 or 3.*

- **Diane:** *Well she needs to learn you can't get your own way. How's she going to learn? Her Mom should be really cross with her for doing all that stuff.*

When we discussed the pictures the children felt that they were really good at showing how angry Sophie was and Evan had a pragmatic question:

- **Jody:** *When she roared a red roar that was brilliant! She's like a dragon!*
- **Claire:** *The pictures and the colours kind of get angrier and angrier too.*
- **Evan:** *Why did she not want to give her sister a turn? It's only an old gorilla toy!*

When we had explored a series of books about different emotions I began to introduce the children to the artists and we compared Max from *Where the Wild Things Are*, with 'angry' Arthur and with 'really angry' Sophie. We examined the pictures and the different styles of illustrations and the children discussed their preferences.

- **Kayleen:** *Remember Max? He wasn't half as bad as Sophie, and his Mum sent him off to a scary monsters' island!*
- **Sam:** *No he only had a dream about that! He didn't really go!*
- **Kayleen:** *He did! You could even see him in the photos with the monsters!*
- **Thomas:** *They're not photos – they're drawings.*
- **Marie:** *I think the Sophie one….[Molly Bang] ….had fun with her paints.*
- **Emily:** *Angry Arthur nearly destroyed the whole world and he didn't get into that much trouble.*
- **Olwen:** *All their Mams were kind and gentle.*

The children were quickly involved in comparing not just the characters and their expressions of feelings, but were beginning to look at how the artist had created images that manipulated their feelings towards the characters.

Gradually I got to know the children better. This particular class had two little boys who disliked sitting still for any length of time. I have written elsewhere (Roche 2007, 2011, and in McDonagh *et. al.* 2012) about the learning I gained from giving these children time and space to settle into school life on their terms, and how successfully they did so. Both children were articulate and deep thinkers. Both were deeply philosophical children and both benefited hugely from having opportunities to discuss picturebooks in class.

Children as theorists and philosophers and critical thinkers

I prepared some of the following material for the NCCA, Aistear Podcasts on doing CT&BT (Roche 2011): the material is reproduced here with permission from NCCA. Some of this material is also drawn from my doctoral work (Roche 2007).

Depending on what source you use, you will find many different definitions of what constitutes critical thinking. I particularly like a paper written by Facione (2010) in which he states that critical thinking is 'thinking that has a purpose (proving a point, interpreting what something means, solving a problem)' and that 'critical thinking can be a collaborative, non-competitive endeavour' (np). We must think critically *about* something. It is not something that can be done in the abstract.

When we are using picturebooks to stimulate dialogue and critical thinking we need to be aware, however, that there are particular skills and dispositions that we are seeking to develop and nurture in children. Drawing on the work of Robert Fisher (2006), we would hope that children would be encouraged to develop what he calls 'the habits of intelligent behaviour' which include being curious, collaborative, critical, creative and caring (Fisher 2006, cited in Jones and Hodson 2006, pp 33–4).

CT&BT can involve children in 'philosophising'. According to Fisher (2006), philosophical dialogue develops the kinds of thinking that children may not get to use in other lessons including, he says, philosophical intelligence, the capacity to ask and seek answers to existential questions. Children ask existential questions and issue philosophical statements all the time. We need to be alert and ready to hear them so as to appreciate the richness (and sometimes the unintended humour).

Some years ago I read bedtime stories to my two nieces Moya (5) and Harriet (3) when they were on a visit. Next morning at breakfast Harriet suddenly looked up from contemplating her cereal and said: 'Auntie Mary, are we real or are we like, made up people in a story?' Here is a tiny fraction of several examples:

- *Heidi (pupil 7): Once I was watching a robin and a crow in my garden. Do robins know who they are? Do they know who crows are? Like, do they both know that they're both birds?*
- *Peter (adult relative): I came in an hour after I had put Eamon (about 4 years old) to bed and he was staring at the ceiling, sucking his thumb. I patted him on the chest and asked him what he was thinking and he said, 'Do you think your last breath is an inhalation or exhalation?' I asked 'What do you think?' he answered: 'Exhalation, because it would be after you took in your last breath'.*
- *Jean (retired teacher): I remember being asked to supervise a class of Junior Infants in the computer room one day while the teacher was out briefly. They were busy enjoying tangrams. The children were working in pairs. I moseyed around listening in. Two boys were naming the shapes as they flicked them into place. They were totally oblivious to the fact that I was behind them. When they came to the trapezoidal shape one child asked the other what that was called. He replied 'I'm not sure...I think it's called a canoe...I don't know why I think that but I think it is...I'm not sure'. I remember thinking this guy is ahead of the posse when it comes to language skills. The little incidentals of teaching! Had the teacher insisted on silence while they were working look what I'd have missed!*
- *Kate (retired teacher): My 3 year old daughter and I were passing a field of cows when she turned to me and said: 'Do cows not have any toilet training? They just do their toilet anywhere!' On another occasion, a local lad from the town was visiting the neighbouring farm. He was driving a tractor, wearing a leather jacket and sunglasses. My son (4) watched him for a few moments and then said 'I'd say he thinks hisself is sexy'.*
- *Eimer (retired teacher): a friend's two small children were engrossed in something in the garden. Their mother investigated. It was an earthworm. One child said: 'Oh let's have him as a pet'. The mother said 'Ah no, lovey, I think he's happier where he is'. The other child said 'And he wouldn't be happier where he isn't....'*

Encouraging further questions and developing a dialogue around children's questions could lead to important educational experiences for children, because philosophy begins in curiosity. Einstein is reputed to have said that curiosity is more important than knowledge since it is needed to generate knowledge. Philosophical enquiry develops questioning skills and builds on children's natural curiosity. It also provides a means for children to develop discussion skills – the capacity to engage in thoughtful conversations with others. In Roche (2000) I wrote about how I have learned to recognise children's utterance as potentially worthy of philosophical enquiry:

One day, recently, I began to eavesdrop on the chatter going on in the little queue waiting for corrections at my desk:

- *'What if we were tall enough to reach that top shelf?'*
- *'That'd be cool!'*
- *'Yeah, what if we were as big as houses and people like our Dads and Mums and Miss were like mice?' (They chortled delightedly at the very notion).*
- *'Yeah, we could carry them around in our pockets ...or in our lunch box!' (More laughs).*
- *'Then we'd hear them munching away. Hey you! Teeny tiny Dad! Leave some for me!'*
- *'We'd have to mind them from cats and stuff...'*
- *'S'posin they got lost! ...You go to a cop and say ...Hey! I've lost my Mum ...An' he'd be thinking that you were lost!'*
- *'But the cops'd be tweenchy too!'...*
- *'Oh wow!'*

I regret to say that in my pre-MA Ed days I would quite likely have said 'Oh, come on Boys! Don't be silly!' The idea of arranging to have a classroom discussion around the idea of giant-sized children and microscopic adults would never have occurred to me. (Roche 2000 p 77)

While I was not setting out to do 'philosophy' per se with my classes, CT&BT shares many of the skills and dispositions that are endorsed by the 'Philosophy for Children' approach. Fisher's (2007) 'habits of intelligent behaviour' mentioned earlier, fit well with themes of well-being, identity and belonging, communicating, exploring and thinking, and with dispositions such as curiosity, perseverance, respectfulness, confidence and risk-taking. Such themes and dispositions are woven through many preschool and early learning programmes. CT&BT also consolidates and builds on principles such as seeing each child's uniqueness; seeing children as citizens; supporting children to form relationships; recognising children's need to engage in active learning through relevant and meaningful experiences, and, importantly, adults sharing the lead in learning with children.

In the dialogue excerpts about colours that we saw earlier, we can see where children were developing as thinkers. Each child had a unique viewpoint. We can see where sometimes one child's idea contributed to another's and perhaps even where one child's thinking scaffolded another's. This often happened: One day we held a discussion following our reading of *Oi! Get off Our Train,* John Burningham's story about a little boy who dreams of taking endangered animals for a ride to safety on his train. Following the story a child introduced the idea of the animals' feelings about their plight. Denis disagreed:

- **Denis:** *Animals don't have feelings*
- **Anna:** *I disagree, Denis. They do. Cos if you kick an animal they scream.*
- **Rory:** *I was thinking the same thing as Anna!*
- **Denis:** *Well.... They only have little feelings...*
- **Con:** *I disagree cos animals have very big feelings to protect their babies!*
- **Alex:** *I agree that Con is really, really good at talking... and listening ...and I think that actually, Con, you know everything.*

- **Con:** *Yes, I do. Thank you, Alex, for saying that.*
- **Alex:** *Don't even mention it.* (Roche 2007 p 206)

Here the children were using their learned conventions of polite language usage along with some sophisticated big ideas about whether animals have feelings or not. Informal ordinary conversation appears to play as significant a role in enabling children to think critically as does the more formal setting of discrete classroom discussion. Within the context of ordinary conversational exchanges, the relationship between my students and me, and between my students and each other, is enhanced through the development of trust and the existence of a spirit of dialogue (Bohm 1998). The children also appear to be developing communicative competence (Dillon 1994) which includes:

> … improving our expressiveness, learning various rules of discourse and acquiring complex abilities of interaction. We learn to talk better. … We learn the intellectual, procedural and social rules and conventions … we develop in the moral culture of discussion … we experience personal growth, considered apart from academic learning … in discussion our personal involvement is deeper and more significant to us.
>
> (p 9)

The picturebook discussions also created a context in the classroom for peer tutoring, where, despite being the youngest student, Jim soon emerged as a natural 'tutor':

- **Owen:** *Jim, do you know what you were saying about ants and greenflies? Is that true?*
- **Jim:** *Yes. The ants act like shepherds with the greenflies as their sheep. They need the sticky stuff that the greenflies produce: it's really quite fascinating. Actually, I have it on a video. I'll bring it in.*

To me this is an example of a child scaffolding another child's development and learning. In classroom discussions, some children, like Jim, operate at the upper level of their ZPD (Vygotsky 1978), so in the discussion circle situation Jim's excellent communicative competence could be seen as supporting other children's ability to participate, sometimes above their actual ability. Morehouse (1999) also asserts that more articulate children act as scaffolds (Bruner 1960) for less articulate children in the discussion.

Campbell (2001) asserts that in classroom discussions

> … even children who exhibit a restricted linguistic code can portray an urgency and a potency which honours the quality of their thoughts, their thinking resonates with a sense of seeking, with mutual scaffolding and empathy, and frequently with refreshing subversiveness.
>
> (p 1)

Rogoff (1990) drawing on Vygotsky's (1978) theory of social communication and learning suggests that children's participation in communicative processes is the foundation on which they build understanding:

> As children listen to the views and understanding of others, and stretch their concepts to find a common ground; as they collaborate and argue with others, consider

new alternatives, and recast their ideas to communicate or to convince, they advance their ideas in the process of participation. It is a matter of social engagement that leaves the individual changed.

(p 95)

By the middle of the second term the children appeared to be confident in their relationship with me and often came to me informally for a chat. These episodes afforded opportunities to further develop a caring relationship, particularly with children like Owen, a shy and nervous child yet a very creative thinker, adept at verbal reasoning. I gave these conversations high priority for enabling the children to develop their critical thinking and celebrate their natural curiosity about the world.

- **Owen:** *Teacher, I'd say my cat can definitely think.*
- **Me:** *Really? How did you find that out?*
- **Owen:** *See, I watch her all the time – when she's not looking. I'd say she thinks about loads of things.*
- **Me:** *That's interesting … like what, for example?*
- **Owen:** *Well … anything really, like catching mice or butterflies and playing and getting food off me.*
- **Me:** *Wow. She sounds really clever. I used to have a cat too.*
- **Owen:** *Did you? Do you still have her?*
- **Me:** *No, she ran away one night and we never saw her again. Your cat sounds like she's very smart, though.*

Cadwell (1997) says that language links us to the world and to others and that, through dialogue, shared meanings are shaped and our singular perspectives are enriched (p 62). My 'singular perspective' was enriched by this child's passionate belief in his cat's ability to think. From this conversation a topic emerged later that week, about whether or not animals could think, and a significant discussion ensued. Oakeshott (1959) suggests that when people are having a conversation they are not engaged in enquiry or debate. He considers conversation as 'an unrehearsed intellectual adventure' and that educators have a responsibility to provide contexts for such intellectual adventures.

Oakeshott (op. cit.) also argues that both poetic and practical language can be found in varying proportions at all stages of development of children. This was frequently manifested in our conversations as we saw in Chapter 4 with Sarah's story about the rich farmer's daughter who died of a broken heart over a 'commoner' and Jim's chat about spiders. Another example was when, following a discussion about Eric Carle's *The Bad-Tempered Ladybird*, Max told the class that 'ladybirds had a special smell' and that he always knew where they were. He told me that there was a big 'nest' of them under his hedge. His mum later told me that he lay for hours looking under a hedge and brought lots of ladybirds for her to see. When we researched ladybirds we discovered that ladybirds emit a foul odour as a deterrent to predators. Like Jim and many other children, Max scaffolded my learning as well as that of the whole class.

Besides the utter pleasure of the conversations, it also demonstrated to me the high level of thinking on each child's part. Jim and Max were high achievers both verbally and in written activities. Some children fared badly in standardised reading and Maths tests, yet excelled in verbal reasoning and thinking. Each episode is another example of why I feel that a didactic pedagogical manner and whole class formal instruction can often be unjust, in that it can serve to deny the intelligence of children who need a more dialogical engagement with knowledge, and time to come to know on their own terms rather than terms dictated by strict adherence to subject coverage. Didacticism excludes children from being seen as significant and unique. It places children in the category of Other (different from me) whereas I try to see children as others (like me, but different in their uniqueness). I have learned to value ordinary conversation, and such ordinary conversation, I believe arises from the very particular teacher-pupil relationship that emerges in classrooms where regular discussions are held.

Challenging norms

One day we had a fire drill. The infants always found such interruptions alarming. There was the unexpected interruption to routine, the loud noise of the alarm and the fright of leaving without coats or bags. Silence and straight lines were demanded as we filed to our respective meeting points. As our school was developing from a 'greenfield' situation, the principal naturally, was very anxious that strict procedures needed to be created and observed by staff and children alike. Eddy was terrified by all this tension. Suddenly he asked anxiously, 'Yeah, well, what's so good about straight lines anyway?' I saw that he was very frightened by the general air of tension. I explained that teachers needed to make certain that all the children in each class were safe if ever a real fire happened; that children had to hear the roll-call; and that it was much faster to count people if they weren't all moving around. Eddy said, 'Oh, OK, I get it now'. In Roche (2007, 2011), I explained how Eddy's question lingered in my consciousness, and I found that I began to ask myself: what is so good about straight lines? Why are uniformity and compliance to rules so synonymous with schooling? Suddenly I found myself questioning many of the norms upon which primary education is frequently premised and, like Eddy, I wished for rational answers that made sense (Roche 2011 p 333).

Bruner (1996) suggested that schools are valuable and extraordinary places 'for getting a sense of how to use the mind, how to deal with authority, how to treat others' (p 78). They are frequently places in which there can be 'antidialogical actions', according to Burbules (1993). In light of Eddy's question about 'straight lines', I began to reflect that straight lines and uniforms have overtones of behaviourism and teach us, perhaps, that in dealing with authority it is often 'safest' to obey uncritically. But obeying uncritically denies children the opportunity to voice their uniqueness as thinkers.

Young children as curious and unique thinkers

- **Emma (4):** *(at the beach): Hey! The sea in my jar is gone all watery – where's the blue gone?*
- **Sarah (4):** *Why do rainbows only go down at the ends? It makes them look sad.*
- **Emma (4):** *(looking at a sheet of music): Wow that music is full of little smiles!*
- **Sarah (5):** *(Looking out the window and seeing some of the neighbouring farmer's bullocks leaping down a path to a meadow after the winter indoors): Look! They're dancing! I bet you it's because they are so excited because they can smell that it's Spring!*

As adults who have had any kind of sustained contact with small children we know, and we saw some examples earlier, that they are natural enquirers (But *why*, Mummy?) and philosophers. However, they are often also theorists claiming 'I know why x happens... it's because...'

- *Emma (4): The sea is only blue when it's with all the rest of it: if you trap a bit in a jar it gets a bit sad and maybe that's what makes it go watery.*
- *Sarah (4): Maybe the rainbow likes hiding behind the rain.*

I daresay that each one of us could add many more examples of small children's fascinating questions – questions that deal with physics, ethics, justice, chemistry, 'infinity and beyond' – and equally fascinating theories of how the world works. Small children and not-so-small children are constantly trying to make meaning and sense of the world and we saw existential questions about the nature of reality, and some very sophisticated pondering about last breaths, and what 'sexy' means, earlier in this chapter. Sometimes children provide their own reasons for why things are the way they are. When they do, I believe they are philosophising.

When it comes to CT&BT time, discussing the picturebook before, during and after the read-aloud can provide opportunities for the children to philosophise, and to construct meaning for themselves about the world and their place in it. We have seen in earlier chapters that a lot of research indicates how children's responses, both questions and comments as they listen to stories being read to them, are a critical aspect of the interactive process. Studies show that this interaction is essential for vocabulary building, language acquisition, understanding conventions of text, and developing thinking skills. We saw this in Chapter 4 when we examined how George learned some new words.

Fisher (2006 in Jones and Hodson 2006 pp 33–47) speaks about the importance of philosophical dialogue in early childhood education. He stated that human intelligence is primarily developed through speaking and listening. He argued that the quality of our lives depends on the quality of our thinking and on our ability to communicate and discuss what we think with others. He suggested that talk is intrinsic to literacy and to our ability to form relationships with others, and that talk is the foundation of both verbal and emotional intelligence. If we take any of that seriously, perhaps we can see that there is a real need to provide space for authentic dialogue in the classroom. Not only is it beneficial to cognitive and affective development, it is often great fun.

In many busy infant classrooms children do not have many opportunities to have discussions and there is an anecdote told about a child who was asked by his mother what he had learned in school that day and he replied 'nothing because the teacher wouldn't stop talking'. We have seen how several studies (from Flanders 1970 to Mercer 2000 to Alexander 2010) show that most of the talk in a classroom is teacher-talk and most of that talk is in the form of questions. And, unfortunately, studies show that most of those questions are closed 'one right answer' kinds of questions. However, CT&BT can provide opportunities for discussions around open-ended comments and questions, giving teachers and children alike, new insights.

More on children as theorists

During a workshop in school one day when I told colleagues about the many occasions when small children have surprised me by theorising, one teacher looked a little incredulous. When I explained that one meaning of 'theorising' is 'making a claim to knowledge and giving a description and an explanation' and gave her some examples I had come across (we shall look at some in a moment), she said, 'Well in that case, I think my David (3) has a theory of how to catch naughty boys'. She told an anecdote about how local children waited for her husband to come home from work; gave him time to get changed, and then when they judged he was at dinner, they knocked on the door claiming their football had gone into the back garden. He duly got up to fetch it and as he rooted about looking for it they ran away laughing. Little David was upset because his dad was angry and later, at bedtime, he told his mum that he 'knew' how to catch bad boys. 'You put a sticky lolly on the footpath and then the bad boys will walk on it and get stuck and Daddy can catch them'. He had a description and an explanation for his claim that he knew how to catch bad boys. Children use their prior knowledge combined with their imagination to come up with explanations for the way things work or the way things might work, as Emma did when her jar of seawater didn't look blue and as Sarah did when she figured out why rainbows looked sad.

By exposing children to rich texts and pictures and then by creating a culture of enquiry by asking 'I wonder why' questions we encourage them to think critically and to offer explanations for their thinking. Children could be encouraged to ask questions and to speculate: I wonder why the illustrator shows us the boy's back rather than his face; I wonder why that illustration has a frame around it and this one doesn't; I wonder why the illustrator put a cage on the title page. Teachers or parents could ask inferential questions: 'why do you think the boy looks sad?' or invite predictions 'I wonder what might happen next', or 'I wonder what the little girl will do now'. When they do that, parents and teachers are providing children with opportunities to hypothesise and theorise and philosophise.

CT&BT offers the children the opportunity to speak in class without the burden of answering a teacher-directed closed question. With the teacher's omnipotent role relaxed, the children are given the opportunity 'to speak, to listen, to reflect, to have an opinion, to make a statement, to ask a question and to be listened to' (Donnelly 1994 p 7). We must encourage and support the children 'to go from the particular to the general and ultimately towards a concept' (op. cit. p 8). The children are dependent, Donnelly says, on their own personal histories of their senses and their knowledge which is sometimes based on concrete experiences, and also sometimes, on their imaginations, to explore and define a thought, a question, or an idea. To use language is, in itself, she says, an abstract activity (p 8). Also by asking children to question, to give reasons for opinions, to think critically, creatively and abstractly we are effectively leading out or drawing out from them what is tacit and innate.

Fisher (1995), discussing the 'Philosophy for Children' programme, states that classroom discussion can serve a very valuable role in making our tacit knowledge known to us. When we articulate this tacit knowledge it ceases to be what Whitehead (1932) called 'inert knowledge'. Bringing this tacit knowledge to mind through talking, can, states Fisher, become a very powerful strategy for thinking and learning. He equates it with the Socratic tradition of teaching which begins with a 'seeming ignorance and proceeds through dialogue to a revealed understanding' (Fisher 1995 p 3). Building on Whitehead (1932) and Polanyi (1959), he postulates that we may even not know what we mean until we hear what we say, and we saw a small child saying something like that earlier. He goes on to state that talking and thinking are very closely linked with the attempts children make to reflect on and extract meaning from experience. Talking to learn in this way, he adds, helps the children through a sort of *'cognitive apprenticeship'*, and philosophy with children provides contexts for this to happen (1995 pp 4–55). Fisher (2009) states 'through creative dialogue children learn how to become co-constructors of new ideas, new meanings and better worlds' (p 200).

Giving children *time* to think is crucial too. Having conducted research on 'wait-time' for over 20 years, Mary Budd Rowe (1986) concluded that teachers wait less than one second for a reply to a question and less than a second to react or respond to a student's answer by posing another question. From my trawl of other papers on 'wait-time' it would appear that things have not changed dramatically in the intervening decades. It takes time to speak, to listen, to question, and to ponder. Listening actively as others speak builds reciprocity of respect and a sense of community. Many teachers who use this kind of dialogical pedagogy attest that the process of doing this work with a class builds up trust within the community of the classroom.

Children as knowers: Alex and Charlie

I was amazed by what my infants knew! I've been teaching infants for years and I suppose I just never let them talk enough before. The stuff they said about their souls… amazing! I couldn't believe they knew all that! (Teacher of 20 years' experience cited in Roche 2007, Appendix B.1)

Haynes (2002) argues for teaching children to think and to philosophise as a means towards encouraging 'the cultivation of reasonableness' and suggests that children should be encouraged to participate in society from an early age, in 'contexts that are meaningful to them such as families, schools and other settings where they have a stake' (p 6).

At the beginning of this book we also saw how, as well as being underpinned by certain ontological assumptions, CT&BT is grounded in a particular epistemological assumption about what constitutes knowledge and who is considered a knower in a classroom. I have documented elsewhere (Roche 2000, 2007, 2011) how, for many years I thought a teacher's main job was to impart knowledge. Knowledge was a thing – out there somewhere – and I saw my function as capturing it, and transmitting or delivering it into their heads. To do this kind of 'teaching' you need two things: a dominant active talker and passive listeners. What kind of learning is going on in such a class? Learning to be bored stiff? Learning to despise schooling? Learning in spite of the 'teaching'?

Austin *et al.* (2003), discussing schooling as a cultural and institutional practice, examine classroom talk, arguing that there is now a substantial body of research from 'a variety of traditions' that shows that teachers have been found to take more and longer turns at talk and to ask lots of questions with IRE (initiation, response, evaluation) being the dominant form of interaction. This three-part sequence, they say, restrains students' opportunities to speak. With a high level of teacher-directedness, student knowledge is placed they say, in a very ambiguous position and student knowledge is little used, valued or developed in such interactive settings (op. cit. pp 5–6). My view of teaching before I engaged in classroom discussion and CT&BT would appear to have been rooted in values of corporatism and traditionalism as regards my practice, yet I held values deep down that viewed education in a more progressive and transformative light. It took me over 20 years, however, to transform my practice from a monologic to a dialogic one. Children like Alex and Charlie taught me. Neither of these two boys were passive listeners. They were active, restless, inquisitive and talkative (see Roche 2007, 2011b; McDonagh *et al.* 2012, pp 39–42; NCCA 2011).

Alex's story

Alex was a restless child and who seemed to hate doing any work that involved a pencil. One day our CT&BT topic, 'What would happen if you left your teddy out in the rain?' was based on a readaloud of McKee's *Elmer and The Lost Teddy* and on an activity suggested by the oral language development cards that accompanied our reading scheme. These cards anticipated that the children would arrive at a series of words to describe various kinds of 'wetness'. After a few suggestions as to how the teddy might feel (emotionally rather than physically), Rory suggested that '*Your teddy might get robbed if you left it out all night*'. We were now zooming off on the wonderful tangent of 'robbed teddies'. People sat up and got really interested. Then Alex produced his claim to knowledge, his description and his explanation: Alex's theory of how to catch a robber.

- **Alex:** *Well anyway, I know how to catch a robber. See, you dig a hole, right? And you put a blanket over it and then put some dirt on the blanket and the robber won't see it and he'll step on it and fall into the hole. That way you'll get your teddy back and then you could call the police and they'd take him away.*

Alex had a theory: his claim to knowledge was 'I know how to catch a robber!', he then went on to provide a *description* of digging the trap and an *explanation* of why the trap would work. As I grew to know him better, I realised that school regimes simply had not suited Alex. He was intelligent and proud, and possibly felt a sense of failure because of his lack of fine-motor skills. His coping mechanisms, for whenever a writing activity was introduced, appeared to take the form of developing avoidance strategies. However, CT&BT gave him the opportunity to demonstrate his excellence in talking and thinking. In Roche (2007) I explain how I introduced the children gradually to the language of 'I agree with X because … and I disagree with X because …'. This seemed to pay off in Alex's case. As time went on and our picturebooks discussions developed into regular events, children began to affirm him with comments such as 'Alex, I think you're really good at talking' and he began to settle down even more. Meanwhile, with a larger triangular pencil and rubber grip, and plenty of opportunities to scribble, gradually his fine-motor skills improved although he never enjoyed using pencils or crayons.

Charlie's story

Like Alex, Charlie seemed unwilling or unable to sit still. He also appeared to hate fine-motor activities and, whenever they began, he would walk about, open cupboards, and act in a mildly disruptive way. I felt that all he needed was more time to settle down. I introduced the class to CT&BT, and, following a story from Fisher (1999) about a bonny baby contest in the jungle, I asked the children for their thoughts about beauty. Each child said beauty was something visual. I decided to ask the children if they thought beauty could be a smell or a sound or a taste. Charlie was walking around but was obviously listening to what the others said, because he suddenly sat into the circle and said, 'I actually know what the most beautiful *sound* in the world is' and he proceeded to tell me that it was the sound of a mummy's voice if a child were lost in a forest (McDonagh *et al.* 2012 p40). I felt that was the day when I finally saw the fine little person he was underneath all the bluster and restlessness. I described this new understanding in Roche (2007 pp 174–5).

Our picturebooks discussions were allowing me to get to know the children as individual thinkers and knowers and I was then able to provide further opportunities for them to develop appropriate ways of learning through enquiry. Because of my newfound knowledge of Alex and Charlie, and their restlessness and love of gross-motor activities, I devised strategies that had them out of their seats and out of doors as much as possible (see also Roche 2007, 2011, 2012).

I have focused on my learning from working with these two children because I want to show that it was through doing CT&BT discussions that I was led towards seeing them as real people, the people with whom I worked every day, and whom I grew to know and respect as patient, tolerant, philosophical and critical citizens. It was always a humbling and informative experience for me to listen to my pupils' thoughts as they wrestled with questions such as why the Little Red Hen's friends wouldn't help her and going on from that to discuss friendship, and falling out with friends, and making up again; listening to them as they tried to decide if Jack was a hero or a villain and their realisation that within most people are 'good bits and bad bits'; watching their fierce concentration as they tried to figure out what was going on in some of the wordless picturebooks; learning to respect their intelligence as they argued; seeing them change their minds as they listened to what others were saying. It was gratifying too to see how they began to work together as a group and show respect and tolerance towards each other. The development of rapport and interpersonal relationships that evolves as class groups engage in CT&BT is something upon which several other teachers have commented, as we saw earlier.

Closed and open questions: maybe he didn't know he was a egg!

Small children are intensely curious as we said already. That is how they learn. But sometimes the 'but why?' questions fade with entry into formal school. Only the teachers' whys are valid it seems. This came home to me when we discussed Daniel Kirk's *Humpty Dumpty*. As well as the picturebook, and several other books that referred to Nursery Rhyme characters, I also had a set of large pictures of nursery rhyme characters. Each poster was 'teacher-proof' in that each had questions on the back. The idea was that the teacher would hold up the card to face the class and read the questions off the back of it. The questions were mostly closed questions such as 'Who is this character?'; 'What colour is Humpty's coat?'; 'How many buttons are on his coat?' and other such closed 'one-right-answer' questions. It struck me that a child who asks questions out of curiosity must be bewildered by these kinds of questions. The child is most probably thinking 'Why on earth is she asking me? Why doesn't she just look at the picture?' Children could soon come to distrust 'teacher' questions, interpreting them perhaps as: 'Hmm... she's actually asking am I listening, or can I count, or do I know my colours'. For example, look what happened when 4 and 5 year olds in my sister's class were asked 'Why do you think Humpty Dumpty was up on that wall?' (a very open-ended question, which offers unlimited scope for possible 'right' answers):

- *Abby: I know Teacher! He has very short little legs and he couldn't see what was making all the noise!*
- *Seán: Yeah. Maybe he couldn't see what was coming so someone had to put him up on the wall.*

- **Ethan:** *Teacher, isn't it very dangerous for a egg to be up on a wall?*
- **Sarah:** *Yeah ...but maybe he didn't know he was a egg!*

So how can we protect or revitalise the curiosity and the 'I wonder whys'? How can we 'set the what-ifs' free once more? In my experience a teaching approach such as CT&BT is one way of restoring importance to philosophising in the classroom. It allows time for pondering, wondering, 'what iff-ing and I wonder why-ing'. Fisher (2006) suggests that a good discussion and thinking session makes links and bridges to real life by encouraging children to draw upon examples from their own experience – or things that they have read about or heard about – experiences that link into their own concerns. The more successful the enquiry, he says, the more it links in to their own concerns and the sorts of things that are not covered by the conventional curriculum. It is one of the great strengths of such an approach, he says, in that it allows children to explore things not otherwise covered and provides opportunities for them to demonstrate their uniquely different intelligences. We saw Mr Gee trying to do this with his class in *Once Upon an Ordinary School Day*. We also saw it clearly demonstrated with children like Alex, Charlie, Owen, Jim, Max and Sarah.

CT&BT in middle-senior primary classrooms

Emancipatory dialogue and benign rebels

When I began discussing picturebooks with 8, 9 and 10 year olds I was immediately struck by the sophistication of the children's reasoning and their willingness to engage with critical thinking. The children in question had been accustomed, since Infant classes, to participating in discussions and there was no problem in getting 'stuck right in'. I could see that the CT&BT programme we had put in place in the school was effective insofar as children were comfortable and at ease in dialogue with each other. There was no element of children being afraid to display their learning and learnedness to others. This is hugely important. In many classrooms children are subdued very quickly by a culture of peer derision and the fear of being called 'loser', 'swot' or 'teacher's pet'.

The dialogic pedagogies that I put into place in my various classrooms find resonance in Bakhtin's ideas about the creation and exchange of meaning. Holquist (2002) suggests that for Bakhtin,

> Existence is ....the event of co-being; it is a vast web of interconnections each and all of which are linked as participants in an event whose totality is so immense that no one of us can ever know it. That event manifests itself in the form of a constant, ceaseless creation and exchange of meaning.
>
> (p 1)

In relation to my students' learning, there was possibly 'a constant ceaseless creation and exchange of meaning' (ibid). When the children were discussing a picturebook, it seemed to me that they were engaged in the co-creation of knowledge in dialogue with each other or with their own thoughts. They were not being told what to say or think: they were not just relying on received wisdom from textbooks. Discrete classroom discussion encouraged the children to be aware of their capacity for originality and critical engagement, and to articulate this awareness (see Roche 2007 pp 51–2).

For example, my 8 and 9 year olds and I had a discussion on animal rights: I read John Burningham's *Oi! Get off Our Train* and Anthony Browne's *Zoo* and then asked the children to discuss their thoughts about animals' rights.

- **Me:** *What about rats? Or guide dogs?*
- **Anne:** *Well, the guide dog is doing a job and he's useful so I'd put him in a different group to the rat 'cos they are just troublesome and if you get a bite of a lady rat you can die …*
- **Aisling:** *I think all animals should have the right to freedom, like us. They shouldn't have to stay in cages for their whole lives. At least we get let out free at 18.*
- **Shaun:** *I've been thinking about rights and I don't think that every single animal should have rights. Some should have rights, not rats, snakes, crocodiles, maybe not wasps. If you made a line you could put those on one side, because they have sharp teeth and they can bite you. Then on the other side you could put lions and tigers and cows and dogs and cats and rabbits and bears. They deserve rights, they're good.*
- **Emma:** *Maybe we give more rights to animals that are cuddly and cute. Like kittens and bunnies and koala bears. It's not the animals – it's us! We're making the rules up.*

Emma's insights were interesting. They corresponded with those of a child from another class who wondered why you wouldn't cry when a goldfish died but you might when a puppy died. 'And they're both pets, really…so why?' The children in that group replied that 'you'd think about your fish differently to how you'd think about your puppy, because maybe fish don't have much personality and puppies have loads'. We then had a debate about why 'fish had no personality'. Again they reasoned that it was on the traits that we humans ascribed to the animals that we judged them.

It mattered little to me that my students' learning from their various dialogical experiences was not quantifiable empirically. What was significant, I felt, was that my students were learning in ways that were life affirming, and the learning opportunities were appropriate to each child's unique way of knowing. I was delighted that the children learned that often situations occur for which no right answers are to be found, and that learning needs to be problematic. I felt that I had found pedagogies that encouraged them to problematise content knowledge as well as their own learning processes. Thus their main subject knowledge became knowledge of their capacity to learn and to think critically.

Here are two excerpts: both following a reading of Poole and Barrett's *The Story of Anne Frank* with two different class groups of 8 and 9 year olds:

- **Brian:** *I was thinking … well … the way we all think can't be forced on us … like we might think it's right to be Catholics but we couldn't make someone be a Catholic, we could bring them to the church but we couldn't force them to believe. You have to be one to really believe … and you can't make anyone else be one unless … they believe … for themselves* (Roche 2007 Appendix C.3.)
- **Kelly:** *I agree with Thomas that freedom would mean doing everything you want even the bad. Well, do you know when you were reading the story [Anne Frank]? Well, you said the Americans joined with Britain to help them against the Germans. Well, in a certain way the Americans when they joined in, they were helping England with freedom, but then that means that they were … against … they were stopping Germany's freedom …if you take sides … it means that sometimes you are stopping someone's freedom … well … a bit …*

- **Paul:** *I disagree with some people and I agree with others, who said that freedom is doing whatever you want, but only in a way. You can only have freedom if you're alone. Because if you were really free to think what you like and say what you like and do what you like it and there were other people around, it could be the baddest thing ever for them because you might want to do all bad things with your freedom … Freedom could be sometimes good but sometimes it could be the baddest thing ever.* (Roche 2007, Appendix C.6.)

The next episode demonstrates that the children developed metacognitive ability as they reflect on their own thinking and evaluate it in the light of new thinking.

In November one year, having done several discussions, I gave the children 'booklets' composed of the transcripts from four discussions dating from early September to the end of October to read and discuss. I saw that they were immediately engrossed and spent the first few minutes quickly scanning the pages for their own contributions. When they found their own name they read their own contributions several times and eagerly showed them each other. Only then did they read through the transcripts.

The children then evaluated their own thinking.

- **Claire:** *Actually it's kind of good to read these again. I wouldn't say what I said there again now though, because when you read what other people said you'd kind of get different feelings about what to say.*
- **Kevin:** *I think the discussion on Yellow Bird was pretty good. I'm kind of amazed at myself… at what I said. It's actually quite sort of … grownup.*
- **Jane:** *I remember after doing that discussion I kept thinking about my feelings and my mind and my soul and wondering about it and stuff. I like what I said here. I'd still agree with it.*
- **Paul:** *I still agree with what I said. It often strikes me when we're on about what the frog said and the toad said and the spider said and…look they're not human! Why are we getting so excited about them? – They're animals for God's sake! …not even real animals…they're made up for a story!*
- **Jenny:** *Yeah but Paul… the point is what's it about … what's the author trying to tell us? … We don't believe the stories, we…think about what the point is.* (Roche 2007 p 255)

I believe the data clearly demonstrate that the children can be critical about their own critical thinking. The data suggest that the children respect the discussions and take them seriously. Paul's contribution was very true to form: he regularly displayed that he was one of the deepest and most lateral thinkers in the class, and he often stated, after some time in discussion, that the suspension of belief he needed to go along with a fiction story had just collapsed. For example, in a discussion about Toad's new Swimsuit (in Lobel 1992) he argued: 'I mean … he's a toad! Why would he need a swimsuit? Frogs don't wear swimsuits!' In the transcript of the *Yellow Bird, Black Spider* discussion, he had said:

- **Paul:** *I don't know why we're all feeing so shocked about the bird eating the spider. That's what birds do…all the time! They eat spiders and worms and cute things like ladybirds. So what's so extraordinary about eating a spider? I think it's because we're looking at that bird as if he's human. He's a bird!* (Roche 2007 Appendix C.9.)

Paul recognised early in his school career that children's fiction is steeped in anthropomorphic imagery. And he was not a fan of the genre. However, Jenny's response to him, as they evaluated the transcripts, shows that Jenny had grasped that the exercise in discussing such stories was an exercise in thinking critically.

When discussions break down

Unlike other methodologies, which focus on the product of 'better thinking', CT&BT discussions are always open-ended processes. There is no artifice, no pre-planned agenda to the discussions other than to want the children to engage critically and respectfully with their own and each others' ideas. There is always the risk of failure and discussions can frequently breakdown. Whenever this happened – when a discussion just failed to 'take off', I would stop it and say 'We don't seem to be in form for talking much today. I wonder why?' and very often *that* would trigger dialogue and I would hear things like: 'well the secretary came in twice'; or 'the milk arrived'; or 'the PA system interrupted'; or 'kids came in to borrow whiteboard markers/paint/crayons' and so on. The children always knew exactly what was wrong. Now and again they would just decide 'We don't really like that story' and then perhaps *that* would also trigger dialogue as to *why* they disliked it. 'Well it's kind of boring'; or 'It's a bit stupid' or, very perceptively, they might say 'Miss, YOU don't even like it'.

However, these were rare occurrences. Most times the dialogue flowed effortlessly.

Another discussion on freedom

The next piece of data is drawn from a discussion on freedom following the reading of Poole and Barrett's *Anne Frank* with another group of 8 and 9 year olds. Neither I nor the children set out with the agenda of discussing freedom. The children's comments on what they understood by freedom came about organically as they responded to the story. It shows me the high level of critical awareness that some children can reach.

- **Kate:** *People deserve freedom: everybody is human, so in that way everybody is the same. It's not fair if one person makes another person do something they don't want to do. No one is more important than anyone else …*
- **Colin:** *I agree that freedom is being able to do whatever you want but you shouldn't have the freedom to kill anyone. Or you shouldn't be able to take over the world and kill people …*
- **Jack:** *I just thought of this when Cian was talking about slaves. I think freedom isn't something you can give to someone. Even if you're a slave owner: because the slave might have freedom already inside themselves and you might be only giving them sort of like … permission or something. Permission doesn't really mean the same thing as freedom …*

The entries in my research diary from that period differ considerably from the kind of rhetoric in the mainstream literatures of critical thinking. I saw that I was living and working with real people, who shared human experiences. Our CT&BT discussions involved us in a genuine sharing of ideas, in a 'constant flow' as Bohm (1998) described.

Feminism and gender awareness

As I continued to explore picturebooks with middle-grade children, I began to see the huge potential these books had for critical literacy. In Chapter 2 we said that critical literacy has to do with 'learning to be curious, sceptical, engaged, and non-complacent' (Luke 1991 p 143). When I read Karlin and Marshall's *Cinderella* to a class of 8-year-old boys in an all-male, inner-city school they had several questions about it:

- **Andy:** *How come the glass slippers didn't disappear with the rest of her clothes?*
- **Jack:** *If the fairy godmother was so magic why didn't she just make her rich and turn the bad sisters into her slaves?*
- **Me:** *Do you think the prince really fell in love with Cinderella?*
- *Chorus of Yesss!*
- **Me:** *If he really loved her then do you think he would have danced with her if he'd seen her in her working rags?*
- **Keith:** *If she went in raggy clothes they might have laughed and [then] that would hurt her feelings.*
- **Barry:** *No way would the prince have danced with her in her raggy clothes...cos his friends would all be mocking him.* (Roche 2000 p 6)

Here Barry seems to have grasped the idea of 'the trophy wife or girlfriend' even at this young age. These children had very pragmatic views and often scoffed at what they considered to be far-fetched solutions to 'problems' in stories. For example, when a colleague asked me to read and discuss the biblical account of Adam and Eve with my class, for her research on classroom discussion, one child said: 'Well, anyway, I know that story just can't be true'. When I asked how he could be so sure he replied 'Simple: snakes don't talk – they only goes ssss!' Similarly when I discussed Fisher's (1999) story of Gelert, a faithful hound who saved a noble baby from a wolf and dies in the process, the children dismissed the story as 'rubbish' on several grounds:

- *Why didn't the Mam and Dad pay a babyminder?*
- *Yeah. What kind of people would go off for the day and leave a dog minding a child?*
- *Why didn't they lock the door?*
- *Even if they only closed the door that would have done cos wolves can't turn knobs!*

Reading Munch's *Paperbag Princess* to a group of 8- and 9-year-old boys and girls led to a really interesting discussion about why most of the 'rescuing' in traditional stories was done by males and nearly all of those rescued were female. Claire and Amy had some reasons:

- **Claire:** *Well I think I know why princes were always the hero! It's clothes! Girls had to wear tight tops that you pulled laces on and big huge skirts and their shoes were high heels and even glass!!! You can't run or climb trees or escape or nothin! But princes wore leggings and flat boots and stuff!*
- **Amy:** *Like what about Barbie now like, and Bratz an things like them ...like, are they trying to get.. small kids to go back to those times? .. dollied up all the time. Like....you'd have to be wonderin about stuff like that...*
- **Helen:** *Remember we were talking about what courage is and what bravery is? Well wearing uncool clothes is brave sometimes. Like when my Mom buys stuff in the charity shop for me I have to be really brave to wear them cos sometimes girls laugh at you.*

We can see how Carrington's (2003) ideas about Diva Starz, mentioned in Chapter 5, could have been very interesting to discuss here, had I been aware of her paper at that time.

Children as 'benign rebels' (Glover 1999)

Glover argued in 1999 that 'we need to teach our children how to think, how to argue and how to analyse'. Moral philosophy has to enter the classroom, he argued (Haynes (2002 p 2).

> My belief is that children actually ask philosophical questions, he said. Children are interested in reasoning. Many children who ask philosophical questions get told by their parents or teachers: 'Oh, don't waste your time thinking about those unanswerable questions. Learn something practical.' But I think that teaching people to think rationally and critically actually can make a difference to peoples' susceptibility to false ideologies, for instance.
>
> (Glover in *Guardian* interview 1999)

Ultimately, Glover argues, communities which stave off atrocities and dictatorship are those which nurture the benign rebel in their children. 'If you look at the people who sheltered Jews under the Nazis, you find a number of things about them. One is that they tended to have different kinds of upbringing from the average person, they tended to be brought up in a non-authoritarian way, brought up to have sympathy with other people and to discuss things rather than just do what they were told,' he said. 'I think that bringing up children in a certain way does help to create a culture in which people are more likely to resist things,' Glover argued. The idea of reintroducing philosophy to schools is one that is gaining momentum in Ireland as arguments for secularising education mount.

An example of pupils being 'benign rebels' –
Will: wasting time in school

My students appeared to enjoy discussions. They often expressed their delight, as in the interchange here:

- **Paul:** *It's fun ... we're thinking about solutions for all kinds of [problems] and for all kinds of reasons and that's fun school work!*
- **Chloe:** *It actually gives your brain energy in it.*
- **Ken:** *It's good because you don't do any like, school work with a pen or a copybook. It's still work but it's fun as well.*
- **Cillian:** *One it's fun, children like it: and two, it brightens up your mind.*
- **Ciara:** *I think sometimes it's a bit of a challenge, because there could be yappers in our class and they have to be quiet as well. But it's also ... good for the teachers because they sit down and listen to what the kids have to think and they could have been learning something earlier in the day that they could be mentioning now and you'd notice that they'd been listening in.*

Will, however, insisted that CT&BT was only fun because it 'wasted school time':

- **Will:** *I love [it] cos it's a bit of fun ... and it's wasting time in school.*
- **Me:** *I'm interested in that word 'wasting'. Is 'waste' the word you wanted to use there?*
- **Will:** *Yeah.*

Other children disagreed with Will's perspectives: Then Alex said:

- **Alex:** *Well OK, you're not working – not like in Maths – you're not doing anything hard, just talking and thinking.*
- **Paul:** *– but thinking is hard work. Listening is hard work. Paying attention is hard work! Well that's what I think, anyway.*

No 'right' answer

Perhaps for Will, areas such as CT&BT, PE, Art and Music, which he also liked, differed from 'ordinary' school work because they allowed for self-expression and were less likely than 'regular' class work to involve a child being requested to provide 'right answers'. Discussing issues in a circle format presents many children, perhaps for the first time, with the opportunity to reach an understanding that for some questions there are no 'right' answers and that, in fact, many answers can be right. It provides a freedom of expression that may not be available in didactic class work. The same dialogue transcript contains the following interaction:

- **Dan:** *When someone talks you can have a new thought …but when you're thinking in Maths, it's different, that doesn't happen.*
- **Me:** *I'm interested in what Dan said about Maths …. that it's a different kind of thinking. I agree, because in Maths you're expected to get a right answer, and there's only one right answer, whereas in Thinking Time there's …*
- **Ciarán:** *(Interrupts) – 'no right answer!'*
- **Me:** *(handing over the microphone) Yes? What do you think?* Laughter from group
- **Ciarán (smiling broadly):** *Well there's no right answer, and it's great! Cos you're allowed to think freely and no one else is allowed to boss you around and it's just … great!* (Roche 2007)

Another example of the awareness of there being 'more than one right answer' occurred in a discussion following the reading of Sheldon and Blythe's *The Whales' Song* in which conflicting views of whaling are presented:

- **Emily:** *Well I've got a bit of a problem here: see, I agree with Lily's Granny that whales are splendid beautiful creatures and they must be protected, but I can also see Uncle Frederick's point of view that whalers have to make their living too. It's terrible hard trying to decide who is right … Maybe they are both right! … Maybe more than one thing can be right at a time! I never thought about that before!*

Participating in a discussion with peers can also offer children the opportunity to reconsider their opinions in light of the beliefs and experiences shared by others.

- **Heidi:** *…when other people say something your ideas change and you actually start thinking more … when you read a story by yourself and you don't do any thinking about it then you don't get the point sometimes, unless they tell it to you, but [in CT&BT] you get the point and other people's points as well.*

- *Jack: [CT&BT] helps you reveal your thoughts. You might have a thought at the start, but by every person speaking you might change it slightly each time and you might end up with something totally different at the end.*

Observers of discussions in my classrooms have frequently expressed surprise at the ease with which children change their views as they assimilate others' ideas. In the dialogue excerpt featured above, Will eventually said:

- *Will: I've actually changed my mind, I disagree with myself: CT&BT is fun but it isn't wasting time, it's using time in a fun way.*
- *Me: Did you feel pressure to change your mind when everyone seemed to disagree with you?*
- *Will: Naw, that's what I thought but after listening to all the points the others made I've changed my mind.*

When I ran a series of workshops for teachers between 2002 and 2004 this particular aspect of my videos – children disagreeing with themselves in the light of perhaps, new critical understanding that had been influenced by others' thinking – often appeared to be one of the most remarked upon aspects. A teacher with 30 years' experience said:

- *Hearing those children change their minds so honestly and matter-of-factly is a humbling experience. I think many adults, [laughing] especially politicians, could learn from them in that respect. I wish I'd seen these videos when I began teaching. It would have changed my style completely.*

My data show children engaging critically with and developing each other's ideas. This resonates with Bohm's (1998) ideas of how he understands dialogue as 'a stream of meaning flowing among and through us and between us' (p 2). He describes how it is possible for new understandings to emerge from the dialogue, which can enable people to create and share meanings together. I like his analogy of these shared meanings acting as a sort of social 'glue' or 'cement that holds people and societies together' (ibid.).

In our CT&BT circles we are not about trying to 'get points' or make 'any particular view prevail' (ibid.), but we are intent on sharing thoughts and making meaning with each other. Observers of my classroom discussions, colleagues who participated in the circle or parents and colleagues who watched videos of discussions are often amazed at the calm way in which disagreement is accepted. They are particularly struck by seeing the children disagreeing with me.

Disagreeing with teacher

As I tried to create a more dialogical classroom I began to see my work as grounded in educative relationships (Roche 2007, 2011). This idea is drawn from several sources, (e.g. Dewey 1934; Freire 1972; McNiff 2000), as well as from my own reflections on practice. I view educative relationships as processes in which people help each other to grow in terms of their own capacity for independent thinking and personal growth, and in which they allow each other to do the same. My influence could be seen as being oriented towards helping myself, my students and my colleagues, to understand that each of us has the capacity for independence of mind and creativity of spirit. As such, the influence that

I exercise is ultimately aimed at enabling others to be free. My practice of encouraging children to exercise their capacity to think for themselves involves helping my students to become free of me. An episode that illustrates this emerging freedom occurred as my Senior Infant class was about to go home following a discussion on 'rainbows and reality' that had lasted for more than an hour and that had amazed me (and two observers) in its intensity and depth. In Roche (2007 p 6) I wrote:

> As he put on his coat 5 year old Eoin said 'Guess what, Teacher, I am going home with just so many questions in my head!' I said that I thought that was good: after all, 'That's what school is for — asking questions and thinking about possible answers.' Aoife, also 5, then said, 'and if you go home with a question and you get an answer to your question, you can always question the answer.'
>
> (Roche 2007 Appendix C.5.)

This last comment really set me thinking. 'Questioning the answer' became a normal practice in my classrooms. I questioned answers and the children questioned answers. In the course of our discussions the children frequently disagreed with me and explained why. My data excerpts bear this out:

- **Paul:** *I think that willpower is just something that you need to do and you're trying to do it, so Teacher, you could be right or you could be wrong.*
- **Deirdre:** *I disagree with Teacher because [the swimsuit] mightn't look funny on someone else: it might only look funny on him.*

I welcome disagreement so long as reasons are provided and our agreed norms of courteous behaviour are complied with. After all I could also reply that 'I disagree with your point because...' Other teachers often feared that allowing children to disagree with the teacher would lead to disrespect and anarchy and all sorts of problems. My experience has been the opposite: in over 20 years of discussions, I never had to reprimand a child for rudeness or disrespect.

Now we have begun to realise that as well as questioning answers we also need to 'question questions'. This realisation came about when I began doing workshops with adolescents, undergraduates and teachers.

CT&BT with post-primary pupils, undergraduates and teachers

Picturebooks are not limited to children. Getting that point across is perhaps one of the most challenging aspects of my work. I have spoken earlier about how frequently only infant and early childhood teachers turn up to workshops. They see the word 'picturebooks' perhaps and assume the workshop only has relevance for the junior classrooms. As we have seen in previous chapters, though, I have used picturebooks in educational contexts at all levels of the system. Picturebooks can also provide food for thought and discussion with older people and can be springboards for exploring issues such as education, gender stereotyping, death and depression. At the end of this book, I have included a sample list of books that could help to help develop dialogue about sensitive issues and topics.

Teachers and student teachers – both primary and post-primary – are generally very open to the idea of tackling contentious or 'sensitive' issues in their classrooms. In all the workshops for teachers that I have held, the only book that caused a ripple of anxiety was Marcus Ewart and Rex Ray's *10,000 Dresses*. Many of the primary teachers, who expressed a view, said they felt insecure around introducing transgender issues and thought that parents would need to be consulted before they would discuss such a topic. Mary (a primary teacher with 15 years' experience) said:

* *That's crazy when you actually stop and think about it. I mean, personally I would have no problem raising this issue. I think parents would be happy enough for me to talk about the Holocaust or death, or global warming or war, but I'd imagine there would be trouble if I read and discussed* 10,000 Dresses. *That's kind of scary actually.*

Some of the other teachers present suggested that one way around any sensitive issue, would be to meet with and inform parents, in advance and outline the rationale for the CT&BT approach. Then, perhaps, through newsletters or updates that would be issued throughout the school year generally, parents could be kept informed about the topics that would be discussed during critical literacy lessons. In that way, they felt, parents could begin to realise that such issues are couched in larger discourses about tolerance and inclusion and social justice and that, as Carrington (2003) said 'our understandings of literacy are always embedded in broader social and economic landscapes' (p 94) and that 'being "literate" is about having the skills and knowledge with which to participate in and transform one's social and cultural context' (p 84).

Summary

We can see now why I have argued throughout that there is no formal template around doing CT&BT. The case studies and examples from practice and from feedback have provided a sense of what's involved. Reiterating that what is needed most of all is a teacher who is open and willing to try this approach to discussing picturebooks, a class-room atmosphere grounded in reciprocity, care and respect and a generous selection of picturebooks. After that, all you need to do is to tailor the CT&BT approach to suit your own context.

Recommended reading

Salisbury, M. and Styles, M. (2012) *Children's Picturebooks*. London: Laurence King Publishing.
Silvey, A. (2012) *Children's Book-a-Day Almanac*. New York: Roaring Book Press.
Sipe, L. (2000) 'Those Two Gingerbread Boys Could be Brothers': how children use intertextual connections during storybook readalouds. *Children's Literature in Education*, 31: 73–90.

Chapter 7

Practical advice

Choosing books; discussion guidelines and cross-curricular ideas

Buying picturebooks for a classroom or nursery could involve quite a large financial outlay so we need to be sure that we are getting the best possible value for our money. When choosing picturebooks for discussion with different age groups, there are several things we need to consider. Let's start with the preschool age group.

What should we look for?

Babies and very young children will respond to both your voice and to the illustrations. You must read aloud in a voice that will keep the child engaged. Remember that we are dealing here in this book with *reading for discussion*. If you are trying to engage a young child actively in a story, then you will read with that in mind, varying your voice and pausing to pose and perhaps answer questions. Picturebooks for younger children will need to be uncluttered and colourful, with illustrations that will attract and hold the small child's attention. Babies respond well to faces of other babies and the *Look Baby! Books* series by Margaret Miller provides a great beginning library. You can use the words in the books or make up your own. Books at this level need to be simple and engaging and your dialogue with the child will provide all that's needed after that.

For example, let's assume you are reading Mem Fox and Judy Horacek's *Where is The Green Sheep?* The cover of the book shows us a picture of three sheep, happily 'holding hands' as they skip down a grassy hillside. The sheep are different colours and they lend themselves to discussion straight away. For example, we could study the cover and then ask: Look at these three sheep. I bet they're going somewhere. I wonder where they are. They aren't in a town are they? We can't see any roads or houses or cars or people around, so maybe they are out in the countryside. Where might they be coming from? Why are they holding hands? They look happy, don't they? There's a red sheep and a yellow sheep and an orange sheep. The title asks 'Where is the GREEN sheep? Hmm ...I wonder where that green sheep could be. Perhaps he's hiding! Do you think the sheep might be hiding? Where, do you think?' Here the child is being encouraged to create her own story. We could then say 'Let's read a little bit and see what the author says'. You could add: 'Mem Fox is the author – she wrote the book: see, her name is here on the cover. I bet *she* knows where the green sheep is. Judy Horacek is the illustrator: her name is here too, look, because she made all those pictures. *She* probably knows where the green sheep is too. *We're going to have to read the book to find out for ourselves, aren't we? Where do you think the green sheep is?'* and so on. Look at all the vocabulary and concepts we have introduced already and the story has yet to begin.

The story starts with a picture of a blue sheep standing in a field smiling out at us (with corresponding opportunities to talk about standing, smiling, face, legs, no tail, blue, wool, grass, flowers and sky): the text says 'Here is the blue sheep'. The next opening shows the red sheep turning a somersault on a hill with the text saying 'And here is the red sheep' (again, there are opportunities here for discussion about what the sheep is doing balancing on one leg, is s/he happy or sad?, the colour red, another hill, more flowers, somersaulting, etc.). On the next opening we see a sheep wallowing ecstatically in a bubble-filled bath. The text is simple and has a good rhythm and has scope for lots of vocabulary – colours, furniture, trains, playgrounds and circuses. Within all of these there are opportunities for adding to the child's knowledge – for example, in the bed scene, we can speak about bedclothes, pillow, counterpane (if that's a word you and the child would use), bookshelf, vase of flowers, books, reading, cosy, sitting up. In the bathroom scene we can speak about bath, water, bubbles, rubber duck, washing, soaking, splashing, etc. Not every child will want this level of detail – or interruption – on the first reading. Some children will just want you to get on with the reading/telling of the story without frills. Subsequent readings could build on any new vocabulary, or you could focus on the rhythm and rhyming aspects when reading. I have given copies of *Where is the Green Sheep?* to several friends and colleagues for reading to their toddlers and in no time at all, some of them have shown me video clips of their children 'reading' the book unaided. When I view these videos, I am amazed by what these children have achieved. Reading and talking about this seemingly simple book involves using a large vocabulary, lots of concepts such as brave/scared; rhyming words like red/bed, clown/down; repeated statement 'here is'; question 'where is the green sheep?' as well as lots of visual clues to aid memory. It is a very clever little book.

Similarly, books like Audrey and Don Wood's *The Napping House*, Margaret Wise Brown and Clement Hurd's classic *Goodnight Moon* and Mem Fox and Jane Dyer's *Time for Bed* lend themselves to similar reading experiences and are perfect for bedtime reading. The Ahlbergs' *Peepo*, Mem Fox and Helen Oxenbury's *Ten Little Fingers and Ten Little Toes*, Penny Dale's *Ten in the Bed*, Laura Joffe Numeroff's series: *If you give a Dog a Donut*, *If You Give a Mouse a Cookie*, *If You Give a Moose a Muffin*, *If You Give a Cat a Cupcake*, *If You Give a Pig a Pancake* are all great for developing vocabulary and for encouraging comprehension skills like prediction – as well as being sheer fun. Lift-the-flap books (like Molly Idle's *Flora and the Flamingo*, Karen Katz's *Peek-a-Baby* or *Where Is Baby's Belly Button?*, Rod Campbell's *Dear Zoo*, or old favourites such as Eric Hill's *Where is Spot?*) provide interactive opportunities as well as enhancing budding prediction skills. Emily Gravett's *Orange, Pear, Apple, Bear* is a perfect book for experimenting with rhyme and change of voice.

Preschool and kindergarten

Preschool and kindergarten children love nursery rhymes, traditional stories and books showing familiar and well-loved objects. Especially good at this stage are books with intertextual references to characters from nursery rhymes or traditional stories. Books such as Janet and Allan Ahlberg's *The Jolly Postman*, *Each Peach Pear Plum*; Colin McNaughton and Emma Chichester Clark's *Have You Ever, Ever, Ever?* and *Not Last*

Night But The Night Before are great for reminding small children of familiar characters and well-known stories as, of course, is David Wiesner's *The Three Pigs*. Likewise, the 'plots' of both John Prater's *Once Upon a Time* and Vivian French and John Prater's *Once Upon a Picnic* are built around the entrances of many recognisable nursery rhyme and traditional story characters. Children love being able to remind you that they *know* these people: when they recognise them, the characters are often greeted as though they are familiar and well-loved old friends. They spot the smallest clues. Towards the end of *Not Last Night But The Night Before,* when George and I were about to find out why Bo Beep and the Three Bears, and the Blind Mice along with many other well-known characters have all rushed in the front door and up the stairs of a bewildered little boy's house, an arm is visible tapping a glass for attention. George said 'Hey, I know who owns that arm. It's the farmer's wife. That's the same as her clothes!' I have to admit, I had not spotted the fabric of her sleeve at all.

Each book should be read in advance and presented to the child when they are receptive and ready. Never 'force' a book on a child. It could lead to the child associating reading with an unpleasant feeling and that is the last thing we want. Instead, each book should be seen as an opportunity to engage the child in discussion and interaction. This is where the magic happens – the child will bond with you and with the reading experience, while effortlessly developing vocabulary and, if the questions you ask are open-ended, the child will begin the process of thinking critically. Important habits, attitudes and values are being laid down; important relationships are being forged; readerly skills such as page-turning and reading from left to right are being developed: turn-taking in conversation is being modelled; vocal tone and inflection when reading are being noted; along with developing visual analysis and verbal ability: a whole vast world of new knowledge is being created.

Beginning school

When choosing books for children in infant classes we should build on the kinds of books listed above. Parents and teachers should choose books that have stimulating texts and images and allow plenty of time for pondering and speculating, for what I call *'what-iffing'* and *'I wonder whying'*. Beginning the process of classroom discussion should be as stress-free and gentle as possible.

Over the past 20 or so years, I have built up a huge library of 'good' picturebooks. These books present philosophical issues, offer concepts for analysis, provide scope for imaginative exploration. At the end of this book, I will provide a list of books that I have found particularly useful for stimulating discussions and dialogue with young children.

Traditional stories

Fisher (2006) suggests that we shouldn't ignore the traditional stories. Nearly all the major traditional fairy-tales are available in picturebook format. One of the reasons traditional fairy-tales continue to be interesting, Fisher says, is because they engage and reflect the key binary concepts, (such as love and hate, beauty and ugliness, fear and courage, life and death) that underpin, fascinate and are relevant to all human lives. Stories that have lasted for centuries often involve powerful concepts. They are strongly involved in children's ways of understanding the world and in engaging their imaginative faculties and so, they can provide a rich stimulus for developing higher order thinking skills.

But sometimes, as we said already, these stories need interrogation. This is where critical literacy begins. According to Harwood (2008 np) 'Critical literacy creates opportunities for children to enter into a dialogue with texts such as Cinderella, and examine issues of power, gender, social class, religion, culture, and race, relating the text to their own world'. What, for example, are the values underpinning the stories of *Beauty and the Beast, Cinderella, Snow White,* etc.? What messages are being sent out to little girls? What are the feminine qualities that are rewarded? What is the reward? What if the Prince displayed the qualities that are demanded of the Princess? It is no harm to present some of the alternative versions of these stories such as *The Paper Bag Princess, Prince Cinders, The Three Little Wolves and the Big Bad Pig.* It should be noted, however, that Alison Lurie (1990) suggests, that contrary to feminist critiques of traditional stories, the traditional stories actually present strong female protagonists rather than passive wives-in-waiting. Why not present both arguments and ask your child or children to decide?

Middle school

Books that challenge gender stereotyping make for interesting discussions: old favourites like Charlotte Zolotow and William Pene du Bois' *William's Doll*; Barrie Wade's *Give a Dog a Name*; Marie Sabine Roger and Anne Sol's *What Are You Playing At?* and Bob Graham's *Crusher is Coming.* Likewise, books that challenge the bullying that often accompanies gender stereotyping are very valuable for classroom discussion around these serious and potentially damaging issues: books such as Tomi de Paola's *Oliver Button is a Sissy* and Harvey Fierstein and Henry Cole's *The Sissy Duckling* and Mary Hoffman and Caroline Binch's *Amazing Grace* provoke very insightful thinking in response to reading them in my classrooms.

Hoose and Tilley's *Hey, Little Ant* was another book that challenged children to think. In the story we get to see a boy's justifications for crushing an ant and the children listening to the story can decide the ending. One of the reasons the boy gives for wanting to crush the ant is: 'Everybody knows an ant can't feel pain'. Following our discussion of the book we examined why a statement that begins 'everybody knows that...' is wrong. This had happened because earlier in the month, when we were discussing homelessness, following a Religious Education lesson on The Good Samaritan, Andrew said 'Well anyway, you should never give money to a homeless person. That's what my Dad says'. When I asked why, he replied: 'Well everybody knows they're only winos and if you give them money they'll just buy more wine to get drunk' and he mimed someone staggering and made the class laugh. I decided we needed to challenge the 'everybody knows' statement there and then.

Later that evening I did an internet search to find more books with that kind of theme and I came across an old picturebook, sadly out of print now, by Jay Williams and Mercer Meyer entitled *Everyone Knows what a Dragon Looks Like.* I managed to get hold of a secondhand copy and it has provided me with some great discussions over the years. It is also a really beautiful book with incredible illustrations and I treasure it. *The Tooth,* a more recent publication by Avi Slodovnick and Manon Gauthier, also challenges homelessness. It is beautifully illustrated and conveys the message that cities can be cold, unforgiving places for the poor. Little Marissa and her mother are going to the dentist and Marissa sees a homeless man. She gives him her tooth to put under his pillow. The book ends with 'Now all he needs is a pillow'. This story has the potential to provide a class with a big question regarding just what is the worth of Marissa's act of compassion. It would have been a good book with which to discuss Andrew's statement.

Senior classes

Picturebooks for senior classes have been discussed in the previous chapters when we spoke about books like *The Island*, *The Composition*, and several books to do with alienation, racism, zenophobia and war. However, we don't always need to have dark subject matter for discussion just because children are older. Shaun Tan's *Rules of Summer* would provide great scope for a discussion on childhood fears and the arbitrary rules imposed on younger children by older friends or siblings. Remember that a book that is quite acceptable in a junior class can provide a completely different level of discussion with older children – think of *Yellow Bird, Black Spider, Once Upon an Ordinary School Day* and *The Three Robbers*, for example.

Practical advice for setting up discussions

As I said earlier, in 2011 I was invited by the National Council for Curriculum and Assessment in Ireland to make some podcasts for the 'Aistear toolkit' – a programme for early years' practitioners (NCCA 2011). Some of the following material is included in the Aistear toolkit (NCCA: Aistear Toolkit 2011) and reproduced with permission here.

From my earliest attempts at classroom discussions (see Roche 2000) I tried to establish routines that would be democratic. I sought methodologies that would allow each child to speak (or not speak), and that would help to begin to develop habits of courteous social behaviour such as listening attentively and responding to others with care. After much trial and error I decided that the circle was one of the best ways for engaging children and that Donnelly's (1994) 'passing the tip' or 'tip around' was a good system for establishing a fair method of turn taking. 'Passing the tip' means simply that each child passes the right to speak to the next child by gently touching their shoulder. We will discuss this further below.

CT&BT – suggestions

With kindergartners you could start as early in the school year as you can by getting the children used to the circle format and to speaking in turns for one round of the circle. I usually began by asking a question such as 'what might be the quietest thing in the world?' (Incidentally, one of the best answers I think I ever got to that question was 'a smile'). We followed this each day with sessions like 'the loudest/biggest/smallest/scariest/happiest/ prettiest thing in the world'. Everybody had an opinion and wanted to share it.

By mid-term to end of term the children should be quite adept at listening, thinking and talking in the discussion circle and you could extend the time gradually. For very young children, or for children who have difficulties staying seated for 30 minutes or more, you could introduce the picturebook prior to seating the children in the circle. Depending on the layout of the room and the number of children in the group, you could simply gather the children round you, or use a visualiser and/or whiteboard and projector. You will need to be patient when beginning this work. The children will take time to adjust from trying to guess what they think you want them to say, to saying what *they* think. Teachers, playschool practitioners and parents all need to realise also:

- that thinking skills needs to be taught as well as 'caught' and they will take time to develop;
- that the behaviours of dialogue and conversation need to be modelled, and again this will take time;
- that the dispositions of critical thinking will develop and evolve gradually as the children feel more confident in presenting their thoughts and see how their thinking is valued.

Introducing the CT&BT approach to the children

- The children need to be made aware that what they are doing is something very precious. Some teachers explain how long ago in Ancient Greece only very wise old men were allowed to do philosophy. They thought that children, especially girl children, were unable to think critically. You then invite the class to prove those Ancient Greeks wrong. You decide how to introduce the approach: you know your class or your child best.
- You need to emphasise that so precious is this work that you will actually record what is being said (using pen and paper or tape-recorder or video). (Note – if you are video-recording or photographing children *you must have permission*.) Recording has several benefits – and we will deal with these later under 'assessment and evaluation' – but one benefit of recording that needs to be emphasised, is that the children often direct all their remarks to you as teacher. However, gradually, because you are looking down at what you are writing, they may begin to speak 'into the circle' and a more dialogical dimension could then emerge.
- CT&BT needs to be carefully timetabled and will generally need about 40–45 minutes to prepare the room, read the story and allow every child to speak. Contexts vary and scheduling will be easier in a small school than in a large school where timetables for resources such as PE halls and computer rooms must be strictly adhered to. In a multi-grade class the story could be read to the whole class and they could discuss it together, or one class group could be allocated work to do while another group carries out the discussion. You will need to work out for yourself what suits your situation best.

You must realise that for the period of time you are in the circle you are merely a facilitator and equal participant. This is really difficult: you must refrain from making value judgements after children have spoken. If you say something like 'wow that was really interesting!' the chances are that you will get several repeats of that child's utterance. I learned this the hard way. It is important to give adequate time to the discussion so that each child gets a chance to talk. As we said before, wait time is important too – sometimes children need a little time to process what they have just heard and to remember what it was they wished to say. It is also important to remember that while you are 'just another participant' in the circle, you must not pretend to be a child or patronise the children in any way.

Pedagogical framing

Of course, as in all pedagogical work, you will need to have thought about the practical aspects such as: when to timetable the session; how to set up the room; how to organise the routines that will be involved; and then how to negotiate rules of behaviour with the children.

Here are some tips that worked for me:

- I facilitated sessions once a week. Within the constraints of your timetable, perhaps you can only schedule a session for once a fortnight. That is fine, so long as the children know that it is going to be a regular aspect of their schoolwork (even in middle and senior school they tend not to appreciate the fact that this is 'work' – because they often only associate 'work' with pencil and paper).
- Try to pick a time when you are reasonably sure of minimal interruptions. If your school has a PA system, let the PA user/manager know when your discussions are scheduled and perhaps infer that you would appreciate not having any non-urgent announcements made.
- Do not choose a time when children will be coming and going for resource or learning support. Try to minimise other interruptions like milk arriving, roll book, etc.
- Try to ensure the children have all been to the toilet and, if possible, that they have had their morning snack and play time. I chose Wednesdays, and initially I set up the room while the class was in the yard. However, even Junior Infant pupils soon became adept at getting schoolbags and tables stowed and had forming a circle down to a fine art. For a number of years I was lucky enough to have an empty room across the corridor, with chairs already set out in a circle.
- Have the children sit in a circle where they can see each other and touch each other to 'pass the tip' (Donnelly 1994). Passing the tip simply means that after the story has been read and you have issued the invitation to the children to speak, the first speaker has the opportunity to tip the person on their right or left. This determines in which direction the discussion will go. When a child is tipped on the shoulder, they have the opportunity to speak. Then, when they are finished speaking they pass on the tip to the next person. Of course they also have the opportunity to pass, if they are feeling shy or are still thinking or have nothing to say. Some teachers prefer to use a 'talking object' such as a teddy or a soft ball. That's up to you. The children get used to this very quickly. Don't forget to record what the children say. Often in the heat of the discussion you miss some contributions. If you have written them, then later, when you are writing them up properly, you will often see gems that you missed.
- If you are reading the whole story at this time, as well as having the discussion, you can now present the picturebook.
- Read the title and ask what it might be about (hands-up session – select one or two answers).
- Is there a dust cover? Remove it and see if the cover beneath is the same or different. Why is it or why isn't it?
- Examine the endpapers front and back: are they the same or different. Why did the illustrator choose those colours? (again – hands up and select some different people

to respond). Do they tell us anything about the story? (Larry Sipe's book *Storytime* (2008) is a mustread if you want to do more of this kind of work).

- Examine the openings one by one – is there a dedication or acknowledgement – who might this person be? Sometimes, there is a small illustration on the title page that offers us a clue to the story plot.
- Remember – in a good quality picturebook there is not a redundant line or word – they have all been very carefully chosen and positioned.
- Read the story slowly with meaning. The author Mem Fox has some good tips for reading aloud on her webpage – see http://www.memfox.com/reading-magic-and-do-it-like-this
- All of this could be done in an interactive session early in the week as part of literacy work and you could just revise the story briefly for the discussion. My own strategy was to emphasise that the author wanted to tell us something and it was our job to try and find out what that 'something ' was: I began with the question: 'what do you think the author wants to tell us?' (You could even hold a session earlier on 'why do writers write?' or 'why do people write books?')

The more formal discussion can then begin:

- After the first read through, close the book. Allow a moment or two for the children to process what they have heard and seen. Then ask 'does anybody have a question about that story or something interesting to say about that story? WAIT. Then, if there is a volunteer, that child begins by speaking. When she is finished she tips the person to her right or left. That person can speak or pass and tip the next person and so on. When a full circle has been completed and the next person is the first speaker again, you can decide whether to have another circle around or a hands-up. A 'hands-up' presents children who didn't speak the first time to speak now but care is needed so that dominant children do not take over.
- Sometimes a child will merely repeat what another child has said. This is fine. The more articulate children can scaffold less articulate children. However, when this happens it presents you with an opportunity to model the language of 'I agree with X because'. Children must be taught also to give a reason as to why they agree. Therefore the 'because' is very important. Having to provide a reason for why they agree eliminates the danger of children quickly adopting a strategy of agreeing with their 'best friends'. When they are comfortable with the language of 'I agree with X because' you could then introduce 'I disagree with X because...' or 'I partly disagree with X'. These are complex language structures for young children and children can be confused at the beginning and may need some scaffolding from you until they become more adept. If the book has presented a concept like loneliness or courage or beauty or loyalty you could say 'I am interested in the word "beauty", I think I know what it means but maybe we could explore it a bit more – what do you think it means?' and then follow the 'pass of the tip' around again. (Again, I emphasise that you need to have studied the book and the pictures so as to have interesting questions to ask.)
- Ask the children why they think the author decided to write this book. Perhaps she has a reason – perhaps there is some 'message' about life, or school, or boys, or girls, or heroes, or beauty, etc. that she is trying to convey?

Negotiating ground rules

A successful discussion will involve negotiating some ground rules with the children. They will need to see that they must listen and speak with respect and courtesy. On introducing CT&BT for the first time my strategy was to begin by announcing early in the day, that 'later on today we will be doing some very important work'. I would then use the ideas presented earlier to build up a sense of the importance of the work and transmit that I placed huge value on this kind of work. BUT I would add, 'for it to work we will need to do three things really well: we will need to listen very carefully to the story and the questions, we will need to think very hard, and we will need to tell each other what we think'.

Then I would ask what else might we need to do so that we can all hear the story and hear each other?

Here are some rules that children came up with:

* No whispering or mocking people when they were talking.
* No shouting.
* No interrupting.
* No being greedy and talking for ages.
* No messing.
* Everybody gets a go.

You could summarise the children's rules and write them on a chart. Prior to every discussion they should be recalled:

For example, your CT&BT RULES could be summarised as:

* We will listen with care and respect.
* We will think before we speak.
* We will speak with care and respect.
* We will not interrupt each other or make noise while people are speaking
* We can agree or disagree with someone but we will give our reasons.

Listening and the importance of silence

We need to address the issue of silence. Silence is often demanded in traditional didactic lessons. In CT&BT we allow children to choose to be silent or to speak when it is their turn. We do expect silence when others are speaking, so that we can hear what each child is saying and we must model this by remaining silent ourselves. Fisher (2006) talks about 'listening with understanding and empathy, devoting mental energy to attending to what others say, perceiving other points of view and sensing others' emotions' (in Jones and Hodson 2006 p 44). As they get used to doing the discussion children can sometimes stop listening to each other as they begin to formulate a response to a question. It is important therefore to allow time for thinking after asking a question. This applies just as strictly to the teacher as it does to the children.

In my own case, I had to reflect on the importance of my own silence in classroom discussions. Fiumara (1990) speaks about the silence of listening as 'the other side of language' (p 4). From being a teacher who, early in my career, relied heavily on verbal skills in a largely didactic practice (see Roche 2011), I had to learn to take a back seat as regards speaking in classroom discussion. It was probably the most difficult aspect of changing my practice for me – because I am an inveterate talker.

Evaluation and assessment

In many educational contexts teachers are obliged to provide the learning outcomes for children for every lesson they teach. Assessing your picturebook lessons need not be a cause for anxiety. Let's look now at a few examples of how you might assess the children's thinking and discussion.

- Recording is important. Whether you develop a personal 'shorthand' scribble, or use a tape recorder or video camera, recording what the children say allows you to have data for assessment and evaluation: Who did not speak? Who made very interesting points? Who seems to be lacking confidence? Who may have a language processing disorder? Whose attention is limited?
- In your planning for 'oral language development' you will have decided what you wish to focus on each week, fortnight or month. Let's assume that you are focusing on 'developing confidence and competence'. Taking the '*confidence*' aspect you could make a rubric of skills that you wish to emphasise, e.g. Participation – you would look over your weekly transcripts and see if that child contributed or 'passed'; 'Makes eye contact', 'Speaks up', 'Willingness to engage' might be other qualities upon which you might to focus.
- Likewise, if you are focusing on '*competence*' you could design a rubric of the skills you value most such as: 'uses appropriate language', 'communicates well', 'elaborates on ideas', 'articulates thoughts coherently', 'makes relevant contributions to discussion', 'speaks out clearly', 'able to sustain an idea and articulate it', 'understands/processes the question and engages with the ideas', 'speaks in whole sentences', etc. You might focus on 'listening' – again you might have noted that a child or children did not appear to listen as others spoke. Of course you wouldn't be able to either focus on all of these criteria at the same time, nor focus on all of the children. Choose a few children to observe and select one or two criteria, and, over the term or half-term, evaluate them in some other oral language settings also such as 'show and tell' 'our news', etc. Perhaps there is a pattern across different oral language lessons. Should there be cause for concern, you will then have evidence to support it.
- You will also have data for informing your teaching – you can clearly see some elements of oral language on which you might need to focus.
- Another less comfortable aspect of recording – particularly using audio or video – is that it can be employed very effectively to monitor your own participation and behaviour as you sit in the circle. I thought I was silent in the discussions, only speaking when it was my turn. I thought I was refraining from making evaluative comments – and then I watched the videos. It was an uncomfortable and embarrassing experience. There I was interrupting, interfering, silencing children by scowling or tisking, hurrying them along as they paused for thought. I was dreadful. But I used the data to improve my facilitative abilities and so it was an opportunity for genuine reflective practice.

CT&BT is not just an oral language 'lesson': The emphasis throughout is on critical thinking and dialogue. Depending on their ages, children can learn new vocabulary while enjoying the story of *Rosie's Walk* or *The Island* for example. They can also demonstrate their understanding about what new words mean; in *Rosie's Walk* there are words such as mill, beehives, henhouse/chicken coop. They can explore concepts together such as what rich means as they discuss the story of *The Three Robbers* or what being a hero means in *Jack* or *Kate and the Beanstalk*. CT&BT is far more than just a chat about children's own experiences. We want to expand their thinking so that they become used to reading between the lines and thinking outside the box. We want to set some of their 'what ifs' and 'yes buts' free.

Reflective practice – self-evaluation

In advance – ask yourself:

* *How do I ensure that all children have time to think?*
* *How do I ensure that all children will feel safe in offering their ideas?*
* *How do I familiarise myself with the stories and the possible areas/topics for discussion?*
* *Am I surprised by how well or how badly a particular child/group of children did in the discussion?*
* *How many children are not contributing? How can I encourage them to participate more?*
* *Can I involve my local library in this programme? Will they lend books to me for discussion?*

After a discussion:

* *Did I ensure that all children had time to think?*
* *Did I ensure that all children felt safe in offering their ideas?*
* *Did I facilitate or dominate?*
* *Did I listen respectfully and attentively?*
* *What could I improve on in relation to my own participation?*

Cross-curricular work

RE and SPHE

Teachers who worry about finding space within their allotted literacy time for having discussions with their pupils, should remember that picturebooks are hugely versatile and lend themselves easily to cross-curricular topics. Many primary school curricula encourage linkage and integration between subjects. Discussions could be timetabled under RE, SPHE, or English because many picturebooks lend themselves to cross-curricular themes. Here are some books that relate, for example, to the topic of relationships: Melanie Watt's *Scaredy Squirrel Makes a Friend*; Louise Yates' *Frank and Teddy Make Friends*; Tad Hills' *Duck, Duck Goose*; Oliver Jeffers' *The Way Back Home*; Emily Gravett's *Wolf Won't Bite;* Jeanne Willis and Sarah Fox Davies' *Mole's Sunrise;* Kathryn Cave and Chris Riddell's *Something Else;* Mem Fox and Julie Vivas' *Wilfrid Gordon McDonald Partridge;* wordless books like Barbara Lehman's *The Red Book*, Aaron Becker's *The Journey*, Shaun Tan's *The Arrival*, and *The Rules of Summer,* or the old favourite *Little Red Hen* (my favourite version is by Paul Galdone).

Maths

Likewise, there are lots of picturebooks that encourage dialogue about Maths: John Burningham's *The Shopping Basket*; Jon Scieszka and Lane Smith's *Math Curse* (in which Mrs Fibonnaci the teacher proclaims 'You know, you can think of almost everything as a math problem'); Pamela Allen's *Who Sank the Boat?*; Theoni Pappas' *The Adventures of Penrose the Mathematical Cat;* Emily Gravett's *The Rabbit Problem;* Pat Hutchins' *Clocks Clocks and More Clocks;* Mem Fox and Terry Denton's *Night Noises* and so on. There is a huge list of suitable books available for examining the concept of numbers, counting, addition, subtraction, shape, space, money/shopping, time, seasons, months, etc. Dr Patricia Moyer-Packenham, the Director of Math Education Centre, George Mason University, who has compiled a comprehensive list of picturebooks that deal with mathematical themes and concepts, says 'when children can talk about maths concepts, the concepts usually make sense to them' (see http://www.dearteacher.com/math-books).

SESE: science books and nature books

In Chapter 4 I spoke about the lyricism and beauty of books like Karen Wallace and Mike Bostock's *Think of an Eel*. Such books teach concepts like lifecycles, expand vocabulary and present a complete aesthetic experience. Pringle and Lamme (2005) say that children must be given a multitude of opportunities to probe, poke and peek into their own backyards or galaxies far away. These opportunities, they add, can be supported by the wealth of information available in science picture books.

> Picture books about animals, when scientifically accurate, have the advantage of presenting children with close up pictures. A picture book can do a lot that cannot be accomplished in a classroom. The pictures freeze time, so a reader can pore over the details in a way that would never happen if the animal were moving... A story allows the reader to follow an animal's life through time – through seasons, weather, and the quest for survival. ...A book can raise questions, provide experiences for observation and carefully guide readers toward arriving at a valid conclusion... it is important to critically examine the existing books to make sure that the information they contain is correct and that any imbedded messages are valid science content knowledge.
>
> (Pringle and Lamme 2005 p 2)

A book like Ed Young's *Seven Blind Mice* can lead to huge discussion about the importance of accurate research – a must for all scientific endeavours. Isvan Banyai's *Zoom* shows the importance of close looking. Nothing is what it seems to be and this book is fantastic for prediction. Prepare for lots of 'wows!' as children explore the pictures. Maria Frazee's *Roller Coaster* examines motion and forces in a delightful way. Judi and Ron Barrett's *Cloudy with a Chance of Meatballs* offers a zany introduction to a discussion on the study of weather; likewise David Wiesner's *Sector 7* kept a group of my 9 year olds engaged in discussion for over an hour and led to a project on clouds. (The children had long been fans of Wiesner's books since discussing *Three Pigs, Tuesday, Free Fall* and *Flotsam*. They loved looking for and finding the many intertextual visual references in his books.)

The different areas of science – natural, physical, chemical, ecological and so on, are richly explored in a vast range of picturebooks, both fiction and non-fiction. In the US,

Karen Ansberry and Emily Morgan have compiled a comprehensive list of picturebooks that encourage scientific exploration and dialogue. They generously provide links to English Language Arts Common Core Alignment on their website: http://www.pictureperfectscience.com/

History and Social Studies

There are countless picturebooks available that provide rich opportunities to discuss aspects of history and social studies syllabi at all levels of school. Prior to introducing my pupils to the their first study of ancient civilisations we examined and explored what 'a civilisation' or 'culture' meant by reading and discussing Paul Fleischman and Kevin Hawkes' *Weslandia*. This book lends itself hugely to cross-curricular work. You can explore language by learning the meaning of words such as staple crop, tuber, morale, scornful, civilisation; you can examine all the facets of culture – language, clothing, food, music, art, writing system, counting system, currency and so on; the botany of plants and the science of seed dispersal is there for exploration, as are binary and deanery maths and Wesley's new mathematical system.

Music and musical instruments can be examined, as can studying the constellations and there is the philosophical area of how people began to make sense of their existence and purpose on the earth. Then there are the affective areas such as examining what a social outcast means, non-belonging, bullying, isolation and difference. Colonisation is touched on when Wesley begins to win over/control his former tormentors. The art work is superb and led to my class experimenting with drawing using thin black markers. Children can explore how paint and ink are made and how alphabets and writing evolved. The book is rich enough to provide a whole year's work in several curricular areas (for more ideas on using this book see Beth Belinder's excellent cross-curricular linkage in her page on http://www.homeschoolshare.com/weslandia.php

Fleischman has also published a wonderful book called *The Matchbox Diary*. Illustrated beautifully by Bagram Ibatoulline, this book would provide a rich stepping stone to beginning to understand what history is really about. It could provide a springboard to discussion on immigration and provide a way to develop empathy and tolerance of immigrants. Shaun Tan's *The Arrival* would make a good partner for this book as would Amy Hest and P.J. Lynch's *When Jessie Came Across the Sea*. Marcia Williams' *Archie's War* uses the hand-drawn pictures of a fictionalised 10-year-old Archie Albright to tell the story of living in England during the period of the First World War 1914–1918. From a literacy point of view this book is excellent for addressing the issue of 'point-of-view' as we see all the events through Archie's eyes mostly. In my classroom this was the book that encouraged a non-reading boy to become animated about a book.

History is often about how one small event triggers a tsunami of other events. James Flora's (1957/2010) *The Day the Cow Sneezed* is a great way to introduce this idea. Verna Aardema and Leo and Diane Dillon's *Why Mosquitoes Buzz in People's Ears*, and Susan Stevens Crummel and Dorothy Donohoe's *All in One Hour* also deal with this idea of cumulative events. One of my favourite picturebooks is Trinka Hawkes Noble and Tony Ross' *Meanwhile Back at the Ranch*, which tells the story of bored Rancher Hicks who heads off to Sleepy Gulch looking for excitement. Meanwhile, back at the ranch his wife Elna deals with all kinds of amazing happenings. Children love this story. It isn't quite the same cause-and-effect story as the others in this section but it does depict how two closely related people, describing the same day, can tell very different stories.

Elsie Piddock Skips in her Sleep by Eleanor Farjeon and Charlotte Voake is a recent addition to my picturebooks collection. The story was first published in 1937 and provides us with a wonderful vignette of village life in Sussex at the turn of the twentieth century.

Carol Hurst, on her Children's Literature website (www.carolhurst.com) recommends several books for getting children to realise the importance of perspective (Istvan Banyai's *Zoom*); of how history is contextualised (Eve Bunting's *Fly Away Home*); and of how events do not happen in a vacuum (David Macaulay's *Black and White*; Bob Graham's *Silver Buttons*, for example).

There are myriads of books dealing with the topic of colonisation, and I would begin with *The Conquerors* by David McKee which is perfect for beginning to understand the complexity of issues such as cultural influence, coercion, and the colonisation of minds. Jane Yolen and David Shannon's *Encounter* is an excellent resource for beginning to understand how cultures collide when Christopher Columbus arrives in the New World. Another book with this theme and told in a partly allegorical way from the perspective of the colonised is *The Rabbits* by John Marsden and Shaun Tan. Books that deal with the causes of conflict are also plentiful: think of McKee's *Tusk Tusk* and *Six Men*, and Nikolai Popov's *Why?*

Older children can examine books such as *Sadako and the Thousand Paper Cranes* by Eleanor Coerr and Ronald Himler; *My Hiroshima* by Junko Morimoto; and *Faithful Elephants: A True Story of People, Animals and War* by Yukio Tsuchiya and Ted Lewin. Each of these books examines true stories that can allow children an insight into how dreadful events like war impact on helpless individuals and helpless creatures alike. Another 'Holocaust' book, but one with a more joyful message, is Margaret Wild and Julie Vivas' *Let the Celebrations Begin*. Josephine Poole and Angela Barrett's *Anne Frank* provides an excellent introduction to discussions about intolerance and racial hatred as does *The Harmonica* by Tony Johnston and Ron Mazellan. Vladimir Radunsky's *What Does Peace Feel Like* could help children examine and explore all the different possibilities of meaning of the word 'peace', by inviting them to imagine what experiencing peace through the five senses would be like. The book begins and ends with translations of 'peace' into nearly 200 different languages. The central message is that all people have the creative power to imagine and create a more peaceful world by working together. Mary Cowhey's (2006) book: *Black Ants and Buddhists: thinking critically and teaching differently in the primary grades* is a good teacher resource for encouraging thinking about peace.

Citizenship

Citizenship and communal responsibility can be discussed through reading several Dr Seuss' books such as *Yertle the Turtle*, *The Sneetches*, *The Lorax*, *The Butter Battle Book* and *Horton Hears a Who*. These books can lead to discussions arising from questions such as: What is a citizen? What is a community? What is a citizen's responsibility to their community? (See also Libresco *et al.* 2011.)

The creative arts: visual art

Picturebooks that deal with the subject of art include: Martha Althés' *I am an Artist*; Louise Yates' *Dog Loves Drawing*; *Ish* and *The Dot* by Peter Reynolds. I particularly like

A is for Art: an abstract alphabet by Stephen T. Johnson; *The First Drawing* by Mordeci Gerstein; *Henri's Scissors* by Jeanette Winter, and *The Day the Crayons Quit* by Oliver Jeffers. *Little Blue and Little Yellow* by Leo Leoni and James Mayhew's *Katie* series are very useful for discussing colour as is *My Many Coloured Days* by Dr Seuss. *Art and Max* by David Wiesner presents a quirky and philosophical look at art that could lead to some illuminating insights. *The Ink Garden of Brother Theophane* could provide children with a link between RE, Art and History.

Picturebooks are also a rich and valuable resources for looking and responding to art. As I have shown earlier I often spread a variety of books out on tables and asked children to choose books with their favourite kinds of illustrations. They discuss *why* they liked a particular kind of illustration. I invite them to put books with the same kinds of illustrations together. Children quickly recognise the style of artists such as Anthony Browne, Mo Willems, Eric Carle, David McKee, Satoshi Kitamura or P.J. Lynch. They could discuss how they think the artist created the pictures and what medium/colours were used. As well as that, children could research their favourites because many picturebook artists have their own websites. The artists' discussions about art styles can lead to very interesting insights. Jane Doonan's book *Looking at Pictures in Picture Books* is an excellent resource for carrying out a detailed study of the artwork in picturebooks. Olshansky (2008) offers another approach, and, for those who like to read the theory of 'reading' visuals, Gunther Kress and Theo van Leeuwen's (1996) *Reading Images: the grammar of visual design* is a seminal text.

Music

I would begin by reading Kathy Stinson and Dusan Petricic's *The Man with the Violin.* Based on a true incident in Joshua Bell's life it has the added advantage of having lots of internet links both to the incident itself and to Bell's playing. This book allows us to engage in very philosophical thinking and discussion about the transformative power of music and the perception we have of what counts as 'good' music and 'good' musicians.

For young children picturebooks that link with the music curriculum could include: Lloyd Moss and Marjorie Priceman's *Zin, Zin Zin a Violin*; William Lach's *Can You Hear it?* (which links art and music); Raschka's *Charlie Parker Played Be Bop;* Quentin Blake's classic *Mister Magnolia;* and, of course, various versions of the traditional *Pied Piper* story. Other books deal with music more covertly: Posy Simmonds' *Fred* is a story about a lazy cat now deceased who, it turns out, had been leading a double life as Famous Fred – the Elvis of the Cat-World.

As well as reading books about music you can try turning books into musical performances. My pupils and I turned several of Julia Donaldson's books into 'songs' particularly the chorus parts of stories like *The Smartest Giant in Town* and *The Gruffalo*. Michael Rosen and Helen Oxenbury's *We're all Going on a Bear Hunt* just begs for an accompanying 'soundtrack' as does Michael Rosen and Adrian Reynold's *The Bear in the Cave*. Books such as Steve Smallman and Caroline Pedlar's *Don't Wake the Bear, Hare!* and Mo Willems' *That is Not a Good Idea,* and *Don't Let the Pigeon Drive the Bus* lend themselves to choral work. Margaret Read McDonald and Sophie Fatus' *The Farmyard Jamboree* provides endless opportunities for music making and an accompanying readymade soundtrack. We might encourage discussion on why some books lend themselves to a musical interpretation more than others. This might highlight the idea of rhythm, rhyme, repetitive choruses, the onomatopoeic elements, etc.

Drama

With very little expertise a teacher could use virtually all picturebooks as opportunities for drama. The elements of drama such as hot-seating, conscience alley, freeze-framing and thought-tracking, narration, etc. can all be employed to enhance comprehension but again, just as in music above, a caveat prevails: I would encourage teachers to discuss *why* certain books or scenes or characters or events are suited to dramatic interpretation.

Intertextuality and cross-curricular work

When I discussed Kathryn Cave and Chris Riddell's *Something Else* with a group of 9 year olds they made amazing connections to their history syllabus, linking the story with their lesson on Gandhi and also with Anne Frank. I videotaped the discussion and often showed it at workshops and in-service sessions.

In Roche 2007 (p 266) I wrote about how this particular video was received. Colleagues who watched it provided positive (and sometimes poignant) feedback, for example:

- *I have been teaching all my life: I am ready to retire. Why am I only learning this now? This way of encouraging children − people!!! − to think would have made such a difference to my teaching … it's so simple and so powerful. (RD extract from conversation with MR following workshop Aug 2004)*

I also provided a workshop for colleagues from my PhD study group and members of the University of Limerick Department of Education and Professional Studies. During the workshop I asked everybody present (about 15 people) to sit in a circle. I had prepared copies of the Cave and Riddell story and I asked people to read a page or so each and then discuss the story. I was unprepared for the depth of the emotional response. Everyone agreed that the experience provided powerful learning:

- *I was amazed at how powerful an activity the [CT&BT] circle is at promoting a depth of engagement … I can only imagine the huge potential within philosophising with children for children's personal and social development … I believe that the environment you create is critical to the richness of thinking and engagement … I believe also that you are, through your [CT&BT] thinking time, a mediator and gateway to children's innate knowledge and understanding. (PhD colleague)*
- *I would have loved CT&BT time when I was a child: I was a non-sporty child, always thinking and pondering. This would have been so liberating and so wonderful for the 'me' I was back then: to have the space to explore feelings, thoughts, ideas − but that need was not appreciated at that time. (University staff member)*

All agreed that such picturebooks can provide pathways to empathy building, and can encourage dialogue about inclusion, marginalisation and social awareness. Libresco *et al.*'s (2011) *Every Book is a Social Studies Book* provides a solid framework for using picturebooks to build a social studies curriculum that encompasses critical thinking, discussion and opportunities for extension.

Caveats about cross-curricular work and picturebooks

The primary purpose of this book is to encourage *classroom talk and critical thinking*. There are limitless possibilities for cross-curricular work. The most important resource of all is the enthusiasm and passion of the teacher. If you are open-minded and focused on developing a dialogic and a holistic practice you will see opportunities every time you research a picturebook in advance of discussing it with your class. I would caution, however, about finishing a classroom discussion and immediately asking the class to do a task based on the book. This turns the dialogic experience into what children perceive as teacher-focused 'work' and they may eventually stop engaging wholeheartedly in the discussion if they know that, following it, there will be some kind of 'regular school task'.

Dissemination – children, parents, colleagues

I recorded many of the discussions in a fast, personal version of shorthand and later transcribed them. After we had completed four or five discussions I would assemble the transcripts into booklets and give them to children to read. We would then have a chat about what they had said. It was interesting to note that children loved doing this activity, and also, for the most part, held fast to their original points of view. This provided them with a form of self-evaluation as well as an exercise in metacognition. For very young children I read out excerpts of transcripts, ensuring that, over time, each child heard their own statements read aloud. I believe that the children saw this as a form of valuing their thoughts and lifted their efforts accordingly. The recording all began because I was observing what I had promised in the ethical statement of my research. Copies of transcripts were also shared with parents and colleagues, as were videos of discussions.

Researching CT&BT

My research approach was self-study action research, which is a collaborative form of educational enquiry. I had promised my research collaborators – children, parents and colleagues – that I would make my data available to them at all times. My research focused on establishing whether I was improving my practice, in terms of developing my own capacity for critical thinking, for the purposes of enabling my children to develop their capacity for critical thinking. I emphasised that the focus was on *me*, and involved the children as reflectors or mirrors in which I could see my practice reflected. The children's actions could reflect how my practice may have been improving, in relation to the improvement in their own critical capacities. Consequently, I monitored both myself and the children, and traced the concurrent development of critical thinking in myself and in them.

The first group of children who became research participants was a Junior Infant class. I explained to them what I was studying and enlisted their help. I asked them to help me to study how I could make myself a better teacher and, especially, how together we could investigate how to make our discussions better. I also wrote to each child's parents explaining what I was doing and asked for their permission to allow their children to be co-participants in the study. Subsequently with older children I negotiated parental permission in writing and requested my students to be active participants by inviting them to critique my practice as I tried to improve classroom dialogue. I invited them to evaluate transcripts, the methodology of CT&BT, and video recordings of discussions (the last both as a class group and in conjunction with their parents; (see Roche 2007, Appendix B.7.).

I also felt that it was critical to my study that my students did not feel coerced either by me or by their parents into participating in the research so I went to some pains to explain my processes of enquiry to each group of children and to negotiate their consent also. I also negotiated with my school colleagues that they would act as critical friends, observers and evaluators. (Appendix A.6.)

Recording – ethical considerations

If you intend to record children electronically it is necessary to ensure that you make it very clear to all concerned as to how you intend to store, share and use these recordings in the future. I negotiated with the school authorities, the children and their parents that I would from time to time invite observers into my classroom. These observers would at times be asked to evaluate my practice (Roche 2007, Appendices B and H), but they could also be colleagues who wanted to learn about doing classroom discussion. This latter is because I had a special post of responsibility in relation to developing a culture of critical thinking in the school and therefore I had to provide professional development for colleagues. Because I wanted to have the opportunity to video tape our classroom discussions from time to time, I negotiated permission from the school authorities, the children and their parents to record the discussions and also subsequently to show the videos in teaching situations. I promised that I would not let the videos out of my possession. This presented problems for me subsequently at a conference when a colleague requested to video my presentation. I had to refuse on the grounds that I had not negotiated permission for such a scenario from the parents of my students. I subsequently negotiated new permissions which allowed for the judicious dissemination of recordings and for CD-ROMs of classroom discussions to be included with my thesis (Appendices A.4., A.11).

With this in mind I also invited parents to read transcripts and to comment, as well as having video evenings where I showed videos of classroom discussions. The feedback was really valuable to me as there were times when I began to doubt myself and wonder if I were giving too much time to, and placing too much emphasis on, these classroom discussions.

Comments like those below really bolstered my confidence and kept me going when times were hard:

- *We have seen a huge improvement in [P]'s self-confidence, in particular, and his Maths (and attitude to same) has come on in leaps and bounds. You also opened his eyes to new areas of interest – history, science and even politics spring to mind!*
- *This is the first time in five years that E. has actually been happy going to school each day.... You brought out the best in him and saw him as a person in his own right* (Appendix B.8.c.).

In Roche (2007 p 93) I wrote:

When I showed some Thinking Time videos to parents of my students, K's father was reminded of his own schooldays:

- *I am so heartened to see my daughter thinking her way through literature, albeit a children's story. I wish we had been allowed to do that in school: we were told the way we should think about stuff. We had those stripy Shakespeare notes and we had to learn the stuff off by heart. What a waste!*

(Appendix B.7.b.)

I contrasted the freedom to think for themselves that I felt that I was now giving my pupils with the lack of freedom of thought during my own schooldays. I wrote:

> By exercising my positive freedom and critical faculties in providing dialogical peda-gogies that support my educational values, I understand that my students will benefit from their negative freedom – freedom from prescriptive pedagogies that may close down opportunities to critique. Because I believe that both freedom of thought and freedom of speech are among the basic goods of humanity, then the denial of such freedom is, to me, a denial of justice and a negation of care.

(Roche 2007 p 93)

Discussion and high-interest picturebooks for reluctant readers

Many teachers will attest to the power of using good picturebooks to ignite or rekindle a love of reading in children who have experienced a sense of failure to progress at the same rate as their peers.

One such example was Jane, an 11-year-old pupil of my colleague Elaine. Elaine writes:

- *Jane had lost interest in reading. Her teachers had noticed that she was experiencing difficulty when she was around 6 or 7 years of age and she had been screened for dyslexia in first class (age 7). The test showed that there were signs that Jane may have some slight reading problems: she was deemed 'borderline', and, despite not being diagnosed as fully dyslexic, the school decided to intervene and give her the benefit of resource hours in literacy (one-to-one tuition). She availed of these from first to fourth class but, in fifth class, Jane refused to continue with resource hours, stating that there was no point; she knew she was a failure, and she began to completely disengage with involvement in reading'. By sixth class (Elaine's class), she refused to read or to engage in discussions about books.*

(Extract from written correspondence by EM Nov 2013)

Elaine recalls that Jane's motivation and self-esteem had taken a dive and she was miser-able. Knowing that I had a big collection of picturebooks, Elaine asked me to choose some that would have high-interest content suitable for an 11–12 year old. I gave her a wide selection that included some Eve Bunting books like *The Wednesday Surprise* and *Train to Somewhere*, and books such as Jacqueline Woodson and E.B. Lewis' *The Other Side* and *Each Kindness*. I also gave her six of Dosh Archer's *Urgency! Emergency!* series. These are funny and easy to read without being patronising. Elaine is an experienced and wise teacher: she began to create a whole class interest in the books so that several chil-dren were vying for being allowed to read them. Before long Jane was taking them home and was eagerly looking for more. Elaine enlisted the support of Jane's mother who began buying similar books for Jane. Jane was particularly engaged with Eve Bunting's

Train to Somewhere and with Jacqueline Woodson's *The Other Side* and Elaine noticed that she would often discuss them with her friends and recommend them to other children. When these books were then read aloud and discussed in class, she participated publicly for the first time. She realised that her contributions were as valid and as perceptive as other children's and quickly began to regain some of her confidence.

• Elaine felt that the pictures proved to be a huge crutch or scaffold to Jane's comprehension ability. By the end of the year Jane was willing to read the class chapter books. Jane suggested to Elaine that font type and size also had an influence on her ability to read as they researched suitable books together. Elaine concludes that the combination of reading and discussing picturebooks unlocked barriers in Jane's self-belief and put her on the road to developing a love of reading.

(Notes from conversation with Elaine Nov 2013)

Summary

In this chapter we have examined some of the practicalities surrounding doing CT&BT discussions in an early years' or primary classroom. Remember, each parent and each teacher and each set of children vary. There are no templates. It will be necessary for you to create your own 'template' to suit your particular context and you may have to tweak it with each class group you teach. Remember too that children's tastes in books are as varied as they are, and a book that will stimulate creative and critical dialogue with one group may well be dismissed as 'boring' by another.

Recommended reading

Haynes, J. (2002) *Children as Philosophers: learning through enquiry and dialogue in the primary classroom*. London and New York: Routledge Falmer.

Haynes, J. and Murris, K. (2012) *Picturebooks, Pedagogy and Philosophy*. Routledge: London and New York.

Jones, D. and Hodson, P. (eds) (2006) *Unlocking Speaking and Listening*. Abingdon, Oxon: Routledge.

Lewison, M., Leland, C. and Harste, J.C. (2011) *Creating Critical Classrooms: K-8 reading and writing with an edge*. New York and Abingdon, Oxon: Routledge.

Littleton, K. and Mercer, N. (2013) *Interthinking: putting talk to work*. Abingdon, Oxon: Routledge.

McCall, C. (2009) *Transforming Thinking: philosophical inquiry in the primary and secondary classroom*. Abingdon, Oxon: Routledge.

Quinn, V. (1997) *Critical Thinking in Young Minds*. London: David Fulton.

Sipe, L. (2008) *Storytime: young children's literary understanding in the classroom*. New York and London: Teacher's College, Columbia University.

Chapter 8

Conclusion

There are all sorts of picture books. There is a place for them all. There are those with plots and those without plots, stories that are funny and stories that are sad and stories that can be both at once. There are books comprised entirely of a mood that the words, like a piece of poetry, evoke. But in the great variety of books that are picture books, each so different from the others, there is one common gift. Ursula Nordstrom, one of the great children's book editors of our time, called it 'retaining a direct line to one's childhood.' Picture books are written from a child's point of view... the off-center way the world looks to children, to whom the world is new and who are trying to make sense out of everything adults take for granted.

(Zolotow, in Sutton and Parvano, 2011 p 43)

The importance of reading and discussing books with children has been emphasised throughout this book. The centrality of good quality picturebooks to the process has been outlined. The CT&BT approach has been proposed as a way of combining both. But we must return now to the rationale for doing this work. Why discuss picturebooks? Why bother doing this kind of critical literacy work? The answer lies in the values we hold about life, society and our place in it. I believe that, unless we are deeply misanthropic and dystopian, we all want to do what we can to create a better, a more just, a more equitable and a fairer world and an approach like CT&BT may provide us with a framework for beginning to set about trying to make a difference for good.

CT&BT is grounded in narrative. There are the narratives, both visual and textual, that we find in the picturebooks we read; the narratives we construct to make sense of the books for ourselves; and the narratives we construct to explain our understanding to others. Stories matter. Sipe (2008) reminds us that thinkers from many academic disciplines have 'pondered the meaning that stories can have for our lives' and he argues that story may be one of the most powerful ways we have of 'imposing order and meaning on our world'. He states that 'we know that experience shapes language (and literature) but language (and literature) can also shape experience' and suggests that narrative is a crucial factor in the formation of identity 'to the extent that the human mind may be understood as a mechanism for turning the raw data of day-to-day experience into narratives' (p 247).

Narrative and metacognition

Bruner (1986) recognised the relevance of narrative for metacognition (thinking about thinking) and in (1996 p 149) suggested that 'we live most of our lives in a world constructed according to the rules and devices of narrative'. Bruner (1996 p 147) says that 'We live in a sea of stories and, like the fish who (according to the proverb) will be the last to discover water we have our own difficulties grasping what it is like to swim in stories'. Bruner argues that we have three main strategies for solving this problem: contrast, confrontation and metacognition (ibid.).

Contrast means that we listen to different or contrasting versions of the same event or sequence of events and we compare them with the intention of understanding how the different or contrasting versions can be equally coherent, and how the one can inform the other, so that a more richly textured understanding is possible. Think of children comparing different versions of the *Three Little Pigs* story, for example. They are able to make sense of Wiesner's version because they have heard several other versions and, during our discussions, they listen to each other's interpretations and add them to their own growing understanding. Similarly, the different accounts of *The Little Red Hen* story allow children who discuss them to expand and extend their knowledge and understanding. Small children can make sense of Mo Willems' *Goldilocks and the Three Dinosaurs* if they already know the Three Bears version. They would also need to understand irony as they negotiate the double meanings in most of the dinosaurs' utterances.

Bruner's second device, *confrontation*, is where the knower must examine their own version of reality in the light of superior claims made by other people defending a different version of reality or in the light of new evidence that they acquire for themselves or new ways they develop to make sense of reality. This happens all the time in discussions: we have seen several examples scattered throughout this book, where, after listening to what others have said, they change their minds. We have heard children claim, 'I actually disagree with myself now because…'

Finally, there is *metacognition*, which Bruner considers an essential pedagogic strategy. This is where learners reflect, not only on their view of reality, with the intention of changing or deepening it, but also how they came to know it in the first place. Again, throughout this book we have seen a variety of examples of children thinking about their thinking and 'putting two and two together'.

Examples

Look at the transcript following a reading of both Anthony Browne's *Zoo* and John Burningham's *Oi! Get Off Our Train*. It gives us a good example of 'contrast'.

- **L:** *I think that actually the two books are related because they're both about cruelty to animals in a way except that in the Zoo book the Zoo is trying to protect the animals and zoos are not really bad. They don't try to do actually harm to the animals … I mean, they try to keep them from getting extinct.*
- **P:** *I think they're related, both stories. They both try to explain to some people that animals are not actually safe at all. They're not safe in zoos. They're protected but that's not the same as saying they're safe. People don't treat them well. In the wild, animals have everything they need to live. But when they're in captivity, they can't get what they need because they can't make themselves understood to humans. Humans can't understand what animals really need. Even parrots that are trained to talk can't tell people what they need. The only way that animals would be really safe and protected is if humans became extinct.*

- ***K:*** *I didn't find them related at first. I found that they both are trying to mention how mean and cruel people are being. Maybe the authors are trying to get us to think so that when we grow up we can stop what greedy people do to animals and we might try to make people find other ways to get keys for their pianos and fur for their fur coats.*

In another discussion, following a reading of *Something Else* (Cave and Riddell 1995) 9-year-old Conor said that the story reminded him of Gandhi in our History syllabus. When I asked him to explain how he arrived at this conclusion he said:

- *Well first I thought that it was a story about animals but then I heard what Cian said and I thought 'Hang on there's more to that story' and then I was thinking it reminded me of another story – well it's not really a story it's something true – it reminded me of Gandhi and the part when he was not allowed to sit in the first class carriage even though he had a ticket… well I suddenly thought that in a way Gandhi was like Something Else…*

Similarly throughout all our discussions, we can see evidence of 'confrontation'. I have had experiences where children would frequently say 'First I was thinking X and now I have kind of changed my mind and I think Y'; sometimes children expressed surprise like Conor did above and they would say 'Whoo! I never knew I knew that until I sort of thought it and said it at the same time'. One or two children have said 'I'll pass because I don't really have any thought yet' or 'I don't know enough yet. I need to think some more'. Sometimes as I later transcribed my scribbled notes from discussions I found myself intrigued by something a child said and I would type it and discuss it with the child next day. They nearly always had an explanation. As I said in Chapter 7, one of the practices I used in order to encourage reflection and metacognition was to type several transcripts and present them to the children in booklet form for their perusal. This was often very enlightening – some would hold fast to their views, and others would say 'Oh, I've been thinking about that since and I kind of disagree with myself now because now I know that…'

In Chapter 6 we saw several examples of children examining transcripts, evaluating their contributions and deciding if they still agreed or disagreed with them.

Metacognition, according to Bruner (op. cit. p 148) converts ontological arguments about the nature of reality into epistemological ones about how we can know and provides us with another strategy for personal and interpersonal negotiation of meaning. Metacognitive activities that ask students to reflect on what they know, what they care about, and what they are able to do, help learners develop an awareness of themselves as learners. We saw an example in Conor's deliberations about *Something Else*, above. CT&BT helps to develop a culture of metacognition in a classroom. The very fact of having to justify their stances and explain their view points, means that children are automatically being given opportunities to become metacognitive learners.

Our lives are lived in and explained by narrative

In her essay in Meek's (1974) *The Cool Web*, Barbara Hardy says:

> …the qualities which fictional narrative shares with that inner and outer storytelling that plays a major role in our sleeping and waking lives. For we dream in narrative,

daydream in narrative, remember, anticipate, hope, despair, believe, doubt, plan, revise, criticize, construct, gossip, learn, hate and love in narrative. In order to live we make up stories about others, and ourselves about the personal as well as the social past and future.

(p 13)

Reading aloud and discussing stories with children affords them greater opportunities to build their own narratives and explanations for the ways things are and how they might imagine things differently. Sipe (2008) agrees and suggests that reading stories (narratives) to children and discussing them encourage them to think for themselves when he says:

The ability to imagine a different society may be partly based on the ability to impose a new narrative construction on the social facts at our disposal: to tell *a different story*. If this is the case, then reading stories to children is a profoundly political, transformative action...realistic fiction, then, may provide young children with greater opportunities to discuss these issues than other genres.

(pp 246–7, emphasis in original)

Maxine Greene takes a similar view when she urges us to become more aware; she talks about living more consciously. In *Landscapes of Learning* (1978a) Greene urges us to think more deeply, to become more 'wide-awake' and, using a metaphor from Virginia Woolf, to 'break though the cotton-wool of daily existence'. She exhorts us not to accept things as they are but to imagine how they could be otherwise. Reading Greene (1988) led me to try to come to an understanding for myself of what an education for freedom entailed. Educating for freedom means, for me, that I must do what I can to encourage myself (alongside, and in relation with, my students) to come to an awareness of the many points of view there can be, and the multiple ways that exist for interpreting our worlds. To be free, I believe, is to be able to think and speak for oneself; to be able to engage the world in an ongoing conversation; and to value the power and meaning that new points of view bring to the collective search for fulfilment. I was enabled by Greene (1978, 1988) to understand that freedom requires a refusal to accede to the given, that it entails a reaching for new possibilities and potentials and a resistance to the objectification of people.

The activities that compose learning not only engage us in our own quests for answers and for meanings; they also serve to initiate us into the communities of scholarship and (if our perspectives widen sufficiently) into the human community, in its largest and richest sense ... Teachers who are alienated, passive, and unquestioning cannot make such initiations possible for those around. Nor can teachers who take the social reality surrounding them for granted and simply accede to them.

(Greene 1978 p 3)

I believe that we owe it to our children to help them become critical and caring citizens. We want to heighten their awareness of social issues and deepen their understanding of themselves as active agents in the world. We want to engage their moral imagination and encourage them to be social beings who think independently and who maintain their philosophical and intellectual curiosity throughout their lives. We want them to be competent, confident readers and writers who see literacy as empowering and liberating.

We want them to have a lifelong love of reading and gain endless hours of pleasure from it. Through reading and discussing picturebooks with them from their earliest days, we hope to provide them with what Luke (1991) calls 'equality of educational possibility'.

> …as teachers of literacy we need to look beyond a continual and exclusive concern with 'new' and better methods in order to rethink from a social and cultural perspective the consequences of our instruction, whether with elementary school children, secondary students, or adults and immigrant second language learners. Who gets what kind of competence from our teaching? To what ends? What kinds of literate subjects does our pedagogy produce? Fitted to what kind of society?
>
> (Ibid.)

These are the kinds of questions that keep me going in my work to promote CT&BT as a form of dialogic teaching for improving critical literacy. Dialogic teaching has been defined by Mercer and Littleton (2007) as the kind of classroom teaching where teachers and children alike make substantial and significant contributions through which children's thinking on particular ideas and or themes is moved forward. Based on my own experience, I would add that this kind of teaching moves the teacher's ideas forward also.

On the dialogic teaching website: http://www.robinalexander.org.uk/index.php/dialogic-teaching/ dialogic teaching is described as that which 'harnesses the power of talk to stimulate and extend students' thinking and advance their learning and understanding' (np). Dialogic teaching, says Alexander (op. cit.):

> …empowers the student for lifelong learning and active citizenship. Dialogic teaching is not just any old talk. It is as distinct from the question-answer and listen-tell routines of traditional teaching as it is from the casual conversation of informal discussion.
>
> (Alexander np)

I would argue, however, that informal chat and conversation may be required to oil the wheels of dialogue by building relationships. When my pupils and I (or my own children and I, or my nephew George and I, or the nursery school children and I, or fellow teachers and I) are engaged in lively verbal interaction I cannot say: 'This is dialogue, and this is discussion, and this is only conversation'. I do value informal or 'ordinary conversation' (Noddings 2002 p 126) for its role in developing relational knowledge and interpersonal relationships, but I suggest that when my students and I talk together, all these elements are often present, interweaving through each other. However, as I said in earlier chapters, an overall 'spirit of dialogue' remains throughout. In our CT&BT circles we are not about trying to 'get points' or make 'any particular view prevail' (Bohm 1998 p 2), but are rather, intent on sharing thoughts and making meaning with each other.

Alexander (ibid.) lists several required conditions for dialogic teaching to thrive:

* *interactions* which encourage students to think, and to think in different ways
* *questions* which invite much more than simple recall
* *answers* which are justified, followed up and built upon rather than merely received
* *feedback* which informs and leads thinking forward as well as encourages
* *contributions* which are extended rather than fragmented

- *exchanges* which chain together into coherent and deepening lines of enquiry
- *discussion and argumentation* which probe and challenge rather than unquestioningly accept
- *professional engagement with subject matter* which liberates classroom discourse from the safe and conventional
- *classroom organisation, climate and relationships* which make all this possible. (op. cit.)

I think I would put Alexander's last point first. CT&BT depends for its success on a classroom or nursery or home environment that is grounded in good relationships of the kind that Noddings (1992) called caring – where respect and care are reciprocal. As we have said already, the whole concept of dialogic teaching is based on ontological and epistemological values where children are seen as real people with the capacity to think critically and where knowledge is seen as a dynamic and evolutionary process. Teachers who live such values in their practice have an educative influence in the learning of others: they create the kind of classroom environment where children feel safe and free to offer opinions, agree and disagree respectfully with each other and with their teacher.

Alexander's conditions as criteria for determining if CT&BT can be viewed as dialogic teaching

1.   **Interactions** which encourage students to think, and to think in different ways

Over the years children have demonstrated their willingness to participate in discussions and to demonstrate their ability to think 'outside the box'. For example, look at what 3–4 year olds had to say about 'things that have no feelings' following a reading of Molly Bang's *When Sophie Gets Angry – Really Really Angry*:

- *Me: I wonder if there is anything that doesn't have any feelings at all?*
- *Cian: Scarecrows don't have feelings but they can make crows feel scared.*
- *Michael: I don't think a leaf has any feelings – it's empty and it has nothing in it.*
- *Cathal: I disagree: it has leaf stuff in it! And on telly it said plants can feel afraid if you're cutting them.*
- *Emma: My Nana talks to her plants and she said they like it and they have …em…leaves and things …so the ones she has might have feelings!*

When asked to list things that made them wonder following a reading of Anita Ganeri's *I Wonder Why The Wind Blows and Other Questions About Our Planet* some 5–6 year olds said:

- *Amy: I have a million thousand 'I wonder whys' after reading that!*
- *Cam: I wonder how the clouds stay up in the sky. Cos they're full of rain and if you had even this size (sandwich bag) full of rain that would be heavy!*
- *H: I often wonder why God put hundreds of people into the world.*
- *Ke: I have another wonder then. I wonder when people talk all different languages to God – does he understand them? What language does he speak? (Laughs) Heavenish!*

Transcript based on a reading of *Oi! Get Off Our Train* by John Burmingham with 5–6 year olds:

- **Me:** *Tell me what you think of this story. Who'd like to start?*
- **M:** *The saddest was the sea-lion.*
- **KO'M:** *I think it's saddest about the bird with the long legs because they were going to take out all the water from his… wet place for farms and then he won't have enough to drink and he'll die!*
- **Me:** *The wet place is called a marsh.*
- **Ka:** *The saddest of all, I think, is the polar bear, because men will cut off all his fur and then he'll get very frozen and cold and then turn to ice!*
- **A:** *I thought it was a bit sad, the bit about the seal … he might die if he doesn't have fish to eat and his water is one of the things to keep him alive. He really needs clean water full with lots of yummy fish. That's what I think!*
- **Cam:** *I agree with A – and if somebody cutted down all the trees then the animals might get pumped into the ground.*
- **Me:** *What do you mean by pumped into the ground, Cam?*
- **Cam:** *Do you know what size those …things for …those …trees cutting down tractors are? They're huge and huge and really big with fat wheels and they have very, very sharp …dangerous… tools. They would roll on top of animals and that's how …they'd be flat …maybe - or dead anyway!*

Older children (7–8) discussing animals rights and our responsibilities to them, following reading Anthony Browne's *Zoo* and John Burningham's *Oi! Get Off Our Train* made some very insightful comments:

- **P:** *… In the wild, animals have everything they need to live. But when they're in captivity, they can't get what they need because they can't make themselves understood to humans. Humans can't understand what animals really need. Even parrots that are trained to talk can't tell people what they need. The only way that animals would be really safe and protected is if humans became extinct.*
- **Kn:** *I seriously agree with P. He is right. If we were extinct they'd be able to live. The zoo is not really for looking after animals. If they were free to do whatever they wanted that would be different but they're not. We're just using them….like objects.*
- **T:** *I agree with L a little bit and I disagree with him a little bit and I agree and disagree with P too. Sometimes maybe zoos could be good. They can help some animals to be safe. …But I also think that it's good to be out running free. I agree with P too, that people are the worst enemies of some animals but I disagree with him because they're also the best friends of other animals.*
- **Ce:** *I actually changed my mind about what I said before. Now I think that animals should be free …well not the dangerous ones, only the nice ones.* (For full transcript see Roche 2007 Appendix C1)

Following a reading of Josephine Poole and Angela Barrett's *Anne Frank*, some 8–9 year olds said:

- **Ey:** *Say if a child grew up in a country like that, it would be awful; no one could have an opinion or anything.*
- **A:** *I agree with Ey. It is very important for people to have their opinions. That's the only way to get rid of guys like Hitler, all the other countries should have joined up and helped….who was he fighting? Anne and her family were German….so, was he fighting his own country, I don't get it…*

- *Se: I was thinking as well that it takes very little to start a war. Remember a while back we were talking about stereotyping? Well I'd say wars can start from stereotyping people, because that can lead to hatred and hatred can lead to war. It's like judging a book by its cover and not looking inside....some people think all Irish people are lazy and drunk and always fighting, and we know they're not...people get a bad name...like if our Junior Infants were out somewhere and they were messing and they had their uniform on and then people might say...'oh, ..that's a very bad school'...well they shouldn't: They should check it out for themselves. Hitler persuaded all the people to go against the Jews. The people should have asked, 'where's the proof that the Jews are all bad'?*
- *V: I was wondering, right? Say now she was one year old and people were going against the Jews...would they have hurt her even though she was only one? Would no one have said 'Stop'?* (For full transcript see Roche 2007 Appendix C3)

Some 9 year olds decided that 'freedom' was the theme of Dosh and Mike Archer's *Yellow Bird, Black Spider:*

- *Jk: Teacher, I need to go next cos I'm bursting to speak! I think freedom isn't something you can give to someone...you might be only giving them ...emmm ...sort of ...like... permission or something. Permission doesn't really mean the same thing as freedom. Like, say, if you gave us all the permission to jump up on the tables and shout, we would still sort of have to decide what to do, cos like, you might be after going nuts. (Laughter)*
- *Hi: Yeah, I agree: freedom can be inside you. Freedom means you have to make your own choices of doing stuff....not all the time: sometimes you have to do other stuff that you mightn't want like work or school. And I agree with Jk, you would have to decide whether to do what the teacher said or not if it was something like jumping up on the tables, because that might not be very safe and the principal certainly wouldn't want it either.*
- *Jr: I agree with Ts and with A too. You can think what you like but you can't always say what you think....freedom would be thinking and saying what you like...You can be free and not free in lots of other ways too...like if you're a child you're free to play on the grass but not on the road. So the road stops your freedom if you're a child. But a road can be a freedom to someone else ...like if someone was driving going away on their holidays...*
- *Gn: I think freedom is to have our lives for ourselves, not to have anyone to own us... It's something inside us that tells us killing is bad and its called shame. If we killed someone we couldn't live with ourselves.*
- *Dd: Freedom means everyone has choices. They can choose what they want and what they don't want. Most people don't want to kill, it's very unlikely anyway. Something inside us stops us from killing others. We have that inside us all the time and it helps us to make choices.*
- *Ca: ...Another thing...you know how we're free, here, to speak? Well everyone should be free to speak.... but not to talk when other people are speaking. Say, em....if people here didn't listen, say they kept talking all the time....that wouldn't really be like ...freedom, it would just be plain rudeness and bad manners and then you'd have to give out to them. But that wouldn't be stopping their freedom, it would be stopping their rudeness and it would be helping other people's freedom...the ones what wanted to keep speaking and giving their opinion.* (For full transcript see Roche 2007 Appendix C6)

2. **Questions** which invite much more than simple recall

CT&BT discussions usually begin with open-ended questions that offer possibilities for pondering, hypothesising, speculating, evaluating and debating. These are considered higher-order questions. Lower-order or closed questions simply demand recalling or demonstrating basic comprehension. However, in order to differentiate for children who may have learning difficulties, sometimes it is necessary to ask the basic recall questions so as to provide them with feelings of success.

3. **Answers** which are justified, followed up and built upon rather than merely received

If we examine any of the transcripts referred to throughout this book, we can see examples of children providing explanations and justifications for their points of view.

4. **Feedback** which informs and leads thinking forward as well as encourages

In CT&BT discussions children are continuously being given feedback by peers as they agree and disagree with each other. Children frequently say I *agree with N because* ; or *I disagree with N because*; or *I kind of agree a little bit and disagree a little bit with N because...* They also received feedback when I would sometimes request further clarification or an extension of what they had said. Children participating in our discussions also received feedback when other children would build on their ideas and extend them even further. They can sometimes even receive very complimentary feedback at times from each other. In my own classes I have had many experiences of children turning to one another and saying 'That's a really good thought' or 'That's a brilliant idea!' Other teachers have had similar experiences (see evaluations in Roche 2000, 2007, Appendices). The fact that their discussions were transcribed or otherwise recorded, and that I engaged in discussion with the children about their discussions, also constituted positive feedback. The fact that time was given to the discussions, that books were chosen and bought with care, were, I believe, also a form of feedback and endorsement. The fact that parents spoke so often and so warmly of the discussions gave *me* very positive feedback also

5. **Contributions** which are extended rather than fragmented

This point relates somewhat to the feedback section above. When a child's ideas are extended by the teacher or by other children several things can happen: they receive feedback; they are afforded an opportunity for reflection and metacognition, and their intrinsic and extrinsic motivation are developed. This relates to Dweck's (1999) ideas about self-theories. The increased sense of confidence gained, can lead children to make further contributions to the discussion as they elaborate or develop their thinking. I have had frequent examples where children arrived back in class after lunchbreak, or next morning, or even after a weekend, and said 'I've been thinking about our discussion on x and what I said and now I think...' Car-pool parents have commented frequently on how discussions continued in the back seat of the car as they drove home. Contributions which are extended allow children to engage in further knowledge creation and could be seen as relating to Bruner's (1996) theories of narrative construction as outlined earlier in this chapter.

6. **Exchanges** which chain together into coherent and deepening lines of enquiry

Children who hold firm points of view and who have these points of view challenged by peers can often seek out extra knowledge in order to reinforce their stances – and sometimes reform their stances. I had an example of this when 8-year-old Jenny tried to prove in a discussion about fast food (that led, interestingly from a reading of Dr Seuss' *The Lorax*) that McDonald's food was nutritionally sound. A few days later she announced that she 'kind of still agreed with herself, but that we should only have fast-food as a treat because it had a lot of fat and salt'. It appeared that she had researched the topic and spoken to her mum and her Auntie who had helped her refine her ideas.

I described earlier how reading picturebooks illustrated by certain artists (e.g. Satoshi Kitamura) led to children becoming familiar with this artist's work and wanting to read more by him. This was true of several authors also. A love of the work of David Wiesner, Shaun Tan, Anthony Browne, Chris van Allsburg and others, became reasons for children to engage in further enquiry about these authors' work. Topics introduced by these authors and others also led to further enquiry. For example, reading and rereading Paul Fleischman's *Weslandia* led to a whole unit of cross-curricular work that began with exploring civilisations, but that led to artwork and music and creative writing also. And we saw in an earlier chapter how reading *Think of an Eel* led to a fascination with eels and their lifecycle.

The intertextual nature of picturebooks is another reason why children become deeply engaged with a topic. This can lead to new lines of enquiry as well as deepening existing ones. This is especially true for older children where historical topics such as the Holocaust or social topics such as immigration or racism can easily be cross-curricularly extended.

7. **Discussion and argumentation** which probe and challenge rather than unquestioningly accept

CT&BT discussions generally take 45–60 minutes and, now and again, have lasted for 80–90 minutes. In Roche (2007) I wrote:

> A significant example of my children thinking for themselves occurred in the discussion that followed reading aloud Simon James' *Dear Greenpeace* with a Senior Infant class of 5– 6 year olds (See Appendix C. 4.) I consider it to be one of the best discussions I have participated in, and one of the longest. Er (a child who rarely contributed) joined in to talk about his dog. Alberto came in for the Spanish lesson but when he saw the children so rapt and engaged he simply sat into the circle. Yvonne our classroom assistant observed and took notes. Yvonne and Alberto gave me written evaluations later: they were both hugely impressed (full transcript in Appendices H. 5. and H. 6.)

The children began by discussing pets and Eo suggested that his dog made plans to catch his cat.

•   ***Me:*** *I'd like to go back to something Eo said earlier about dogs making plans. I think that's very interesting. Can dogs make plans? Can dogs think?*

- **M:** *Well I think they think about loving their owners and stuff.*
- **Cl:** *I don't think they can think. You need language to think.*
- **Me:** *I wonder about that … about whether or not you need language to think? Can babies think?*
- **M:** *I don't think so, I think they do a lot of feeling and dreaming but as they grow they learn more stuff and then they can think.*
- **Er:** *Well my dog is always thinking about me!*
- **Sh:** *If we put Er's brain in Cl's head, who'd be doing the thinking – Er or Cl?*
- **K:** *We think with our brain so Cl would have Er's thoughts and memories and dreams.*
- **I:** *I don't think so. I think that for a little time it would be mostly Er's thoughts but then it would start to be Cl's thoughts.*
- **Er:** *I think every bit of us can think, even our skin, because our skin gets itchy even when we're asleep.*
- **Mr:** *Yeah cos if our skin didn't think, we wouldn't be able to turn in the bed at night.*

The discussion engaged all of the children for over an hour. Yvonne subsequently wrote:

- *[this] was the most amazing conversation I ever heard in a group of children in all my years caring for children … it was the most thought-provoking morning… they started talking about their pets and whether they could think … this led on to a conversation about human thoughts and brains … they discussed if their brain slept or not … Alberto … felt the same as I did … amazed that children of such a young age could have so much knowledge.*

Throughout this book there have been several examples of children exhibiting their capacity for critical, creative, original and abstract thinking.

8. **Professional engagement with subject matter** which liberates classroom discourse from the safe and the conventional

I have provided several examples of discussions where children have said that they disagree with me: I wrote in Roche (2007 p 76) that 'Questioning the answer has become a normal practice in my classrooms. I question answers and the children question answers. In the course of our discussions the children frequently disagree with me and explain why. My data excerpts (below) bear this out.

- **Paul:** *I think that willpower is just something that you need to do and you're trying to do it, so Teacher, you could be right or you could be wrong' (following a reading of Lobel's Frog and Toad story about 'Willpower').*
- **Chloe:** *I disagree with Teacher because the story said 'you look funny in the swimsuit', not 'the swimsuit looks funny on you'.*

Children often interrupted other lessons:

- *[Maths lesson] Teacher I can think of better ways of doing that problem.*
- *[RE lesson] I don't get it. How can Jesus be seated at the right hand of the Father if Jesus is the human form of God? Does the Father have hands?*
- *[RE lesson] Where was God when the big bang happened?*

- *[Maths lesson] I think I know two more different ways of doing that!*
- *[English* Charlotte's Web*] I can think of about twenty more things that Charlotte could have done to help Wilbur!* (see also Roche 2011 p 332)

Disequilibrium

If you introduce CT&BT into your teaching you must be prepared for some discomfort and disequilibrium when your taken-for-granted pedagogical assumptions might face serious scrutiny. The following account is an example of my own professional learning or as Alexander (op. cit.) puts it: my 'professional engagement with subject matter:

> RSE is one of the core resources for the Social and Personal Health Education curriculum. One of the lessons for third class – which, in our school, was called the 'sensitive content lesson' and which involved notifying parents in advance so that they could be prepared for further questions and exploration of the topic – contains information about the growth of the foetus in the uterus and how babies are born. It necessitates the use of the correct anatomical names for parts of the body and so, in an attempt to give the topic the gravitas it deserved, I decided to take my students into the spare room across the corridor where we usually had our weekly CT&BT discussions. The children automatically sat in a circle and I began by reading the preliminary part of the lesson, a poem about new life. I then tried to 'deliver' the rest of the lesson, but was confounded when the children constantly interrupted and discussed babies and pre-natal care and spontaneously shared their experiences of the births of new siblings or cousins.

> My research journal notes for the day show how I became flustered and asked the children to 'please stop interrupting so that I could talk': Suddenly C, looking perplexed, asked

- *But Teacher, I don't get it, like … why did you bring us in here if you don't want us to talk?*

> I answered that I had to teach the lesson and that I had to stick closely to the way it was presented in the teacher's book. C replied:

- *Yeah, but why are we in here so? Why didn't we stay in the class?*

> Heads nodded in assent and CF said:

- *Teacher, like, this is … like, our room for talking; and you're … you're always saying you're just one of us like, one of the listeners - in here.*

> I realised then that I had expected to be able to teach didactically without any challenges simply because 'I had decided'. Suddenly for the very first time I saw that years of experience of classroom dialogue in a circle format meant that the introduction of a didactic practice in that format now needed some preliminary explanation, if not an apology from me. Instead I had simply assumed an authoritarian role and excluded the children – treated them as excluded 'Others' who must listen to me and

absorb information without thinking for themselves. I clearly saw that thinking critically is a feature of a holistic education practice, not an add-on 'bonus' that I bestow at certain times. I saw that going into a different room 'for thinking' reinforced the reification of critical thinking as a 'thing' we do in Room 15, but not in our classroom, unless I 'allowed' 'it'.

(Roche 2007 p 243)

From an initial feeling of confusion and annoyance at the children's interruptions and their attempts to turn the session into a discussion, I now felt a huge sense of achievement that I had brought these children to a place where hitherto unquestioned norms of didacticism were now being challenged. I thought of Neil Postman and Charles Weingartner (1972) and felt I had turned my teaching into a 'subversive' activity unwittingly and I was very proud of it!

Back in the classroom later I discussed the episode with the children and told them how I'd been taken aback by their involvement. I asked them what they thought would have happened if I had 'taught' the lesson in our own classroom.

- **G:** *Well, we would like, probably have let you talk more, like for longer I suppose.*
- **C** added: *Yeah, but after like, a while, we'd still probably expect that we could interrupt with questions and tell you stuff too.*

Describing this episode in Roche (2007 pp 243–4) I wrote: 'I saw that while I had achieved some small measure of progress, there was still a long way to go'. However, I now see that if I preface a lesson with an explanation of why sometimes I need the cooperation of their silence so as to impart information and assure them that I will then follow through with setting aside time for discussion, I can achieve a far more democratic practice. I realised too, following the episode described above, that my children were not simply 'going though the motions' of discussion: as far as they were concerned they were taking part in real dialogue. This is different to what Elkind and Sweet (1997) referred to as the way in which many students see classroom dialogue as 'filling in the blanks' – a process where, in 'discussion', children try to guess what the teacher wants and supply 'right' answers. They cite their own experience as students and state:

> Our teacher would start to lead a classroom 'discussion', but we had a sinking suspicion that it was just a sham. All she wanted from the class was for us to fill in the blanks of her pre-programmed curriculum. She would fish around from student to student until she got the answer she was looking for. So we kids had to make a choice between sincerely expressing our own thoughts on the subject, at considerable risk to our grade, or simply giving the teacher what she wanted to hear. The 'smarter' kids chose to play it safe. Their reward was the teacher's effusive praise for supplying the 'right' answer.
>
> (Elkind and Sweet 1997 p 1)

Burbules (1993) also speaks about the irony of asking questions to which one already knows the answer, which, he says, only happens in educational contexts (p 98). Holt (1964) similarly showed that children use many strategies in order to provide 'right' answers, or to merely 'survive' in class by pleasing teachers. When I started out to encourage children to be better critical and creative thinkers, I wanted to provide my children with a more authentic experience, to engage them in what I understood by genuine dialogue. I wanted to encourage them to be thinkers rather than 'teacher pleasers' or providers of 'right' answers. I wanted them especially to begin to realise that often there are no right answers, and that social problems can often arise because of contesting rights.

I believe that I have adequately demonstrated that the CT&BT approach complies with the criteria for dialogical pedagogy.

Dialogic teaching

Alexander (2006 p38) describes dialogic teaching as being the kind of teaching that is collective, supportive and genuinely reciprocal: a form of teaching that involves thoughtfully structured extended exchanges to build understanding; and where children's own words, ideas, speculations and arguments feature prominently. I hope I have managed to convince readers that simply promoting books and reading is not enough: for CT&BT to be successful, teachers, parents and caregivers must engage in dialogic teaching using picturebooks as stimuli.

As we said earlier, our children need to be able to enjoy literature, to be competent in reading and comprehending what they read, to have the skills to express themselves verbally and in writing; they also need to be able to think for themselves and be critical enough to take what is good from any reading material and discard what is not. Literacy is about far more than reading, writing and talking: it is inherently culturally, socially and politically value-laden. Like Harwood (2011 np) I feel that the addition of critical literacy is 'theoretically defensible and pedagogically necessary to prepare young children for the ever-changing literate world'. Children need to be able to unearth and examine the messages often contained within texts. The social world of children must provide the context for literacy instruction and learning so that this kind of engagement with reading will allow them to deal with key issues in their lives that will lead to them seeing literacy as empowering. The texts we choose must reflect their realities as well as others' realities. If the children in our classrooms are from culturally diverse backgrounds the picturebooks we choose should reflect that reality.

The texts we select for discussion must be examined closely by the teacher so that she is aware of possible bias, or overt and covert ideology. In a review published online in May 2013 in *Inis* the magazine of Children's Books Ireland, I wrote the following review of Ahlberg and Ingman's (2013) *Hooray for Bread* (reprinted with permission):

> This book has all the hallmarks of a traditional read-aloud favourite: a refrain that can be roared out, rhyme and rhythm, understandable language, a great topic in the life-cycle of a loaf of bread, and beautiful, deceptively simple illustrations. What's not to like? The book has a traditional and nostalgic feel to it. There is a sense of harking back to old-style values of order and peace and 'all's right with the world'. Early in the morning, the baker bakes a loaf. He samples it crusty and warm from the oven. After his wife has eaten some, the baker's son gets a lovely sandwich. The baker's wife and baby then head out for a walk in the park. Children will learn about a traditional family, about a day that is ordered and sequenced through mealtimes, about meals that can be made from bread, about animals and pets. Details matter in every

picture. At one point, the loaf sits on a plate happily humming to itself while dreaming of earlier days in a sunny cornfield. In the kitchen, outside the window, in the garden and around the edges of the park, a host of details wait to be explored and discussed. Ingman's clever illustrations have a hazy, lazy appeal. He transmits a sense of warmth and harmony, using simple lines and pastel colours. We see smiling slices of bread, ecstatic ducks, beans with tiny legs, birdies wearing hats. Wholesomeness and comfort abound – or do they? Perhaps some caution is needed because it would appear that a very gendered, white, 'traditional' set of values is being reinforced. What assumptions are being made? Which readers are being positioned as outsiders? How many children will not see their reality reflected in this depiction of 'ordinary' family life?

Thinking together

Shor (1992) explains that traditionally, school knowledge is assumed to be produced separate from students, who are asked only to memorise what the teacher orders. Consequently, the act of knowing is often reduced into transference of existing knowledge, with the teacher as specialist in this transference. In this way the qualities of critical reflection, problematising, and uncertainty, which are all qualities needed for learning, are ignored in favour of absorbing others' knowledge.

However, while a certain amount of preparation is important – such as choosing the picturebook carefully and thoroughly examining it and familiarising yourself with it, as outlined above – I must also emphasise that we must never sit into a discussion with any agenda other than seeking critical thinking and talking. We must not dominate the discussion or lead it in a certain direction. Granted, if children are going completely off on a tangent we might try gently bringing them back on task. However, when I sit into a discussion group with children I have no planned responses when I talk to them, other than to allow them to critique and discuss whatever picturebook has been chosen. Our interactions evolve dialogically in response to the ideas and the spontaneous contributions of each member of the group. There is no seeking of closure or right answers. I know that if I were to stand outside the group and direct or control it from without, in an authoritarian manner, and seek a product called 'knowledge' which could then be turned into 'activities' that my children call 'school work', it would not work. It 'works' because I am in the circle, as one-in-relation-with-my-students, enjoying the exciting co-creation of ideas, sharing our knowledge with each other, and as Murris (2000) said: 'thinking with one big head'.

Some picturebooks arranged by topic

Education:

- *Once Upon an Ordinary School Day* (Colin McNaughton and Satoshi Kitamura)
- *Thank You Mr Falker* (Patricia Polacco)
- *The Wednesday Surprise* (Eve Bunting)
- *The Composition* (Antonio Skarmeta and Alfonso Ruano)
- *I Hate School* (Jeanne Willis and Tony Ross)

Separation and fear:

- *The Wolf* (Margaret Barbelet and Jane Tanner)
- *What If* (Anthony Browne)
- *Hansel and Gretel* (Anthony Browne)
- *The Rumor* (Monique Felix)
- *The Tunnel* (Anthony Browne)

Relationships:

- *Fox* (Margaret Wild and Ron Brooks)
- *Farther* (Grahame Baker-Smith)
- *John Brown Rose and The Midnight Cat* (Jenny Wagner and Ron Brooks)
- *My Dad* (Anthony Browne)
- *My Mum* (Anthony Browne)
- *The Trouble with Mum* (Babette Cole)
- *Gorilla* (Anthony Browne)
- *Voices in the Park* (Anthony Browne)
- *A Bad Case of Stripes* (David Shannon)
- *Little Blue and Little Yellow* (Leo Lionni)
- *Scaredy Squirrel Makes a Friend* (Melanie Watt)
- *Grandpa* (John Burningham)
- *Maia and What Matters* (Tine Mortier and Kaatje Vermeire)
- *Rules of Summer* (Shaun Tan)
- *The Lost Thing* (Shaun Tan)
- *So Much* (Trish Cooke and Helen Oxenbury)
- *There's Going to be a Baby* (Helen Oxenbury)

- *The Red Book* (Barbara Lehman)
- *Bluebird* (Bob Staake)
- *Wild* (Emily Hughes)
- *Each Kindness* (Jacqueline Woodson and E.B. Lewis)
- *The Tunnel* (Anthony Browne)
- *Look What I've Got* (Anthony Browne)
- *Denver* (David McKee)
- *I Like to be Little* (Charlotte Zolotov and Eric Blegvad)
- *Extra Yarn* (Mac Barnett and Jon Klassen)
- *Voices in the Park* (Anthony Browne)

Illness and death:

- *Grandpa* (John Burningham)
- *Maia and What Matters* (Tine Mortier and Kaatje Vermeire)
- *Duck, Death and the Tulip* (Wolf Erlbruch)
- *Farther* (Grahame Baker–Smith)
- *Faithful Elephants* (Yukio Tsuchiya and Ted Lewin)

Censorship, fundamentalism, intolerance:

- *Tusk Tusk* (David McKee)
- *The Conquerors* (David McKee)
- *Why?* (Nikolai Popov)
- *The Rabbits* (John Marsden and Shaun Tan)
- *The Composition* (Antonio Skarmeta and Alfonso Ruano)
- *Rose Blanche* (Roberto Innocenti and Ian McEwan)
- *Star of Fear, Star of Hope* (Jo Hoestlandt and Johanna Kang)
- *My Hiroshima* (Junko Morimoto)
- *Let the Celebrations Begin* (Margaret Wild and Julie Vivas)
- *The Tricycle* (Elisa Amado and Alfonso Ruano)

Gender:

- *Crusher is Coming* (Bob Graham)
- *The Sissy Duckling* (Harvey Fierstein and Henry Cole)
- *Oliver Button is a Sissy* (Tomie de Paola)
- *I'm Glad I'm a Boy! I'm Glad I'm a Girl!* (Whitney Darrow)
- *William's Doll* (Charlotte Zolotow and William Pene du Bois)
- *Piggybook* (Anthony Browne)
- *Prince Cinders* (Babette Cole)
- *Kate and the Beanstalk* (Mary Pope Osborne and Giselle Potter)
- *10,000 Dresses* (Marcus Ewart and Rex Ray)
- *Princess Smartypants* (Babette Cole)
- *Princess Smartypants Breaks the Rules* (Babette Cole)
- *The Paperbag Princess* (Robert Munsch and Michael Martchenko)

Racism and immigration:

- *The Arrival* (Shaun Tan)
- *Amazing Grace* (Mary Hoffman and Caroline Binch)
- *The Colours of Home* (Mary Hoffman and Karin Littlewood)
- *The Other Side* (Jacqueline Woodson and E.B. Lewis)
- *The Matchbox Diary* (Paul Fleischman and Bagram Ibatoulline)
- *When Jessie Came Across The Sea* (Amy Hest and P.J. Lynch)
- *Here I am* (Patti Kim and Sonia Sanchez)

Anxiety and depression:

- *The Red Tree* (Shaun Tan)
- *Why Are You So Sad?* (Beth Andrews and Nicole Wong)
- *Silly Billy* (Anthony Browne)
- *Darkness Slipped in* (Ella Burfoot)
- *The Huge Bag of Worries* (Virginia Ironside and Frank Rodgers)

Homelessness:

- *Fly Away Home* (Eve Bunting)
- *The Tooth* (Avi Slodovnick and Manon Gauthier)

Nature:

- *The Tin Forest* (Helen Ward and Wayne Andersen)
- *The Storm* (Charlotte Zolotov and Margaret Bloy Graham)
- *Think of an Eel* (Karen Wallace and Mike Bostock)
- *River Story* (Meredith Hooper and Bee Willey)
- *First the Egg* (Laura Vaccaro Seeger)
- *The Lorax* (Dr Seuss)
- *Oi! Get Off Our Train* (John Burningham)
- *Zoo* (Anthony Browne)

Interesting points of view:

- *Really Really Big Questions about Me* (Stephen Law and Marc Aspinall)
- *Let's Do Nothing!* (Tony Fucile)
- *Where Does Tuesday Go?* (Janeen Brian and Michael King)
- *The World According to Warren* (Craig Silvey and Sonia Martinez)

Bibliography

Alexander, R. (nd) Dialogic Teaching website. Online, available at: http://www.robinalexander. org.uk/index.php/dialogic-teaching/ (accessed Jan 2014).

Alexander, R. (2006) *Towards Dialogic Teaching: rethinking classroom talk*. 3rd ed. UK: Dialogos Ltd.

Alexander, R. (2010) Speaking but not listening? Accountable talk in an unaccountable context. *Literacy*, Nov 2010, 44 (3): 103–11.

Ambrose, G. and Harris, P. (2008) *The Fundamentals of Graphic Design*. Lausanne: AVA Publishing.

Ansberry, K. and Morgan, E. (nd) Picture books to encourage scientific dialogue. Online, available at http://www.pictureperfectscience.com/ (accessed Jan 2014).

Arizpe, E. and Styles, M. (2003) *Children Reading Pictures: interpreting visual texts*. London: RoutledgeFalmer.

Austin, H., Dwyer, B. and Freebody, P. (2003) *Schooling the Child: the making of students in classrooms*. London and New York: RoutledgeFalmer.

Ayers, W. (nd) *Teaching*. Online, available at: http://billayers.wordpress.com/teaching/ (accessed Jan 2014).

Baddeley, P. and Eddershaw, C. (1994) *Not So Simple Picture Books: developing responses to literature with 4 to 12 year olds*. Stoke-on-Trent: Trentham Books.

Bader, B. (1976) *American Picture Books: from Noah's Ark to the Beast Within*. New York: Macmillan.

Bakhtin, M. (1981) *The Dialogic Imagination*. Austin: University of Texas Press.

Ball, S. (2003) The teacher's soul and the terrors of performativity. *Journal of Education Policy*, 18 (2): 215–28.

Belinder, B. (nd) Cross-curricular linkage for *Weslandia*. Online, available at: http://www.home-schoolshare.com/weslandia.php (accessed Jan 2014).

Benhabib, S. (1987) 'The generalized and the concrete other' in E.F. Kittay and D.T. Myers (eds) *Women and Moral Theory*. Totowa, New Jersey: Rowman and Littlefield (pp 154–77).

Bergman, R. (2004) Caring for the ethical ideal: Nel Noddings on moral education. *Journal of Moral Education*, 33 (2) June 2004.

Berk, L. and Winsler, A. (1995) *Scaffolding Children's Learning: Vygotsky and early childhood education*. Washington, DC: National Association for the Education of Young Children.

Biemiller, A. (1999) *Language and reading success*. Cambridge, MA: Brookline.

Biemiller, A. and Boote, C. (2006) An effective method for building meaning vocabulary in primary grades. *Journal of Educational Psychology*, 98: 44–62.

Bohm, D. (1998) On dialogue. *Thinking: The Journal of Philosophy for Children*, 14 (1): 2–7.

Bohm, D. (2004) *On Dialogue*. London and New York: Routledge Classics.

Booker, K. (2012) Using picturebooks to empower and inspire readers and writers in the upper primary classroom. *Literacy Learning: the Middle Years*, 20 (2): i–xiv.

Boyd, M. and Galda, L. (2011) *Real Talk in Elementary Classrooms: effective oral language practice*. New York: The Guildford Press.

Brandt, R. (1993) On teaching for understanding: a conversation with Howard Gardner. *Educational Leadership*, 50 (7): 4–7.

Bromley, K. (2007) Nine things every teacher should know about words and vocabulary instruction. *Journal of Adolescent & Adult Literacy*, 50 (7): 528–37.

Brookfield, S. (2012) *Teaching for Critical Thinking: tools and techniques to help students question their assumptions*. San Francisco: Jossey-Bass.

Brown, M. (2013) *Children miss out on reading*. Online, available at: http://www.theguardian.com/books/2013/jul/06/children-miss-out-on-reading (accessed 10 July 2013).

Browne, A. (nd) cited in *Sharing and enjoying picture books: tips for foundation stage and key stage one teachers*. Online, available at: http://fileserver.booktrust.org.uk/usr/resources/421/sharing-picture-books-leaflet_1.pdf (accessed Dec 2013).

Browne, A. (2009) *Developing Language and Literacy 3-8*. 3rd ed. Los Angeles and London: Sage.

Bruner, J. (1960) *The Process of Education*. Cambridge, MA: Harvard University Press.

Bruner, J. (1986) *Actual Minds, Possible Worlds*. Cambridge, MA: Harvard University Press.

Bruner, J. (1996) *The Culture of Education*. Cambridge, MA: Harvard University Press.

Bruner, J. (2002) *Making Stories: law, literature, life*. New York: Farrar, Straus and Giroux.

Buber, M. (1965) *I and Thou*. 2nd ed. (Trans R.G. Smith). New York: Scribner.

Burbules, N. (1993) *Dialogue in Teaching: theory and practice*. New York: Teachers' Press.

Cadwell, L. B. (1997) *Bringing Reggio Emilia Home: an innovative approach to early childhood education*. New York: Teachers College Press.

Campbell, E.M. (2001) *Thinking Time as a Context for Moral Enquiry*. St Patrick's College, Dublin: Unpublished M.Ed. thesis.

Campbell, R. (2001) *Read-Alouds With Young Children*. Newark, Delaware: International Reading Association.

Carrington, V. (2003) 'I'm in a bad mood. Let's go shopping': Interactive dolls, consumer culture and a 'glocalized' model of literacy. *Journal of Early Childhood Literacy*, April 2003, 3: 83–98.

Cashore, K. (2003) Humor, simplicity, and experimentation in the picture books of Jon Agee. *Children's Literature in Education*, 34: 147–81.

Chall, J.S., Jacobs, V.A. and Baldwin, L.E. (1990) *The Reading Crisis: why poor children fall behind*. Cambridge, MA: Harvard University Press.

Chapin, H. (1978) *Flowers are Red*. 'Living Suite' Album. Elektra.

Chaskin, R.J. and Rauner, D. M (1995). Youth and caring: An introduction. *Phi Delta Kappan*, 76 (9): 667–74.

Clay, M. (1991) *Becoming Literate: the construction of inner control*. Portsmouth, NH: Heinemann.

Coles, R. (1986) *The Political Life of Children*. Boston, MA: Houghton Mifflin.

Coles, R. (1989) *The Call of Stories: teaching and the moral imagination*. Boston, MA: Houghton Mifflin.

Comber, B. (2001) 'Critical literacies and local action: teacher knowledge and a new research agenda', in B. Comber and A. Simpson (eds) *Negotiating Critical Literacies in Classrooms*. New Jersey: Erlbaum (pp 271–82).

Comber, B. (2003) 'Critical literacy: power and pleasure with language in the early years', in V. Vasquez and B. Comber (eds) *Critical Perspectives in literacy: demonstrations of curricular possibilities* (pp 4–18). Handout for a pre-convention institute of the International Reading Association, Orlando, FL. (Reprinted from The *Australian Journal of Language and Literacy*, 2001, 24 (3): 168–81.)

Courtney, A., Gleeson, M.et al. (2009) *Building Bridges of Understanding: a strategic approach to children's comprehension development*. Limerick. MIC: Curriculum Development Unit.

Cowhey, M. (2006) *Black Ants and Buddhists: thinking critically and teaching differently in the primary grades*. Portland, Maine: Stenhouse Publishers.

Crawford, K. (1996) Vygotskian approaches to human development in the information era. *Educational Studies in Mathematics*, (31): 43–62.

Cremin, T., Comber, B. and Wolf, S. (2007) Editorial. *Literacy*, 41 (2), July 2007.

Crystal, D. (2005) *How Language Works*. London and New York: Penguin.

Dadds, M. (2001) The politics of pedagogy, teachers and teaching. *Theory and Practice*, 7(1): 43–58.

Dawes, L. (2005) *Teaching Speaking and Listening in the Primary School*. London: Taylor and Francis: David Fulton Publishers.

Dawes, L. and Sams, C. (2004) *Talkbox: speaking and listening activities for learning at Key Stage 1 (ages 6-8)*. London: David Fulton.

Dewey, J. (1910) *How We Think*. Boston, MA: DC Heath and Co., Publishers.

Dewey, J. (1934) *How We Think: A restatement of the relation of reflective thinking to the educative process*. Chicago, IL: Henry Regnery.

Dewey, J. (1963) *Experience and Education*. New York: Collier Books.

Dillon, J.T. (1994) *Using Discussions in the Classroom*. Buckingham: Open University Press.

Dombey, H. (2009) Research with a focus on the teaching and learning of reading in the pre-school and primary years. NATE/UKLA. Online, available at: http://www.ite.org.uk/ite_research/research_primary_focus/ (accessed Nov 2013).

Dombey, H. (2013) Synthetic phonics is not enough: teaching young children to read and write in English. Paper presented at 18th European Conference on Reading, Jonkoping Sweden, August 2013.

Doonan, J. (1993) *Looking at Pictures in Picturebooks*. Stroud. Thimble Press.

Donnelly, P. (1994) *Thinking Time, Philosophy with Children: the educational, psychological and philosophical rationale for doing philosophy with primary school children*. Milton Keynes: Open University. M Ed. Unpublished thesis.

Dresang, E.T. and McClelland, K. (1996) Radical changes. *Book Links*, 5(6): 40–6.

Dweck, C. S. (1999) *Self Theories: their role in motivation, personality, and development*. Hove: Psychology Press, Taylor and Francis Group.

Eccleshare, J. (ed) (2009) *1001 Childrens' Books You Must Read Before You Grow Up*. London: Cassell Illustrated.

Edwards, K. (2013) *We Love Picture Books*. Online, available at: http://www.sevenstories.org.uk/news/latestnews/we-love-picture-books (accessed Dec 2013).

Egan, K. (1989) *Teaching as Storytelling*. Chicago, IL: University of Chicago Press.

Egoff, S.A. (1981) *Thursday's Child: trends and patterns in contemporary children's literature*. Chicago, IL: American Library Association.

Elkind, D.H. and Sweet, F. (1997) *Ethical Reasoning and the Art of Classroom Dialogue*. Online, available at: http://www.goodcharacter.com/Article_3.html (accessed March 2014).

Erickson, F. (1993) 'Transformation and school success: the politics and culture of educational achievement', in E. Jacob and C. Jordan (eds) *Minority Education*: anthropological perspectives. Norwood, N.J: Ablex (pp 27–51).

Evans, J. (ed.) (1998) *What's in the Picture: responding to illustrations in picture books*. London: Paul Chapman.

Evans, J. (2004) *Literacy Moves On: using popular culture, new technologies and critical literacy in the primary classroom*. Abingdon, Oxon: Taylor and Francis.

Evans, J. (2009) *Talking Beyond the Page: reading and responding to picturebooks*. London: Routledge.

Facione, P.A. *Critical Thinking: what it is and why it counts*. Online, available at: http://www.slideshare.net/adindasafrini/critical-thinking-what-it-is-and-why-it-counts (accessed Jan 2014).

Farren, M. (2006) *How Do I Create a Pedagogy of the Unique through a Web of Betweeness?* Unpublished PhD thesis. University of Bath. Online, available at: http://www.actionresearch.net/living/farren.shtml (accessed Jan 2014).

Fillmore, L.W. and Snow, C. (2000) *What Teachers Need to Know about Language*. McHenry, IL and Washington, DC: Delta Systems and Center for Applied Linguistics.

Fisher, R. (1995) *Teaching Children to Think*. Cheltenham: Stanley Thornes.

Fisher R. (1999) *First Stories for Thinking*. Oxford: Nash Pollock.

Fisher, R. (2000) *First Poems for Thinking*. Oxford: Nash Pollock.

Fisher, R. (2006) 'Talking to think: why children need philosophical discussion', in D. Jones and P. Hodson (eds) *Unlocking Speaking and Listening*. Abingdon, Oxon: Routledge.

Fisher, R. (2009) *Creative Dialogue: talk for thinking in the classroom.* Abingdon, Oxon: Routledge.

Fiumara, G. (1990) trans. Charles Lambert. *The Other Side of Language: a philosophy of listening.* London and New York. Routledge.

Flanders, N. (1970) *Analyzing Teacher Behaviour.* University of Michigan. Addison-Wesley.

Foster, J. (1993) *Twinkle Twinkle Chocolate Bar.* Oxford: Oxford University Press.

Fox, M. (2008) *Reading Magic: why reading aloud to our children will change their Lives forever.* Orlando, New York and London: Harcourt.

Fox, M. *Like Mud, Not Fireworks: the place of passion in the development of literacy.* Available online at: http://www.memfox.com/like-mud-not-fireworks.html (accessed Sept 2013).

Freire, P (1972) *Pedagogy of the Oppressed.* Harmondsworth and New York: Penguin Books.

Fromm, E. (1979) *To Have Or To Be.* London: Abacus.

Gamble, N. (2013) *Exploring Children's Literature.* 3rd ed. London and Thousand Oaks, CA: Sage.

Gee, J.P (1993) 'Postmodernism and literacies', in C. Lankshear and P MacLaren (eds) *Critical Literacy: politics, praxis and the postmodern.* Albany, NY: SUNY Press.

Glenn, M. (2006) Working with collaborative projects: my living theory of a holistic educational practice. Unpublished PhD Thesis. University of Limerick. Online, available at: http://www.eari.ie (accessed Nov 2013).

Goldstone, B.P. (2002) Whaz up with our books? Changing picture book codes and teaching implications. *The Reading Teacher,* 55: 362–69.

Gollapudi, A. (2004) Unravelling the invisible seam: text andi in Maurice Sendak's Higglety Pigglety Pop! *Children's Literature,* 32: 112–33.

Goodman, K.S. (1980) 'Barpie was proving his kump', in Y.M. Goodman, C.L. Burke and B. Sherman, *Strategies in Reading: Focus on Comprehension.* New York: Holt Reinhart.

Goodman, Y. (1998) 'Foreword: The making of meaning through the picture book', in J. Evans (ed.) *What's in the Picture: responding to illustrations in picture books.* London: Paul Chapman.

Government of Ireland (1999) *Primary School Curriculum.* Dublin: Stationery Office.

Graham, J. (1990) *Pictures on the Page.* Sheffield: NACE.

Greene, M. (1978) Teaching: the question of personal reality. *Teachers College Record,* 80 (1): 23–35.

Greene, M. (1978a) *Landscapes of Learning.* New York: Teachers College Press.

Greene, M. (1988) *The Dialectic of Freedom: the John Dewey Lecture Series.* New York: Teachers College Press.

Griffiths, M. (2003) *Action for Social Justice in Education.* Maidenhead: Open University Press.

Guardian (1999) 'Into the garden of good and evil: an interview with Jonathan Glover'. Online, available at: http://www.theguardian.com/theguardian/1999/oct/13/features11.g2 (accessed Nov 2013).

Guardian (2000) 'Portrait of the artist as a gorilla: Anthony Browne explains his surrealist children's style to Julia Eccleshare'. Online, available at: http://www.theguardian.com/books/2000/jul/29/booksforchildrenandteenagers? (accessed Nov 2013).

Guardian (2010) 'Many parents failing to read to children, survey shows'. Online, available at: http://www.theguardian.com/education/2010/apr/30/children-parents-reading-stories (accessed Oct 2013).

Guardian (2013a) 'Children miss out on reading'. Online, available at: http://www.guardian.co.uk/books/2013/jul/06/children-miss-out-on-reading (accessed July 2013).

Guardian (2013b) 'Philip Pullman: Loosening the chains of the imagination'. Online, available at: http://www.theguardian.com/lifeandstyle/2013/aug/23/philip-pullman-dark-materials-children (accessed August 2013).

Guppy, P. and Hughes, M. (1999) *The Development of Independent Reading.* Buckingham: Open University Press in A. Browne (2009) *Developing Language and Literacy 3-8.* 3rd ed. Los Angeles and London: Sage.

Hall, K. (2003) *Listening to Stephen Read: multiple perspectives on literacy.* Buckingham and Philadelphia: Open University Press.

Hall, K. (2004) *Literacy and Schooling: towards renewal in primary education policy*. Ashgate: Aldershot.

Hall, N. (1987) *The Emergence of Literacy*. Portsmouth, NH: Heinemann.

Halliday, M.A.K. (1993) Towards a language-based theory of learning. *Linguistics and Education*, 5: 93–116.

Hardy, B. (1974) 'Narrative as a primary act of the mind', in M. Meek (ed.) *The Cool Web: the pattern of children's reading*. London: The Bodley Head.

Harste, J., Woodward, V. and Burke, C. (1984) *Language Stories and Literacy Lessons*. Portsmouth, NH: Heinemann.

Harste, J.C. (2006) *Understanding Reading: multiple perspectives, multiple insights*. Online, available at: http://phpindiana.edu/~harste/wrkprg/ (accessed August 2013).

Hart, B. and Risley, T. (1995) *Meaningful Differences in the Everyday Experience of Young American Children*. Baltimore: Paul H. Brookes Publishing Co.

Harwood, D. (Fall, 2008) Deconstructing and reconstructing Cinderella: theoretical defense of critical literacy for young children. *Language and Literacy Journal*, 10 (2) n/p.

Hateley, E. (2009) Magritte and cultural capital: the surreal world of Anthony Browne. *Lion and the Unicorn*, 33 (3): 324–48.

Haven, K.F. (2007) *Story Proof: the science behind the startling power of story*. Westport, CT: Libraries Unlimited.

Haynes, J. (2002) *Children as Philosophers: learning through enquiry and dialogue in the primary classroom*. London and New York: Routledge Falmer.

Haynes, J. and Murris, K. (2012) *Picturebooks, Pedagogy and Philosophy*. Routledge: London and New York.

Hoffman, J.L. (2010) Looking back and looking forward: lessons learned from Early Reading First. *Childhood Education*, 87 (1): 8–16.

Hoffman, J.L. (2011) Coconstructing meaning: interactive literary discussions in kindergarten read-alouds. *The Reading Teacher*, 65 (3): 183–94.

Hollindale, P. (2011) *The Hidden Teacher: ideology and children's reading*. Stroud: Thimble Press.

Holt, J. (1964) *How Children Fail*. London: Penguin.

Honig, A. (2007) Oral language development. *Early Childhood Development and Care*, 177, (6 & 7): 581–613.

Holquist, M. (2002) *Dialogism: Bakhtin and his world*. 2nd ed. London and New York: Routledge.

Hunt, P. (ed.) (1999, 2009) *Understanding Children's Literature*. Abingdon, Oxon: Routledge.

Hunter, M. (1992) *The Pied Piper Syndrome*. New York: HarperCollins.

Hurst, C. (nd) Children's Literature. Online, available at: http:// www.carolhurst.com (accessed Jan 2014).

Isbell, R., Sobol, J., Lindauer, L. and Lowrance, A. (2004) The effects of storytelling and story reading on the oral language complexity and story comprehension of young children. *Early Childhood Education Journal*, 32 (3).

Iser, W. (1988) 'The reading process: a phenomenological approach', in D. Lodge (ed.) *Modern Criticism and Thought: A reader*. London: Longman.

Janis, I.L. (1972) *Victims of Groupthink*. New York: Houghton Mifflin.

Jalongo, M.R. and Sobolak, M. J. (2011) Supporting young children's vocabulary growth: the challenges, the benefits, and evidence-based strategies. *Early Childhood Education Journal*, 38: 421–29.

Janks, H. (2010) *Literacy and Power*. New York and Abingdon, Oxon: Routledge.

Jeffers, O. (nd) Interview: Online, available at: http://www.booktrust.org.uk/books/children/illustrators/interviews/143 (accessed Jan 2013).

Jewett, P and Smith, K. (2003) Becoming critical: moving toward a critical literacy pedagogy. An argument for critical literacy. *Action in Teacher Education*, 25 (3).

Johnston, A. and Frazee, M. (2011) *Why We're Still in Love with Picture Books (Even Though They're Supposed to Be Dead)* Online: available at: http://archive.hbook.com/magazine/articles/2011/may11_frazee.asp (accessed July 2013).

Jones, N. (nd) cited in *Sharing and Enjoying Picture Books: tips for foundation stage and key stage one teachers*. Online, available at: http://fileserver.booktrust.org.uk/usr/resources/421/sharing-picture-books-leaflet_1.pdf (accessed Dec 2013).

Jones, D. and Hodson, P. (eds) (2006) *Unlocking Speaking and Listening*. Abingdon, Oxon: Routledge.

Kaderavek, J.N. and Justice, L.M. (2004) Embedded-explicit emergent literacy intervention II: Goal selection and implementation in the early childhood classroom. *Language, Speech, and Hearing Services in Schools*, 35: 212–28.

Kirkland, L.D. and Patterson, J. (2005) Developing oral language in primary classrooms. *Early Childhood Education Journal*, 32: 6: 391–5.

Kohl, H. (2007) *Should We Burn Babar? Essays on Children's Literature and the Power of Stories*. New York: The New Press.

Kress, G. and Van Leeuwen, T. (1996) *Reading Images: the grammar of visual design*. New York: Routledge.

Leland, C.H., Harste, J.C. and Huber, K.R. (2005) Out of the box: critical literacy in a first-grade classroom. *Language Arts*, 82 (4) March 2005.

Leland, C., Lewison, M. and Harste, J. (2013) *Teaching Children's Literature: it's critical!* New York and London: Routledge.

Lever, R. and Sénéchal, M. (2011) 'Discussing stories: How a dialogue reading intervention improves kindergarteners' oral narrative construction'. *Journal of Experimental Child Psychology*, 108: 1–24.

Lewis, D. (2001) *Reading Contemporary Picturebooks: picturing text*. Abingdon, Oxon: Routledge.

Lewison, M., Leland, C. and Harste, J.C. (2011) *Creating Critical Classrooms: K-8 reading and writing with an edge*. New York and Abingdon, Oxon: Routledge.

Libresco, A.S., Balantic, J. and Kipling, J.C. (2011) *Every Book is a Social Studies Book: how to meet standards with picture books, K-6*. Santa Barbara, CA: Libraries Unlimited.

Lin, Q. (2001) Toward a caring-centered multicultural education within the social justice context. *Education* 122 (1): 107–14.

Lindfors, J. (1999) *Children's Inquiry: using language to make sense of the world*. New York: Teachers College Press.

Lipman, M. (1977) *Discovering Philosophy*. 2nd ed. Englewood Cliffs, NJ: Prentice Hall.

Lipman, M. (1982) Philosophy for Children. *Thinking, The Journal of Philosophy for Children*, 3 (4): 35–44.

Littleton, K. and Mercer, N. (2013) *Interthinking: putting talk to work*. Abingdon, Oxon: Routledge.

Lowry, L. (1997) *Look*. Horn Book Magazine article ,1 March 1997. Online, available at: http://www.hbook.com/1997/03/choosing-books/horn-book-magazine/look/#_ (accessed Jan 2014).

Luke, A. (1991) Literacies as social practices. *English Education*, 23 (3): 131–47.

Luke, A. and Freebody, P. (1997) 'Shaping the social practices of reading', in S. Muspratt., A. Luke and P Freebody (eds) *Constructing Critical Literacies: teaching and learning textual practice*. Cresskill, NJ: Hampton Press, pp 185–225.

Luke, A. and Freebody, P. (1999) A map of possible practices: Further notes on the 'four resources' model. *Practically Primary*, 4 (2): 5–8.

Lurie, A. (1990) *Don't Tell the Grown-Ups: the subversive power of children's literature*. New York: Little Brown and Co.

Maagerø, E. and Østbye, G.L. (2012) Do worlds have corners? When children's picture books invite philosophical questions. *Children's Literature in Education*, (2012) 43: 323–37.

Macaulay, D. (1991) *Caldecott Acceptance Speech*. Online, available at: http://hmhbooks.com/davidmacaulay/words.html# (accessed Jan 2013).

Mackey, M. (2012) (ed.) Picturebooks and Literary Understanding in Honour of Lawrence Sipe. New York and London: Springer.

McAlister, A.R. and Cornwell, T.B. (2010) Children's brand symbolism understanding: links to theory of mind and executive functioning. *Psychology & Marketing*, 27(3): 203–28.

McCall, C. (2009) *Transforming Thinking: philosophical inquiry in the primary and secondary classroom*. Abingdon, Oxon: Routledge.

McClay, J. (2000) "Wait a second . . ." Negotiating complex narratives in black and white. *Children's Literature in Education*, 31 (2).

McDonagh, C., Roche, M., Sullivan, B. and Glenn, M. (2012) *Enhancing Practice through Classroom Research: a teacher's guide to professional development*. Abingdon, Oxon: Routledge.

McLaren, P (2002). *Life in Schools: an introduction to critical pedagogy in the foundations of education*. 4th ed. New York: Longman.

McMahon, S. and Raphael, T., with Goatley, V. and Pardo, L. (1997) *The Bookclub Connection: literacy learning and classroom talk*. New York: Teachers College Press, and Newark, DE: International Reading Association.

McNiff, J. (2000) *Action Research in Organisations*. London: Routledge.

McNiff, J. with J. Whitehead (2002) *Action Research: principles and practice*. 2nd ed. London: Routledge Falmer.

McNulty, M. (2003) *Postmodernism in Children's Books*. Postscript to Papers from the 2003 PAC conference. Ed. Beckie Flannagan, Francis Marion University. Online, available at: http://www2.unca.edu/postscript/volumexxi.html (accessed Nov 2013).

Mallett, M. (2006) *The Lyrical Voice in Non-Fiction*. Primary Bookmark series no 3. Leicester: University of Leicester, The English Association.

Marcus, L.S. (ed.) (2012) *Show Me a Story! Why Picture Books Matter: conversations with 21 of the world's most celebrated illustrators*. Somerville, MA: Candlewick Press.

Mason, J. (2002) *Researching Your own Practice: the discipline of noticing*. London and New York: Routledge.

Medwell, J., Wray, D., Poulson, L. and Fox, R. (1998) *The Effective Teachers of Literacy Project*. Exeter: University of Exeter.

Meek, M. (ed.) (1974) *The Cool Web: the patterns of children's reading*. London: The Bodley Head.

Meek, M. (1982) *Learning to Read*. London: The Bodley Head.

Meek, M. (1988) *How Texts Teach What Children Learn*. Stroud, Glos: Thimble Press.

Meek, M. (1991) *On Being Literate*. Portsmouth NH. Heinemann

Meek, M. (2004) in D. Taylor (2004) PROFILE: Yetta Goodman, Maxine Greene, Louise Rosenblatt, and Margaret Meek Spencer: Language, Literacy, and Politics. *Language Arts*, 81 (4) March 2004: 344–51.

Mercer, N. (2000) *Words and Minds*. London and New York: Routledge.

Mercer, N. and Littleton, K. (2007) *Dialogue and the Development of Children's Thinking: a sociocultural approach*. Abingdon, Oxon: Routledge.

Michaels, W. and Walsh, M. (1990) *Up and Away: using picture books*. Oxford: Oxford University Press.

Miller, D. (2009) *The Book Whisperer: awakening the inner reader in every child*. San Fransisco. Jossey-Bass.

Moebius, W. (1986) Introduction to picturebook codes. *Word and Image*, 2 (2): 141–58.

Moebius, W. (2011) 'Picture book', in P. Nel and L. Paul (2011) *Keywords for Children's Literature*. New York and London: New York University Press, pp 169–73.

Morehouse, R. (1999) *Philosophical Inquiry in a Classroom Situation: A case study with broader implications*. Paper delivered at 5th International Conference on Philosophy in Practice, Wadham College, Oxford, July 1999.

Moyer-Packenham, P. (nd) Picture books for teaching Maths. Online, available at: http://www.dearteacher.com/math-books (accessed Jan 2014).

Murphy, B. (2004) Practice in Irish infant classrooms in the context of the Irish primary school curriculum (1999): insights from a study of curriculum implementation. *International Journal of Early Years Education*, 12 (3) October 2004: 245–59.

Murris, K. (2000) Can children do philosophy? *Journal of Philosophy of Education*, Summer 2000: 261–80.

National Council for Curriculum and Assessment (NCCA). Aistear Toolkit: *Interactions: Children's Thinking and Talking*. Online, available at: http://action.ncca.ie/resource/Childrens-thinking-and-talkiing/65 (accessed Jan 2014).

Nel, P. and Paul, L. (2011) *Keywords for Children's Literature*. New York and London: New York University Press.

Nikolajeva, M. (2010) 'Interpretative codes and implied readers of children's picturebooks', in Teresa Colomer, Bettina Kümmerling- Meibauer and Cecilia Silva-Diáz (eds) *New Directions in Picturebook Research*. New York: Routledge, pp 27–40.

Nicolajeva, M. and Scott, C. (2006) *How Picturebooks Work*. New York and London: Garland.

Nikola-Lisa, W. (1994) Play, panache, pastiche: postmodern impulses in contemporary picture-books. *Children's Literature Association Quarterly*, 19 (1): 35–40.

Noblit, G.W., Rogers, D. and McCadden, B. (1995) In the meantime: the possibilities of caring. *Phi Delta Kappan*, L6 (9): 680–5.

Noddings, N. (1988) An ethic of caring and its implications for instructional arrangements. *American Journal of Education*, 96 (2): 215–30.

Noddings, N. (1992) *The Challenge to Care in Schools; an alternative approach to education*. New York: Teachers College Press.

Noddings, N. (2002) *Educating Moral People: a caring approach to character education*. New York: Teachers College Press.

Noddings, N. (2006) *Critical Lessons: what our schools should teach*. New York: Cambridge University Press.

Nodelman, P. (1988) *Words about Pictures: the narrative art of children's picture books*. Athens, GA: University of Georgia Press.

Oakeshott, M. (1959) *The Voice of Poetry in the Conversation of Mankind*. London: Bowes and Bowes.

OECD (2011) PISA in Focus. (10 November). Online, available at: http://www.oecd.org/pisa/49012097.pdf (accessed August 2013).

Office for Standards in Education (OfSTED) (2012) *Moving Literacy Forward*. HMI. 15 March 2012. London: OfSTED publications.

O'Donohue, J. (2003). *Divine Beauty: the invisible embrace*. London: Transworld Publishers.

Pantaleo, S. (2002) Grade 1 students met David Wiesner's Three Pigs. *Journal of Children's Literature*, 28 (2) Fall 2002.

Pantaleo, S. (2004) Young children and Radical Change characteristics in picture books. *The Reading Teacher*, 58 (2) October 2004.

Pantaleo, S. (2005) Reading young children's visual texts. *Early Childhood Research & Practice*. Online, available at: http://ecrp.uiuc.edu/v7n1/pantaleo.html (accessed Jan 2014).

Pantaleo, S. (2005a) Young children engage with the metafictive in picture books. *Australian Journal of Language and Literacy*, 28, (1): 19–37.

Pantaleo, S. (2007) 'Everything comes from seeing things': narrative and illustrative play in black and white. *Children's Literature in Education*, (2007) 38: 45–58.

Parkes, B. (1998) 'Nursery children using illustrations in shared readings and rereading', in J. Evans (1998) *What's in the Picture: responding to illustrations in picture books*. London: Paul Chapman, pp 44–57.

Paul, L. (1998) *Reading Otherways*. Stroud: Thimble Press.

Peirce, C. S. (1931–58) *Collected Writings* (8 Vols.) (Eds Charles Hartshorne, Paul Weiss and Arthur W Burks). Cambridge, MA: Harvard University Press.

Polanyi, M. (1959) *Personal Knowledge: towards a post critical philosophy*. London: Routledge.

Postman, N. and Weingartner, C. (1972) *Teaching as a Subversive Activity*. Penguin Education: Harmondsworth.

Pringle, R. and Lamme, L. (2005) Picture storybooks and science learning. *Reading Horizons*, (46) 1.

Quinn, V. (1997) *Critical Thinking in Young Minds*. London: D. Fulton.

Rand Reading Study Group (2002) *Reading for Understanding: toward an RandD program in reading comprehension*. Santa Monica, CA: RAND.

Roche, M. (2000) *How can I improve my practice so as to help my pupils to philosophise?* Unpublished MA Ed. Dissertation. UWE, Bristol.

Roche, M. (2007) *Towards a Living Theory of Caring Pedagogy: interrogating my practice to nurture a critical, emancipatory and just community of enquiry.* Unpublished PhD Thesis. University of Limerick. Online, available at: http://www.eari.ie (accessed July 2013).

Roche, M. (2010) 'Critical Thinking and Book Talk': Using picturebooks to promote discussion and critical thinking in the classroom. *Reading News* (Conference Edition). Dublin. Reading Association of Ireland. Autumn 2010.

Roche, M. (2011) Creating a dialogical and critical classroom: reflection and action to improve practice. *Educational Action Research*, 19 (3): 327–43.

Roche, M. (2011a) *Review of Shareen, N. (2011): Good Little Wolf.* Published in Inis, Sept 2011. Online, available at: http://www.inismagazine.ie/profile/156.

Roche, M. (2011b) Notes for Aistear (NCCA) Podcasts, (in National Council for Curriculum and Assessment (NCCA). Aistear Toolkit: *Interactions: Children's Thinking and Talking.* Online, available at: http://action.ncca.ie/resource/Childrens-thinking-and-talkiing/65 (accessed Jan 2014).

Roche, M. (2012) Critical Thinking and Book Talk: Exploring the Potential of Picturebooks for Developing Oral Language, Critical Thinking and Critical Literacy. Reading Association of Ireland Conference, *From Literacy Research to Classroom Practice: Insights and Inspiration*, Dublin, Sept 2012.

Roche, M. (2013) *Creating a distinct space for a dialogical approach to literacy: a challenge and an opportunity.* 37th Annual Conf Reading Association, Ireland Sept 2013.

Roche, M. (2013a) Review of *Maia and What Matters* in Inis, the Magazine of CBI, Dec 2013. Online, available at: http://www.inismagazine.ie/profile/156 (accessed Jan 2014).

Roche, M. (2013b) *Review of Hooray for Bread* in Inis, the Magazine of CBI, May 2013. Online, available at: http://www.inismagazine.ie/profile/156 (accessed Jan 2014).

Rogoff, B. (1990) *Apprenticeship in Thinking: cognitive development in social context.* Oxford: Oxford University Press.

Rose, J. (2006) Independent Review of the Teaching of Early Reading. London: DfES.

Rosenblatt, L. (1938) *Literature as Exploration.* New York: D. Appleton-Century.

Rosenblatt, L. (1978) *The Reader, The Text, The Poem: the transactional theory of the literary work.* Carbondale, IL: Southern Illinois University Press.

Rowe, M.B. (1986) Wait-time: slowing down may be a way of speeding up. *Journal of Teacher Education*, Jan 1986. Online, available at: http://ahsqilt.wikispaces.com/file/view/Wait+Time.pdf (accessed Jan 2013).

RTE (2012) 'Survey suggests one in five parents do not read to their children'. Online, available at: http://www.rte.ie/news/2012/0726/330664-eason-reading-survey/ (accessed Aug 2013).

Rubin, P. C. and Wilson, L. (1995) Enhancing language skills in four- and five-year-olds. *Interaction* (Spring 1995) Canadian Child Care Federation.

Russell, B. (1932/ 1997) *Education and the Social Order.* London: Unwin Paperbacks.

Salisbury, M. and Styles, M. (2012) *Children's Picturebooks.* London: Laurence King Publishing.

Sanders, J.S. (2009) The critical reader in children's metafiction. *The Lion and the Unicorn*, 33 (3): 349–61.

Sanders, S.J. (2013) Chaperoning words: meaning-making in comics and picture books. *Children's Literature*, 41: 57–90.

Schaefer, L. (2013) Online, available at: http://mrschureads.blogspot.ie/2013/12/author-lola-schaefer.html.

Seeger, P (1963) *Little Boxes.* 'We Shall Overcome' Album. Columbia Records.

Serafini, F. (2012) Taking full advantage of children's literature. *The Reading Teacher*, 65 (7): 457–9.

Shermis, S. (1999) *Reflective Thought, Critical Thinking.* Online, available at: http://www.ericdigests.org/2000-3/thought.htm (accessed Jan 2014).

Shor, I. (1992) *Empowering Education: critical teaching for social change.* London and Chicago: University of Chicago Press.

Shor, I. (1999) *'What is critical literacy?'* in I. Shor and C. Pari (eds) (1999) *Critical Literacy in Action.* Portsmouth, NH: Heinemann Press (see also http://www.lesley.edu/journal-pedagogy-pluralism-practice/ira-shor/critical-literacy/).

Shor, I. and Pari, C. (eds) (1999) *Critical Literacy in Action*. Portsmouth, NH: Heinemann Press.

Shore, C. and Wright, S. (1999) Audit culture and anthropology: neo-liberalism in British higher education. *The Journal of the Royal Anthropological Institute*, 5 (4): 557–75.

Shulman, L. (1986) Those who understand: knowledge growth in teaching. *Educational Researcher*, 15 (2): 4–14.

Silvey, A. (2012) *Children's Book-a-Day Almanac*. New York: Roaring Book Press.

Sipe, L. (2000) 'Those Two Gingerbread Boys Could be Brothers': How children use intertextual connections during storybook readalouds. *Children's Literature in Education*, 31: 73–90.

Sipe, L. (2008) *Storytime: young children's literary understanding in the classroom*. New York and London: Teacher's College, Columbia University.

Sipe, L. (2012) in M. Mackey (ed.) *Picturebooks and Literary Understanding in Honour of Lawrence Sipe*. New York, London: Springer.

Sipe, L. and Brightman, A.E. (2009) *Journal of Literacy Research*, 41: 68–103.

Sipe, L. and McGuire, C. (2006) Picturebook endpapers: resources for literary and aesthetic interpretation. *Children's Literature in Education*, 37 (4) December 2006: 291–304.

Smith, F. (1979) *Reading Without Nonsense*. New York: Teacher College Press, cited in M. Meek (1988) *How Texts Teach What Children Learn*. Stroud, Glos: Thimble Press.

Snow, C. (1998) Language and literacy development interview with ECT staff. *Early Childhood Today*, Aug 1998. Online, available at: http://www.scholastic.com/teachers/article/ect-interview-catherine-snow-language-and-literacy-development (accessed Jan 2013).

Snow, C.E. (2001) 'Preventing reading difficulties in young children: precursors and fallout', in T. Loveless (ed.) *The Great Curriculum Debate: Politics and education reform*. Washington, DC: Brookings Institution Press, pp 229–46.

Snow, C. (2013) Prerequisites to reading: vocabulary or knowledge? *Reading News: Newsletter of Reading association of Ireland*, Summer 2013, Educational Research Centre. St Patrick's College, Dublin.

Snow, C. (2013a) *Promoting classroom discussion to improve reading comprehension: results from the implementation of Word Generation in grades 6–8*. Paper presented at 37th Annual Conference RAI. Language Literacy and Literature: Reimagining Teaching and Learning. MIE, Dublin, Sept 2013.

Stanovitch, K. (1986) Matthew effects in reading: some consequences of individual differences in the acquisition of literacy. *Reading Research Quarterly*, Fall XXI-4: 360–407.

Stephens, J. (1992) *Language and Ideology in Children's Fiction*. White Plains, NY: Longman.

Stephens, J. and Watson, K. (eds) (1994) *From Picture Book to Literary Theory*. Sydney, NSW: St Clair Press.

Stevens, L.P and Bean, T.W (2007) *Critical Literacy: context, research, and practice in the K-12 Classroom*. Thousand Oaks, CA and London: Sage.

Stevenson, D. (1994) 'If You Read This Last Sentence, It Won't Tell You Anything': Postmodernism, self-referentiality, and the Stinky Cheese Man. *Children's Literature Association Quarterly*, 19: 32–4 (Spring, 1994).

Stewig, John W. (1995) *Looking at Picture Books*. Fort Atkinson, WI: Highsmith Press.

Straub, S. and Dell' Antonia, K.J. (2006) Reading, Toddlers and Twos. Naperville, IL: Sourcebooks Inc.

Sullivan, A. and Brown, M. (2013) *Social Inequalities in Cognitive Scores at Age 16: the role of reading*. CLS Working Paper Series. London: Institute of Education.

Sutton, R. (1994) 'The Big Picture' in *The Bulletin of the Center for Children's Books*, October 1992, 46(2).

Sutton, R. and Parvano, M.V. (2010) *A Family of Readers*. Somerville, MA. Candlewick Press.

Tan, S. (2002) *Picture Books: Who are They For?* Online, available at: http://www.shauntan.net/images/whypicbooks.pdf (accessed Jan 2014).

Tan, S. (2010) *Words and Pictures: an intimate distance*. Lingua Franca, Radio National ABC, 2010. Online, available at: http://www.shauntan.net/images/essayLinguaFranca.pdf (accessed Jan 2014).

Taylor, D. (2004) Profile: Yetta Goodman, Maxine Greene, Louise Rosenblatt, and Margaret Meek Spencer: Language, literacy, and politics. *Language Arts*, 81 (4): 344–51.

Topping, K.J. and Trickey, S. (2007). Impact of philosophical enquiry on school students' interactive behaviour. *International Journal of Thinking Skills and Creativity*, 2(2): 73–84 (see http://sapere.org.uk/Portals/0/SAPERE%20P4C%20Research%20map%20-%20first%20draft%20June%202011.pdf

Trelease, J. (2006, 2013) *The Read-Aloud Handbook*. NY, Toronto, London: Penguin.

Trickey. S. and Topping K.J. (2004) Philosophy for children: a systematic review. *Research Papers in Education*, 19 (3): 365–80.

Trifonas, P.P. (2002) *Semiosis and the Picture-Book: on method and the cross-medial relation of lexical and visual narrative texts*. Online, available at: http://french.chass.utoronto.ca/as-sa/ASSA-11-12/article4en.html (accessed Dec 2013).

Vasquez, V. (2007) Using the everyday to engage in critical literacy with young children. *The NERA Journal* (2007), 43 (2).

Vasquez, V. (2010) *Getting Beyond 'I like the book': creating space for critical literacy in K–6 Classrooms*. Newark, DE: International Reading Association.

Vygotsky, L.S. (1978). *Mind and Society: The development of higher mental processes*. Cambridge, MA: Harvard University Press.

Wells, G. (1986) *The Meaning Makers: Children learning language and using language to learn*. Portsmouth, NH: Heinemann.

Wells, G. (1997) 'Commentary: learning to be literate: reconciling convention and invention', in S. McMahon and T. Raphael, with V. Goatley and L. Pardo (1997) *The Bookclub Connection: literacy learning and classroom talk*. New York: Teachers College Press, and Newark, DE: International Reading Association.

Wells, G. (2001) 'The case for dialogic inquiry', in G. Wells (ed.) *Action, Talk and Text: learning and teaching through inquiry*. New York: Teachers College Press.

Wells, G. (2003) 'Children talk their way into literacy', in J.R. García (ed.) *Enseñar a escribir sin prisas… pero con sentido*. Sevilla, Spain: Publicaciones del M.C.E.P, pp 54–76. Online, available at: http://people.ucsc.edu/~gwells/Files/Papers_Folder/Talk-Literacy.pdf (accessed Aug 2013).

Wertsch, J.V. (1988) *Vygotsky and the Social Formation of Mind*. Cambridge, MA. Harvard University Press

Whitehead, A. N. (1932) *The Aims of Education and Other Essays*. London: Williams and Norgate Ltd.

Whitehead, J. (1989) Creating a living educational theory from questions of the kind, 'How Do I Improve my Practice?' *Cambridge Journal of Education*, 19 (1): 41–52.

Whitehead, J. (2012) *To Know is Not Enough. Or is it?* Online, available at: http://www.actionresearch.net/writings/jack/jwaera12noffke200212.pdf (accessed Jan 2014).

Wilkie-Stibbs, C. (2005) 'Intertextuality and the child reader', in P. Hunt (ed.) *Understanding Children's Literature*. 2nd ed. New York: Routledge, pp 168–79.

Wolfenbarger, C. and Sipe, L. (2007) A unique visual and literary art form: recent research on picturebooks. *Language Arts*, 83 (3): 273–80.

Woods, K. (2011) *Education: The Basics*. Abingdon Oxon: Routledge.

Zevenbergen, A. and Whitehurst, G. (2003) 'Dialogic reading: a shared picture book reading intervention for preschoolers', in A. Van Kleeck, S.A. Stahl, and E.B. Bauer (eds) *On Reading Books to Children: Parents and teachers*. Mahwah, NJ: Lawrence Erlbaum.

Zucker, T., Cabell, S., Justice, L., Pentimonti, J. and Kaderavek, J. (2013) The role of frequent, interactive prekindergarten shared reading in the longitudinal development of language and literacy skills. *Developmental Psychology*, 49 (8): 1425–39.

Referenced picturebooks

Note: Many of the publication dates below are for reissues of older books. Books are listed in the order in which they appear in each chapter.

Introduction

Pookie (1946, Collins) I. Wallace
The Adventures of Fingerling (1960, Lutterworth) Dick Laan
Puss in Boots (c.1950, Blackie's Easy to Read Books)

Chapter 1

Once Upon an Ordinary School Day (2004, Andersen Press) Colin McNaughton and Satoshi Kitamura
The Wolf (1992, Macmillan) Margaret Barbelet and Jane Tanner
Gorilla (1983, Julia McRae; 2008, Walker Books) Anthony Browne
Zoo (1999, Red Fox) Anthony Browne
Oi! Get Off Our Train (1989, Red Fox) John Burningham
The Tunnel (1992, Walker Books) Anthony Browne
Penguin (2007, Candlewick Press) Polly Dunbar
Yellow Bird, Black Spider (2004, Bloomsbury) Dosh and Mike Archer

Chapter 2

Little Red Hen (2001, Houghton Mifflin) Paul Galdone
Jack and the Beanstalk (1974, Houghton Mifflin) Paul Galdone
The Princess and the Pea (2005, Penguin) Lauren Child
Cinderella (1978, Houghton Mifflin) Paul Galdone
The Widow's Broom (1992, Houghton Mifflin) Chris Van Allsburg
Once Upon an Ordinary School Day (2004, Andersen Press) Colin McNaughton and Satoshi Kitamura
The Wolf (1992, Macmillan) Margaret Barbelet and Jane Tanner
Angry Arthur (1982, Andersen Press) Hiawyn Oram and Satoshi Kitamura
Lily Takes a Walk (1988, Picture Corgi) Satoshi Kitamura
Sheep in Wolves' Clothing (1997, Red Fox) Satoshi Kitamura
Comic Adventures of Boots (2011, Andersen Press reprint) Satoshi Kitamura

Chapter 3

Once Upon an Ordinary School Day (2004, Andersen Press) Colin McNaughton and Satoshi Kitamura

The Three Robbers (1962/2009, Phaidon) Tomi Ungerer

Archie's War (2009, Walker Books) Marcia Williams

War Game (2006, Pavilion Children's Books) Michael Foreman

Faithful Elephants (1988, Houghton Mifflin) Yukio Tsuchiya and Ted Lewin

When Jessie Came across the Sea (1999, Walker Books) Amy Hest and P.J. Lynch

The Arrival (2006, Hodder Children's Books) Shaun Tan

The Island (2008, Allyn & Unwin) Armin Greder

Tusk Tusk (2006, Andersen Press) David McKee

The Conquerors (2004, Andersen Press) David McKee

The Matchbox Diary (2013, Candlewick Press) Paul Fleischman and Bagram Ibatoulline

The Whales' Song (1997, Puffin Books) Dyan Sheldon and Gary Blythe

The Colour of Home (2002, Frances Lincoln) Mary Hoffman and Karin Littleton

The Ink Garden of Brother Theophane (2010, Charlesbridge) C.M. Millen and Andrea Wisnewski

The First Drawing (2013, Little, Brown and Co.) Mordicai Gerstein

Maia and What Matters (2013, Book Island) Tine Mortier and Kaatje Vermeire

The Magic Bed (2007, Red Fox) John Burningham

Twinkle Twinkle Chocolate Bar (1993, Oxford University Press) John Foster

The Troll (2009, Macmillan) Julian Donaldson and David Roberts

Time for Bed (2010 Houghton Mifflin) Mem Fox and Jane Dyer

I'm as Quick as a Cricket (2004, Child's Play International) Audrey and Don Wood

Kate and the Beanstalk (2000, Atheneum) Mary Pope Osborne and Giselle Potter

A Dark, Dark Tale (1992, Picture Puffin) Ruth Brown

The Smartest Giant in Town (2002, Macmillan) Julia Donaldson and Axel Scheffler

Rosie's Walk (2009, Simon & Schuster) Pat Hutchins

Something Else (1995, Picture Puffins) Kathryn Cave and Chris Riddell

The Black Book of Colours (2010, Walker Books) Menena Cottin and Rosana Faria

Chapter 4

Kate and the Beanstalk (2000, Atheneum) Mary Pope Osborne and Giselle Potter

Rosie's Walk (2009, Simon & Schuster) Pat Hutchins

Frog and Toad Collection (2004, Harper Collins) Arnold Lobel

Time for Bed (2010, Houghton Mifflin) Mem Fox and Jane Dyer

Think of an Eel (1993, Walker Books/2004, Candlewick Press) Karen Wallace and Mike Bostock

The Island (2008, Allyn & Unwin) Armin Greder

The Widow's Broom (1992, Houghton Mifflin) Chris Van Allsburg

Rose Blanche (2004, Red Fox) Ian McEwan and Roberto Innocenti

The Composition (2003, Groundwood Books) Antonio Skarmeta and Alfonso Ruano

Fly Away Home (1991/2012, Houghton Mifflin) Eve Bunting and Ronald Himler

Faithful Elephants (1988, Houghton Mifflin) Yukio Tsuchiya and Ted Lewin

Anne Frank (2005, Hutchinson) Fiona Poole and Angela Barrett)

Piggybook (1990/2008 Walker Books new ed.) Anthony Browne

Something Else (1995, Picture Puffins) Kathryn Cave and Chris Riddell

Tusk Tusk (2006, Andersen Press) David McKee

War and Peas (2002, Andersen Press) Michael Foreman

Yellow Bird, Black Spider (2004, Bloomsbury) Dosh and Mike Archer

Chapter 5

Once Upon an Ordinary School Day (2004, Andersen Press) Colin McNaughton and Satoshi Kitamura
Yellow Bird, Black Spider (2004, Bloomsbury) Dosh and Mike Archer
Think of an Eel (1993, Walker Books/2004 Candlewick Press) Karen Wallace and Mike Bostock
Gentleman Jim (1980, Jonathan Cape) Raymond Briggs
When The Wind Blows (1982, Penguin) Raymond Briggs
The Tin-Pot Foreign General and the Iron Lady (1984, Hamilton) Raymond Briggs
Ethel and Ernest (1998, Jonathan Cape) Raymond Briggs
My Hiroshima (1992, Puffin Picture Books) Junko Morimoto
The Composition (2003, Groundwood Books) Antonio Skarmeta and Alfonso Ruano
The Island (2008, Allyn & Unwin) Armin Greder
The Black Book of Colours (2010, Walker Books) Menena Cottin and Rosana Faria
Time for Bed (2010, Houghton Mifflin) Mem Fox and Jane Dyer
Feathers and Fools (2000, HMH Books for Young Readers) Mem Fox and Nicholas Wilton
The Red Tree (2010, Hodder Children's Books) Shaun Tan
The Matchbox Diary (2013, Candlewick Press) Paul Fleischman and Bagram Ibatoulline
Fox (2008, Allen & Unwin) Margaret Wild and Ron Brooks
This is not my Hat (2012, Walker Books) Jon Klassen
The Lion and The Mouse (2011, Walker Books) Jerry Pinkney
Flotsam (2012, Andersen) David Wiesner
Bluebird (2013, Random House) Bob Staacke
Journey (2013, Walker Books) Aaron Becker
The Wolf (1992 Macmillan) Margaret Barbelet and Jane Tanner
When Jessie Came across the Sea (1999, Walker Books) Amy Hest and P.J. Lynch
The Whales' Song (1997, Puffin Books) Dyan Sheldon and Gary Blythe
Zoo (1999, Red Fox) Anthony Browne
Gorilla (1983, McRae; 2008, Walker Books) Anthony Browne
Hansel and Gretel (2008, Walker Books) Anthony Browne
Weslandia (2007, Walker Books) Paul Flesichman and Kevin Hawkes
The First Christmas (2009, Puffin reissue) Jan Pienkowski
Jamie O'Rourke and the Pooka (2002, Puffin reissue) Tomie de Paola
The Three Robbers (1962/2009, Phaidon) Tomi Ungerer
Where the Wild Things Are (2000, Red Fox new edition) Maurice Sendak
In the Night Kitchen (2001, Red Fox new edition) Maurice Sendak
We are in a Book (2010, Hyperion Books) Mo Willems
It's a Book! (2012, Macmillan) Lane Smith
Harold and the Purple Crayon (1955/2012 Essential Picture Book Classics) Crockett Johnson
Bear Hunt (1994/2010 Puffin re-issue) Anthony Browne
The Pencil (2009, Walker Books) Allan Ahlberg and Bruce Ingman
Dog Loves Drawing (2012, Red Fox) Louise Yates
Bad Day at Riverbend (1999, Houghton Mifflin) Chris Van Allsburg
Open This Little Book (2012, Chronicle Books) Jesse Klausmeier and Suzy Lee
No Bears (2013, Walker Books) Meg McKinlay and Lelia Rudge
Wolves (2006 Macmillan) Emily Gravett
Warning: Do Not Open This Book! (2013, Attria Books) Adam Lehrhaupt and Matthew Forsythe
The Stinky Cheese Man and Other Fairly Stupid Tales (1993, Puffin) John Scieszka and Lane Smith
Black and White (1991, Houghton Mifflin) David Macaulay
The Three Pigs (2012, Andersen Press) David Wiesner
Voices in the Park (1999, Corgi) Anthony Browne
Frog and Toad Collection (2004, Harper Collins) Arnold Lobel

Each Peach Pear Plum (1999, Viking Kestrel) Janet and Allan Ahlberg
Not Last Night but the Night Before (2010, Walker Books) Colin McNaughton and Emma Chichester Clark
Kate and the Beanstalk (2000, Atheneum) Mary Pope Osborne and Giselle Potter
Princess Smartypants (1996, Picture Puffin) Babette Cole
Prince Cinders (1997, Picture Puffin) Babette Cole
The Three Little Wolves and The Big Bad Pig (2003, Egmont) Eugene Trivizas and Helen Oxenbury
The Frog Prince, Continued (1992, Picture Puffin) John Scieszka and Steve Johnson
The Very Smart Pea and the Princess to be (2011, Dragonfly Books) Mini Grey
The True Story of the Three Little Pigs (1991, Picture Puffin) John Scieszka and Lane Smith
Little Mouse's Big Book of Fears (2008, Macmillan) Emily Gravett
Good Little Wolf (2011, Jonathan Cape) Nadia Shareen
Billy Where Have all Your Friends Gone? (2005, Discovery Publ) Declan Carville and Sarah Roche
My Dad (2003, Random House) Anthony Browne
Thank You Mr Falker (2012, Penguin Putnam) Patricia Polacco
My Hiroshima (1992, Puffin Picture Books) Junko Morimoto
Ethel and Ernest (1998, Jonathan Cape) Raymond Briggs
The Sad Book (2011, Walker Books) Michael Rosen and Quentin Blake
The Tunnel (1992, Walker Books) Anthony Browne
Changes (2008, Walker Books) Anthony Browne
Through the Magic Mirror (2010, Walker Books) Anthony Browne
Rosie's Walk (2009, Simon & Schuster) Pat Hutchins
Free Fall (1991, William Morrow) David Wiesner
Tuesday (1998, Houghton Mifflin) David Wiesner
That is Not a Good Idea (2013, Walker Books) Mo Willems

Chapter 6

Rosie's Walk (2009, Simon & Schuster) Pat Hutchins
The Stranger (1986, Houghton Mifflin) Chris Van Allsburg
The Three Pigs (2012, Andersen Press) David Wiesner
The Black Book of Colours (2010, Walker Books) Menena Cottin and Rosana Faria
Mr Wuffles (2013, Andersen Press) David Wiesner
Sector 7 (2000, Houghton Mifflin) David Wiesner
The Arrival (2007, Hodder Children's Books) Shaun Tan
Journey (2013, Walker Books) Aaron Becker
How to Catch a Star (2005, Harper Collins Children's Books) Oliver Jeffers
Lost and Found (2006, Harper Collins Children's Books) Oliver Jeffers
The Red Book (2004, Houghton Mifflin) Barbara Lehman
Faithful Elephants (1988, Houghton Mifflin) Yukio Tsuchiya and Ted Lewin
My Many Coloured Days (1996, Red Fox) Dr Seuss, Steve Johnson and Lou Fancher
When Sophie Gets Angry – Really Really Angry (2008, Scholastic) Molly Bang
Angry Arthur (1982, Andersen Press) Hiawyn Oram and Satoshi Kitamura
Where the Wild Things Are (2000, Red Fox) Maurice Sendak
The Bad Tempered Ladybird (2010, Puffin reissue) Eric Carle
Elmer and the Lost Teddy (2008, Andersen Press) David McKee
Humpty Dumpty (2001, Scholastic) Daniel Kirk
Oi! Get Off Our Train (1989, Red Fox) John Burningham
Zoo (1999 Red Fox) Anthony Browne
Anne Frank (2005, Hutchinson) Fiona Poole and Angela Barrett)
Frog and Toad Collection: Dragons and Giants (2004 Harper Collins) Arnold Lobel

Yellow Bird, Black Spider (2005, Bloomsbury) Dosh and Mike Archer
Cinderella (1992, Little Brown and Co) Barbara Karlin and James Marshall
The Paperbag Princess (2009, Annick Press) Robert Munsch and Michael Marchenko
The Whales' Song (1997, Puffin Books) Dyan Sheldon and Gary Blythe
10,000 Dresses (2008, Seven Stories Press) Marcus Ewart and Rex Ray

Chapter 7

Where is the Green Sheep? (2009, Wadsworth Publishing; boardbook ed.) Mem Fox and Judy Horacek
The Napping House (2000, Red Wagon Books) Audrey and Don Wood
Goodnight Moon (2007, Harper Festival) Margaret Wise Brown and Clement Hurd
Time for Bed (2010, Houghton Mifflin; boardbook ed.) Mem Fox and Jane Dyer
Peepo (2011, Puffin reissue) Janet and Allan Ahlberg
Ten Little Fingers and Ten Little Toes (2009, Walker Books) Mem Fox and Helen Oxenbury
Ten in the Bed (2007, Walker Books) Penny Dale
If You Give a Dog a Donut (2011, Balzer & Bray/Harperteen) Laura Joffe Numeroff and Felicia Bond
If You Give a Mouse a Cookie (2013, Harper Collins) Laura Joffe Numeroff and Felicia Bond
If You Give a Moose a Muffin (1994, Harper Collins) Laura Joffe Numeroff and Felicia Bond
If You Give a Cat a Cupcake (2000, Laura Geringer Books) Laura Joffe Numeroff and Felicia Bond
If You Give a Pig a Pancake (1998, Scholastic) Laura Joffe Numeroff and Felicia Bond
Flora and the Flamingo (2013, Chronicle) Molly Idle
Peek-a-Baby (2007, Little Simon; boardbook ed.) Karen Katz
Where is Baby's Belly Button? (2002, Little Simon) Karen Katz
Dear Zoo (2010, Macmillan) Rod Campbell
Where is Spot? (2009, Warne) Eric Hill
Apple Pear Orange Bear (2007, Macmillan) Emily Gravett
The Jolly Postman (1999, Puffin) Janet and Allan Ahlberg
Each Peach Pear Plum (1999, Viking Kestrel) Janet and Allan Ahlberg
Have You Ever Ever Ever? (2012, Walker Books) Colin McNaughton and Emma Chichester Clark
Not Last Night but the Night Before (2010, Walker Books) Colin McNaughton and Emma Chichester Clark
The Three Pigs (2012, Andersen Press) David Wiesner
Once Upon a Time (1995, Walker Books) John Prater
Once Upon a Picnic (2008, Walker Books) Vivian French and John Prater
The Paperbag Princess (2009, Annick Press) Robert Munsch and Michael Marchenko
Prince Cinders (1997, Picture Puffin) Babette Cole
The Three Little Wolves and The Big Bad Pig (2003, Egmont) Eugene Trivizas and Helen Oxenbury
William's Doll (1991, Picture Lions) Charlotte Zolotow and William Pene du Bois
Give a Dog a Name (1995, Scholastic Hippo) Barrie Wade
Crusher is Coming (1999, Picture Lions) Bob Graham
Oliver Button is a Sissy (1990, Harcourt) Tomie de Paola
The Sissy Duckling (2002, Simon and Schuster) Harvey Fierstein and Henry Cole
Amazing Grace (2007, Francis Lincoln Children's Books) Mary Hoffman and Caroline Binch
Hey, Little Ant (1998, Tricycle Press) Philip and Hannah Hoose and Debbie Tilley
Everyone Knows What a Dragon Looks Like (1984, Prentice Hall) Jay Williams and Mercer Meyer
The Tooth (2010, Kane/Miller Book Publishers) Avi Slodovnick and Manon Gauthier
The Island (2008, Allen & Unwin) Armin Greder
The Composition (2003, Groundwood Books) Antonio Skarmeta and Alfonso Ruano
Yellow Bird, Black Spider (2005, Bloomsbury) Dosh and Mike Archer
Once Upon an Ordinary School Day (2004, Andersen Press) Colin McNaughton and Satoshi Kitamura

The Three Robbers (1962/2009, Phaidon) Tomi Ungerer
Scaredy Squirrel Makes a Friend (2008, Catnip) Melanie Watt
Frank and Teddy Make Friends (2011, Red Fox) Louise Yates
Duck, Duck Goose (2009, Boxer Books) Tad Hills
The Way Back Home (2008, Harper Collins Children's Books) Oliver Jeffers
Wolf Won't Bite (2012, Macmillan Children's Books) Emily Gravett
Mole's Sunrise (2012, Walker Books) Jeanne Willis and Sarah Fox-Davies
Something Else (1995, Picture Puffins) Kathryn Cave and Chris Riddell
Wilfrid Gordon McDonald Partridge (1987, Puffin) Mem Fox and Julie Vivas
The Red Book (2004, Houghton Mifflin) Barbara Lehman
Journey (2013, Walker Books) Aaron Becker
The Arrival (2007, Hodder Children's Books) Shaun Tan
Little Red Hen (2001, Houghton Mifflin) Paul Galdone
The Shopping Basket (1992, Red Fox) John Burningham
The Maths Curse (1998, Puffin) Jon Scieszka and Lane Smith
Who Sank the Boat? (1988, Puffin) Pamela Allen
The Adventures of Penrose the Mathematical Cat (1997, Wide World US) Theoni Pappas
The Rabbit Problem (2010, Macmillan Children's Books) Emily Gravett
Clocks, Clocks and More Clocks (1994, Atheneum Books) Pat Hutchins
Night Noises (2001, Harcourt Australia) Mem Fox and Terry Denton
Think of an Eel (1993, Walker Books/2004 Candlewick Press) Karen Wallace and Mike Bostock
Seven Blind Mice (2002, Pearson) Ed Young
Zoom (1995, Viking Kestrel) Isvan Banyai
Roller Coaster (2007, Harcourt Children's Books) Maria Frazee
Cloudy with a Chance of Meatballs (2012, Little Simon) Judi and Ron Barrett
Sector 7 (2000, Houghton Mifflin) David Wiesner
The Three Pigs (2012, Andersen Press) David Wiesner
Free Fall (1991, William Morrow) David Wiesner
Tuesday (1998, Houghton Mifflin) David Wiesner
Flotsam (2012, Andersen) David Wiesner
Weslandia (2007, Walker Books) Paul Flesichman and Kevin Hawkes
The Matchbox Diary (2013, Candlewick Press) Paul Fleischman and Bagram Ibatoulline
When Jessie Came Across the Sea (1999, Walker Books) Amy Hest and P.J. Lynch
Archie's War (2009, Walker Books) Marcia Williams
The Day the Cow Sneezed (2010, Enchanted Lion Books) James Flora
Why Mosquitoes Buzz in People's Ears (2002, Penguin) Verna Aardema and Leo and Diane Dillon
All in One Hour (2009, Two Lions) Susan Stevens Crummel and Dorothy Donohoe
Meanwhile Back at the Ranch (2010, Picture Puffin) Trinka Hawkes Noble and Tony Ross
Elsie Piddock Skips in her Sleep (2000, Walker Books) Eleanor Farjeon and Charlotte Voake
Fly Away Home (1991/2012, Houghton Mifflin) Eve Bunting and Ronald Himler
Black and White (1991, Houghton Mifflin) David Macaulay
Silver Buttons (2013, Walker Books) Bob Graham
Rules of Summer (2013, Lothian Children's Books) Shaun Tan
The Conquerors (2004, Andersen Press) David McKee
Encounter (1996, Cengage Learning) Jane Yolen and David Shannon
The Rabbits (2010, Hodder Children's Books) John Marsden and Shaun Tan
Tusk Tusk (2006, Andersen Press) David McKee
Six Men (2011, North South Books) David McKee
Why? (1998, North South Books) Nikolai Popov
Sadako and the Thousand Paper Cranes (2009, Pearson) Eleanor Coerr and Ronald Himler
My Hiroshima (1992, Puffin Picture Books) Junko Morimoto

Faithful Elephants (1988, Houghton Mifflin) Yukio Tsuchiya and Ted Lewin
Let the Celebrations Begin (1996, Orchard Books) Margaret Wild and Julie Vivas
Anne Frank (2005, Hutchinson) Fiona Poole and Angela Barrett
The Harmonica (2010, Charlesbridge) Tony Johnston and Ron Mazellan
What does Peace Feel Like? (2004, Atheneum) Vladimir Radunsky
Yertle the Turtle and Other Stories (2004, HarperCollins Children's Books) Dr Seuss
The Sneetches and Other Stories (2003, HarperCollins Children's Books) Dr Seuss
The Lorax (2010, Harper Collins Children's Books) Dr Seuss
The Butter Battle Book (1984, Random House Books for Young Readers) Dr Seuss
Horton Hears a Who (2008, HarperCollins Children's Books) Dr Seuss
I am an Artist (2013, Macmillan) Martha Althés
Dog Loves Drawing (2012, Jonathan Cape) Louise Yates
Ish (2005, Walker Books) Peter Reynolds
The Dot (2004, Walker Books) Peter Reynolds
A is for Art: an Abstract Alphabet (2008, Paula Wiseman Books) Stephen T. Johnson
The First Drawing (2013, Little, Brown and Co.) Mordicai Gerstein
Henri's Scissors (2013, Beach Lane Books) Jeanette Winter
The Day the Crayons Quit (2013, Harper Collins) Drew Daywalt and Oliver Jeffers
Little Blue and Little Yellow (1996, William Morrow) Leo Lionni
Katie Art Collection (2010, Orchard Books) James Mayhew
My Many Coloured Days (2001, Red Fox) Dr Seuss, Steve Johnson and Lou Fancher
Art and Max (2011, Andersen Press) David Wiesner
The Ink Garden of Brother Theophane (2010, Charlesbridge Publishing) C.M. Millen and Andrea Wisnewski
The Man with the Violin (2013, Annick Press) Kathy Stinson and Dusan Petricic
Zin, Zin Zin a Violin (2000, Aladdin Paperbacks) Lloyd Moss and Marjorie Priceman
Can You Hear it? (2006, Harry N. Abrams, Inc.) William Lach
Charlie Parker Played Be Bop (1997, Orchard Books) Chris Raschka
Mister Magnolia (2010, Red Fox) Quentin Blake
Fred (2014, Andersen) Posy Simmonds
The Smartest Giant in Town (2003, Macmillan Children's Books) Julia Donaldson and Axel Scheffler
The Gruffalo (1999, Macmillan Children's Books) Julia Donaldson and Axel Scheffler
We're all Going on a Bear Hunt (1993, Walker Books) Michael Rosen and Helen Oxenbury
The Bear in the Cave (2009, Bloomsbury Publishing) Michael Rosen and Adrian Reynold
Don't Wake the Bear! Hare! (2011, Little Tiger Press) Steve Smallman and Caroline Pedlar
That is Not a Good Idea (2013, Walker Books) Mo Willems
Don't Let the Pigeon Drive the Bus (2004, Walker Books)
The Farmyard Jamboree (2006, Barefoot Books) Margaret Read McDonald and Sophie Fatus
Something Else (1995, Picture Puffins) Kathryn Cave and Chris Riddell
The Wednesday Surprise (2012, Houghton Mifflin Harcourt reprint) Eve Bunting
Train to Somewhere (2012, Houghton Mifflin Harcourt reprint) Eve Bunting
The Other Side (2001, Penguin Putnam Books) Jacqueline Woodson and E.B. Lewis
Each Kindness (2012, Penguin Putnam Books) Jacqueline Woodson and E.B. Lewis
Urgency! Emergency! **series** (2009, Bloomsbury) Dosh Archer

Conclusion

The Three Pigs (2012, Andersen Press) David Wiesner
Goldilocks and the Three Dinosaurs (2013, Walker Books) Mo Willems
Zoo (1994, Red Fox) Anthony Browne
Oi! Get Off Our Train (1989, Red Fox) John Burningham

Something Else (1995, Picture Puffins) Kathryn Cave and Chris Riddell
When Sophie Gets Angry – Really Really Angry (2008, Scholastic reprint) Molly Bang
I Wonder Why The Wind Blows and Other Questions (1994, Kingfisher Books) Anita Ganeri
Anne Frank (2005, Hutchinson) Fiona Poole and Angela Barrett
Yellow Bird, Black Spider (2005, Bloomsbury) Dosh and Mike Archer
*The Lorax (*2010, Harper Collins Children's Books) Dr Seuss
Weslandia (2007, Walker Books) Paul Flesichman and Kevin Hawkes
Think of an Eel (1993, Walker Books/2004 Candlewick Press) Karen Wallace and Mike Bostock
Dear Greenpeace (1998, Walker Books) Simon James
Hooray for Bread (2014 Walker Books) Allan Ahlberg and Bruce Ingman

Index

Bromley, K. 68–9
Brookfield, S. 29
Brown, M. 8, 68
Browne, A. 12–13, 31, 85, 88, 95, 104, 118, 148, 153; illustrations 87, 94
Bruner, J. 39, 55, 103, 109, 111, 147–8, 149, 156
Buber, M. 10, 19, 47
bullying: challenging 130
Burbules, N. 111, 160
Burningham, J. 57, 96, 108, 118, 148, 152

Cadwell, L.B. 110
Caldecott, R. 83
Campbell, R. 55, 109
caring relationships 10, 152; developing 110
Carle, E. 110
Carrington, V. 91–2, 93, 121, 126
Carville, D. 94
Cashore, K. 88
cause-and-effect stories 139–40
Cave, K. 61, 142, 149
censorship: picturebooks about 163
Chall, J.S. 66
Changes 95
Chaskin, R.J. 10
children: as 'agents of text' 19; as benign rebels 122–3; as real people 19–20, 116, 120; scaffolding by 9, 49, 108–9, 134; as theorists and philosophers and critical thinkers 106–17; when to present books to 129; *see also* kindergarten children; younger children
children as knowers 21, 22, 114–16; Alex's story 115, 116; Charlies's story 115–16
choosing picturebooks 127–31; for infant classes 129; for kindergarten 128–9; for middle school 130–1; for preschoolers 127–9; for senior classes 131; traditional stories 129–30
Cinderella 121
circle format 131, 134, 152
citizenship: discussing 140; promoting active 14, 151
'civilisation': study of 139
Clark, E.C. 94, 128
classroom culture: metafiction and 89–90
classroom dialogue, as 'filling in the blanks' 159–60
classroom discussions 3, 28; break down 120; in CT&BT 8, 67, 156–7; dissemination 143; effect on language skills 66–7; philosophical enquiry through 70; practical advice *see* practical advice for discussions; as 'problem-posing' 21; scaffolding in 109, 134; and tacit knowledge 113; and teacher-pupil relationships 111; *see also* 'educationally productive discussions'
classroom environments 152
classroom practice: picturebook theory and 79–81
classroom talk 114

classrooms: CT&BT in *see* CT&BT in the classroom; as dialogic communities 10; oral language in 73; as replication and repetition settings 2; social relationships within 11
Clay, M. 73
close looking 22, 43, 88, 138
closed questions 9, 112, 116, 155
Cloudy with a Chance of Meatballs 138
co-being: existence and 117
Coerr, E. 140
cognition 90; *see also* metacognition
cognitive apprenticeship 114
cognitive development: interaction and 9, 73; language and 65–6, 71; reading for pleasure and 68
Cole, B. 94
Coles, R. 80
colonisation: study of 139, 140
Comber, B. 2, 7, 12
Come Away from the Water, Shirley 96
communal responsibility: discussing 140
communicative competence: development 61
communicative processes: effect on understanding 109–10
community: building a sense of 114; *see also* democratic and participatory communities; dialogic communities
community of enquiry 22, 47; metafiction and 89–90
complexity of picturebooks 86, 99
comprehension 27–33, 49; critical thinking and 29; defining 27, 32; levels 31; meaning-making and 29, 30–3; transaction and 27; *see also* visual comprehension
comprehension skills 31–2; decontextualising 32; itemising 31; reading aloud and 59
conflict: books dealing with causes 140
confrontation 148; examples 149
The Conquerors 140
'constant flow' of ideas 120
constrained skills 31
consumerist ideology: critique 92–3
contemporary literary theory 96
contentious issues, tackling 126
continuing professional development (CPD), in visual literacy 103
contrast 148; examples 148–9
contributions: extending 155–6
conversation 110, 111, 132; and building relationships 151–2; and critical thinking 109; effect on oral and written language 73; *see also* dialogue
The Cool Web 149
Corbett, P. 55
Cornwell, T.B. 91
Cottin, M. 62
courage: examining 93